CONCEPTIONS OF FAIR PAY

Conceptions of Fair Pay

THEORETICAL PERSPECTIVES AND
EMPIRICAL RESEARCH

Miriam Dornstein

PRAEGER

New York
Westport, Connecticut
London

Library of Congress Cataloging-in-Publication Data

Dornstein, Miriam, 1935–
   Conceptions of fair pay : theoretical perspectives and empirical
research / Miriam Dornstein.
      p.   cm.
   Includes bibliographical references and index.
   ISBN 0-275-93404-7 (alk. paper)
   1. Wage payment systems—Moral and ethical aspects.   2. Pay
equity.   3. Distributive justice.   I. Title.
   HD4926.D67   1991
   331.2'153—dc20   91–8609

British Library Cataloguing in Publication Data is available.

First published in 1991

Praeger Publishers, One Madison Avenue, New York, NY 10010
An imprint of Greenwood Publishing Group, Inc.

Printed in the United States of America

The paper used in this book complies with the Permanent
Paper Standard issued by the National Information Standards
Organization (Z39.48—1984).

10 9 8 7 6 5 4 3 2 1

Copyright Acknowledgment

The author and publisher gratefully acknowledge permission
to use the following copyrighted material:

Excerpts from Elliott Jaques, *Equitable Payment*, 2nd ed.
London: Heinemann Educational Books, 1970.

Contents

Tables

Preface

Organizational behavior theorists as well as compensation theorists agree that an understanding of the subjective pay-fairness perceptions of employees is crucial for understanding their organizational behavior and reactions to given pay schemes; and hardly any textbook on these topics fails to mention this. At the same time, all admit that except perhaps for an exposition of Adams's (1963, 1965) equity theory, they have little to convey to their readers on this topic. While this may have been true to some extent a few years ago, it does not reflect the present situation. From the middle of the 1970s, relevant research and theorizing have gained momentum and a substantial body of materials on the subject is now available. However, many, especially outsiders not intensively involved in researching this issue as well as some insiders, in particular those too involved in following a particular avenue, find it difficult to keep abreast of these new developments. A major reason for this difficulty lies in the great fragmentation of research effort on the subject caused by competing theories and paradigms and sharpened by mutual critiques. Disciplinary divisions, such as that between psychologists and sociologists, have added to the fragmentation which in turn has led to a wide scattering of publications in many books and journals and little cross-referencing between researchers not sharing the same perspective and discipline. A recent book even remarks that geography also emerges as a dividing factor (Deutsch, 1985: 107). True, in the 1980s several volumes appeared that showed clear signs of a willingness to lower the barriers somewhat by publishing works conducted under the influence of a variety of theoretical orientations and by researchers of differing disciplinary affiliations (e.g., Mikula, 1980; Lerner and Lerner, 1981; Greenberg and Cohen, 1982; Messick and Cook, 1983; Bierhoff, Cohen, and Greenberg, 1986; Masters and Smith, 1987). But the main dividing lines were maintained and merely transferred to the publications themselves: The tendency in these compilations is to treat each work as a separate entity with very "loose coupling" among them. Moreover, recent attempts to integrate some to the perspectives are still overshadowed by the existing mutual critiques and their ramifications.

Another major obstacle in the way of those wishing to acquaint themselves with the theoretical and empirical research relating to the subjective pay fairness perceptions of employees, stems from the fact that work on this subject is part and parcel of work on the wider topic of justice in social relations and has no clear and defined identity of its own. While much initial, and even subsequent, work on this topic is based on studies involving monetary rewards and actual or experimentally constructed work settings, and while much of the theorizing leans on examples relating to economic rewards, the subject is always treated in the framework of more general theories of subjective justice perceptions.

This book attempts to overcome the above obstacles: It aims to illuminate the subject of perceived pay fairness and its determinants by drawing on the work done along all major theoretical perspectives and by researchers of varying disciplinary affiliation, not to mention varying geographical location. The task proceeds gradually. The starting point—in Part II—is a description of the initial theoretical formulations, the critiques levelled against them, and the major points of controversy between them (Chapter 2). Chapter 3 is an exposition of recent theoretical developments relating to the major elements emphasized by the various theories, and of recent attempts of integration between the dominant perspectives. Chapter 4 highlights the major points of controversy and open questions arising from prevalent theoretical work, while preparing the ground for a review of available empirical research. Part III is dedicated to this latter task. The chapters in this part are built around major elements in the mainstream theories reviewed. The presentation of materials here follows a pattern that intends to give the reader some idea about the methodologies employed in investigating the issues reviewed. Part IV deals with the conclusions emanating from the empirical findings reviewed in Part III and examines their implications. Chapter 8 summarizes the findings, evaluates them, confronts them with the major questions posed in Chapter 4, and pinpoints the major lacunae left by prevalent research. In Chapter 9 the conclusions drawn from the findings are taken one step further. This chapter examines the tentative implications for wage administration and wage policy emanating from them and thus closes the circle that started in Part I (Chapter 1) with a brief review of the sources of recent interest in the subject among practitioners.

A few words are also in order on what the reader should *not* expect to find in this work. It does not deal with the theory or empirical research involving the behavioral *consequences or reactions* to perceived inequity in pay or that dealing with *procedural justice* defined as the perceived fairness of the *means* used to determine rewards (e.g., Folger and Konovsky, 1989: 115). These are outside the scope goals of this book, which is to illuminate the factors that underlie and determine the perceived fairness of the *amount* of pay employees receive.

Acknowledgments

I wish to acknowledge with thanks the illuminating comments of Abraham Friedman of the Hebrew University of Jerusalem and of Eliezer Rosenstein of the Technion, the Israel Institute of Technology in Haifa, who read earlier drafts of some of the chapters. Thanks are also due to Murray Raveh, who assisted me with English language problems, to Heather Kernoff, who typed the manuscript, and to the Research Authority of Haifa University for their financial assistance in manuscript processing.

Part I   Introduction

1 Recent Interest in the Subject

In today's free-market economies, government control and regulation, collective bargaining, and intrafirm wage administration have become important and inseparable components of the process of wage determination. In a regulated, negotiated, and administered system there is room for a variety of considerations and demands that by definition have no place in a system regulated by impersonal market forces. While the latter is based on the actions of vast numbers of participants acting anonymously and independently of each other and producing results that they may not have foreseen or intended, the former is based on a relatively small and identifiable number of decision makers with a variety of predetermined or imposed aims, acting on behalf of and affecting the lives of large collectivities. Demands and considerations of fairness in pay make little sense in a system subject to impersonal market forces but not where a relatively small number of decision makers play the main role. These, the regulators, negotiators, and administrators, have become the targets, if not the carriers, of such demands which have indeed gained a central place in today's wage determination process.

The issue pervades all the contexts fulfilling a role in wage determination: government economic policy, collective bargaining, and organizational wage administration. The forms and meanings, however, change according to the particular circumstances involved. Here are some important examples.

THE WIDER CONTEXT: GOVERNMENT ECONOMIC POLICY AND COLLECTIVE BARGAINING

Government Economic Policy

Many facets of government economic policy are closely interwoven with the question of fair wages. One of them concerns the national-income distribution and specifically the issue of the relative shares of capital and labor in the national income. The basic argument in this context is that the issue of fair wages cannot be detached from the wider question of labor's fair share in the national income. Specifically, it is argued that wages cannot be fair if labor does not receive its fair share in national income. As such, the issue is hardly ever absent from the agenda. It arises at times of economic change, when the national income is growing or contracting and parties are concerned with the ensuing adjustments in their relative shares. But it is also present when there is little change in the national income but parties are anxious to obtain their fair slice of the cake.

Government anti-inflationary policy is another case in point. Quite often this involves wage restraints or wage freezing. These strategies raise questions about the fairness of the required restraints and their possible impact on labor's total share in the national income, and about the relative share and wage level of specific groups in the economy.

Another arena is government employment policy. A frequent question in this context is if it is fair at times of high unemployment to hold down wages, and even lower the minimum wage level, in order to encourage employment. When inflationary pressures threaten to erode the buying power of wages, the issue becomes extremely urgent.

The subject of fair wages also crops up in relation to minimum-wage legislation. Questions about how a minimum fair wage should be defined arise, and generate others such as what constitutes a fair minimum-living standard for employees. From here it is only a short way to wider arguments, for example, that a fair living standard must *generally* be a major criterion of fairness in wages.

Collective Bargaining and Wage Negotiation

Not all union activities concern wages and not all activity over wages involves questions of fair pay; but fair-pay issues pervade collective bargaining and dominate much of the wage-negotiating process. Unions demand fair wages for their constituents and these demands take on a variety of forms depending on the specific context. For example, in setting wage rates for a particular occupational category, the issue of relativities vis-à-vis other categories is often raised and interpreted in terms of fairness. In setting wages for particular jobs, or rates in an incentive scheme, fairness is often interpreted in terms of payment-for-effort. In requesting pay raises for specific groups, fairness is quite often linked with maintenance of productivity rates or, in other cases, with maintenance of previous relativity to other groups. When costs of living allowances are demanded, fairness is related to a fair standard of living, and so on.

Both the above major contexts—government economic policy and union activity—are in essence political contexts dominated by a system of representation. Considerations and demands about fair wages are brought into the decision-making process by those purporting to represent employees' interests, views, and conceptions. The decision makers here are hardly concerned with the individual employees' views, conceptions, and feelings about the subject. These are sifted through the multiple prisms of collective action, bargaining, and power games, and reach the decision makers in statistical aggregates to be weighted on the scales of political power contests.

In the immediate employment context, however, decision makers cannot afford to look at the individual employee as a statistic. Here he loses his anonymity and becomes an identifiable position holder in a complex work structure that depends for its efficiency on his and his fellow-workers' role performances being adequate. His feelings and perceptions, relating to fairness in pay, insofar that they are perceived to affect his role performance, are of immediate concern to the employing organization and the decision makers shaping the wage policy and wage administration processes. We turn now to a brief review of the factors underlying this concern, specifically some central features of the labor markets and wage-determination processes in modern industrial societies, and the place of organizational wage policies in them.

THE WIDER CONTEXT: MODERN LABOR MARKETS

In today's industrial society, labor markets differ markedly from the classical free-market model. The differences are multiple, including imperfect competition, internal labor markets, and job competition instead of wage competition.

Imperfect Competition and Low Mobility Rates

The classical competitive labor market model presupposes free and frictionless labor mobility: Employees are assumed to act in a system where all jobs are open on the same terms to all potential bidders and where employers are in constant competition with each other over every employee. The employee is assumed to choose the job that offers him the best remuneration, to stay on the job as long as his employer meets the current market rate, and to leave it for a better-paid opening if such is available. In the modern labor markets, however, the reality is otherwise: Mobility rates are far lower than one might expect from the model and show a high degree of selectivity (e.g., Reynolds, 1986). These mobility patterns partly reflect a state of affairs where

> although the majority of workers are vaguely conscious of the job market, they cannot be said to be actively in it. They are sufficiently satisfied with their current jobs or fearful of the uncertainties to be encountered in the movement so that they are not weighing the advantages of other jobs against their own. *Unless ejected from their current jobs they are only passive participants in the market.* Not only by choice but also by necessity is this the case, for many employers . . . prefer not to hire persons employed elsewhere. (Kerr, 1986: 200; emphasis added)

Internal Labor Markets

The above statement about the preferences of employers focuses attention on another facet of modern labor markets reflected in the mobility patterns described and constitutes a major divergence from the classical model: the preference of employers for filling vacancies through internal recruitment rather than external hiring. Researchers (e.g., Doeringer and Piore, 1985) refer to this phenomenon as the internal labor market. Doeringer and Piore (1985) define this as an administrative unit within which the market functions of pricing, allocating, and often training labor are performed. The boundaries and structure of the internal market are determined by a set of institutional rules. These define the "ports of entry"—the hiring job classifications—into the internal market as well as the mobility avenues between jobs. In the overall job structure, entry-port jobs constitute only a small proportion of the total and are typically at the bottom of the wage scale (e.g., Livernash, 1957).

Employers' preference for internal labor markets is due to several factors, including lower turnover and training costs. Both these costs are closely associated with skill specificity. As skill specificity increases there is greater need for intra-organizational training. High turnover rates, however, involve losses of training investments and are therefore shunned by the organization. Internal recruitment not only lowers the losses involved in turnover but also involves a lowering of training costs, especially when there is skill specificity: "In any work place learning and teaching occur automatically, and often at little cost. . . . This is true even when the production process is relatively standard and the required skills fairly general in the economy. When jobs are enterprise specific, the advantages of internal training are even greater" (Doeringer and Piore, 1985: 31–32).

Other costs that employers wish to prevent or lower through internal recruitment are, for example, those incurred in attracting, screening, and assessing the qualifications of new candidates: "The efficiency of internal recruitment and screening derives from the fact that existing employees constitute a readily accessible and knowledgeable source of supply whose skills and behavioral characteristics are well known to management" (p. 31).

Similarly, internal recruitment saves employers high termination costs arising mainly from employee insurance and benefit programs. Some of these (e.g., severance pay and employment insurance) are initiated by workers and deliberately designed to impose termination costs on the employing organization and limit its freedom to initiate termination.

Internal markets thrive because they are preferred not only by employers but also by employees. Employees prefer them because of a series of benefits they offer. They are often associated with large organizations, preferred by employees because they are perceived as more prestigious working places, offer higher average wages, improved working conditions and better indirect compensation, as well as enhanced job security and improved chances of advancement. Internal markets are also considered preferable in terms of equity and due process considerations (e.g., Doeringer and Piore, 1985).

Job Competition Instead of Wage Competition

In the modern labor markets the trainability and long-term potential of employees, or their skills for a career rather than their specific skills, have become a major criterion for selecting employees from the outside market. Thurow (1975) has developed a model of job competition that he contrasts with the usual model of wage competition to explain the dynamics of the resultant labor market. "The key ingredient in the job-competition model is the observation that most cognitive job skills are not acquired before a worker enters the labor market but after he has found employment through on-the-job training programs. . . . Thus, the labor market is not primarily a bidding market for selling existing skills but a training market where training slots must be allocated to different workers" (p. 76). To minimize training costs, employers rank potential workers on the basis of estimated training costs. This leads to labor queues: individuals queued by employers according to their "trainability" for certain jobs. Candidates' trainability is assessed mainly in terms of their background characteristics. Previous work experience and existing skills become important ingredients in the selection process since they imply lower training costs (knowing the first skill lowers the costs of acquiring the second).

In the job competition model, the market is cleared by altering hiring requirements and amount of on-the-job training provided, rather than by wage shifts. Wage competition is thus largely eliminated from the process and employment competition becomes limited to entry jobs. Employers are interested in minimizing the impact of wage competition and employment competition because of their potential impact on internal training and technical change.

> If workers feel that they are training potential wage or employment competitors every time they show another worker how to do their job each man would seek to build his own little monopoly by hoarding skills and information to make himself indispensable. Wage and employment insecurity also means that every man has a vested interest in resisting any technical changes that might reduce his wages or employment opportunities (Thurow, 1975: 81).

Employers are also reluctant to respond to increases in demand of labor by bidding for higher wages since this might lead to demands for higher wages from those already employed by them; they prefer to lower hiring standards. To further insulate themselves from market trends, employers also tend to forbid the unemployed to bid back into their old jobs at lower wages (p. 85).

Partly Insulated Internal Labor Markets

The internal labor market is thus partly insulated from the external labor market in three major respects: job vacancies tend to be filled from within (fluctuations in supply and demand have thus a limited impact on the employing organization since they mainly affect entry jobs usually placed on the lower rungs of employment ladders where they can be dealt with through changes in recruitment requirements); required skills tend to be supplied through internal training (the employing organization is thus not directly exposed to the impact of external fluctuations in skill level supplies); and the internal wage structure tends to be insensitive to wage competition (external wage shifts thus have no direct impact on the wage levels in the organization). Insulation is not total or uniform: it varies, even rather widely, with the specific labor markets faced by the employing organization. But one of its major results is that employing organizations have gained a measure of latitude in wage determination: "in almost all labor markets the work organization is able to vary pay and hiring standards to some extent" (Patten, 1977: 108).

But it is not only the internal labor markets that insulate the wage structure from the economic market forces. A contributing factor is the difficulty of employers to orient themselves according to economic forces in shaping their pay policies: In classical economics, wage levels are determined in each case by the marginal productivity of labor. But, observes Pen (1971) in his economic treatise about income distribution, "in some cases marginal productivity is a vague idea, which leaves room for wage and salary movements that may be most considerable. So large in fact, that the whole economic reasoning drowns in it. . . . This creates considerable room; the policy-makers have a good deal of freedom to fix remuneration" (p. 96). Prominent examples are employees in the civil service, higher managerial echelons, and the professions. For employers, then, wage level "instead of being dictated by the market is a matter of policy" (Reynolds, Masters, and Moser 1986: 188). How do organizations proceed to carry out these policies? What are the considerations that guide them?

THE IMMEDIATE CONTEXT

Considerations in Organizational Pay Policy

Employee Motivation as a Major Pay-Policy Goal. A literature review indicates that pay policies involve a variety of considerations and goals, one being employee motivation. The importance of this goal has increased in recent decades due to several factors. First, guiding concepts have changed: Employing organizations have learned that the link between employee behavior and economic incentives is far more complex than assumed in the economic man model that has in the past guided employee motivation policies, and that much more effort and thought have to be invested in the subject to find suitable solutions. Second, there are the structural changes in labor markets. Internal markets now depend heavily on the willingness of employees to remain in, and to be productive and contributory members of, the organization. Indeed, the whole internal market system would prove a terrible burden if these and especially the last goal were not achieved: A workforce in which heavy investments have been made to train it for the required skills and to retain it in the organization but which did not make the required contributions would be a disaster. Aware of this, wage policy makers pay much attention to employee motivation when shaping pay policies: "Wage and compensation models developed in recent years . . . are related primarily to motivation and behavior in the internal market" (Mahoney, 1979a: 193).

Moreover, concern with employee motivation has been augmented by an additional factor: the proportional increase in the workforce of job occupants whose contributions are difficult to control, monitor and evaluate—the semiprofessionals, the professionals, and the managerial echelons, those whose contributions are mental rather than physical. This difficulty results in a greater need to rely on such employees' *willingness to contribute*. How to achieve this willingness has become a prominent issue in the sphere of wage and compensation policy concerned with employee motivation: "Today the compensation administrator is even more concerned with motivating employees to 'work smarter rather than harder'; this productivity-related goal poses new questions about motivational incentives." (Patten, 1977: 11).

Beyond the recognition that each employee usually has *some* latitude in deciding how much to contribute, and that the contribution of many is not easily assessed— and much therefore depends on their willingness to contribute—it is also recognized that once the tight nexus with the external market has been severed by deliberate policy and union activity, this latitude grows even wider: Employees are protected from harsh disciplinary measures by the unions and by the vested interest of the employing organization in their long-term association with it.

A Fair-Pay Policy as a Means in Employee Motivation. Maintaining a policy of fair or just pay has come to be perceived as an important means of achieving employee motivation (e.g., Mahoney, 1979a). The basic guiding postulate is that the willingness of employees to participate—that is, join the organization and stay with it—and their willingness to contribute will be determined among other things by the perceived fairness of the rewards offered by the organization (e.g., March and Simon, 1958). The link between conceptions of fair pay and willingness to contribute was already revealed in the early phases of behaviorial sciences investigations into employee behavior. A famous example is some of the findings of Roy's (1952, 1954) study. In his participant case study in an industrial enterprise, Roy discovered that employees working under individual incentive plans had clear notions about fair or unfair pay rates and based on these notions divided jobs into "gravy" and "stinkers":

> On stinkers they put forth only minimal effort; either they did not try to achieve a turn-in equal to the base wage rate or they deliberately slowed down. . . . Earnings of $1.00 an hour in relation to a $1.25 quota and an 85 cent base rate were considered worth the effort, while earnings of 95 cents were not. The attitude basic to the "goldbricking" type of restriction was expressed succintly thus: 'They are not going to get much work out of me for this pay' (1954: 436).

The need to introduce a criterion of fairness in devising effective pay structures is widely recognized by pay-policy makers and pay administrators: "Equity forms the building block, the foundation on which pay systems are designed," states the opening chapter of a well known treatise on compensation (Milkovich and Newman, 1984: 8). Even economists have warmed to the idea (e.g., Thurow, 1975). However, the means of achieving a measure of fairness is not perceived as readily available (e.g., Mahoney, 1979a: 194; Patten 1977: 140): "Considerations of equity, or perhaps more correctly considerations of inequity, appear to be central to compensation theory and administration. Unfortunately there is little base in theory or practice for the determination and justification of any equity criterion" (Mahoney, 1979a: 193).

Aiming at Pay Fairness in Actual Practice

Nevertheless, compensation theorists and practitioners continue to seek ways and means of bringing the employing organization somewhat closer to the target of pay fairness even in the absence of a genuine equity criterion. Several such means are considered as capable of this task. These are external and internal wage comparability, job evaluation and job rating, and pay for performance. While these means are widely used in organizations for a variety of purposes they are also considered useful for achieving a measure of pay fairness.

External wage comparability is regarded as a means of achieving a degree of equity vis-á-vis other employees outside the employing organization. The assumption is that wages in the organization should be comparable to those outside it. The focus is on the going rates for comparable work with other employers. This obviously raises the question of which other outside rates are relevant—those in the local community, in the industry, or those in the entire economy and outside it. Often this question is decided by rule of thumb: "If the compensation planner is concerned with the pay of a foreman, he must confine his attention to the pay of foremen in the local community." However, "when considering an appropriate rate of pay for a manager of corporate marketing, the compensation specialist needs to be concerned with *at least the industry*" (Patten, 1977: 166; emphasis added). The rationales for this and similar recommendations are some assumptions about the width of involved employees' horizon:

> For many blue-collar jobs, employees apparently lack knowledge of external comparisons across wide geographical areas. They do not really care, for example, what is being paid in Seattle, Washington, for a job like the one they are performing in Lansing, Michigan. . . . This is not true of a professional-level employee who considers himself as being in the national labor market. (Patten, p. 165)

Dunlop (1957) used the term *wage contour* to accommodate the process of external comparisons. A wage contour is defined as a relatively stable group of wage determining units linked through similarity of product markets, similar sources for labor force, or common labor market organization (custom) and that by virtue of these links have common wage-making characteristics.

Internal wage comparability is considered an important means of achieving equity vis-à-vis other employees within the employing organization. Several authors have analyzed the process of internal comparisons in the wage-determination processes (e.g., Dunlop, 1957; Livernash, 1957). According to Livernash, "in internal wage-rate comparisons . . . any given job is not related to all other jobs in an equally significant manner. Some jobs are closely related as to job significance, others more remotely related" (1957: 147). The key concepts here are *job clusters* and *key rates*. Within a job cluster, wage rates are more closely related to each other than wage rates outside it. Dunlop defines job clusters as a stable group of job classifications or work assignments within a wage-determining unit that are so linked by (1) technology, (2) the administrative organization of the production process, or (3) the social custom that they have common wage-making characteristics. The larger relationships between jobs within a cluster develop round key jobs and their wage rates—the key rates: the job rates for jobs within the job cluster are "pegged" to the key rates.

Job evaluation and job rating are, however, considered a relatively more rational and "scientific" way of establishing an internally fair pay structure than internal comparisons (e.g., Patten, 1977; Mahoney, 1979a; Reynolds et al., 1987). Job evaluation is defined as "a systematic method of appraising the value of each job in relation to other jobs in the organization. . . . Job evaluation places an evaluative value on the job regardless of the incumbent" (Patten, 1977: 197). The process of job evaluation involves a set of steps such as deciding which factors will be used, rating the jobs in terms of the selected factors, grouping the jobs into a limited number of grades, establishing wage anchoring points (lowest and highest wages), and establishing rate curves—the pace of rise for intermediate labor grades.

Pay for performance is considered a means of achieving equity through adjusting the individual's pay to his contributions. Here, attention concentrates on those means that can serve for evaluating these contributions—a variety of measures focusing on employees' inputs such as seniority, education, skill level, or his outputs and performances.

Researchers express doubts about the ability of external and internal pay comparability, job evaluation, and pay for performance to approximate pay policy to the proclaimed goal of achieving a measure of justice in pay. These may be useful tools in many respects but their real usefulness in regard to pay equity is doubtful for several reasons. Regarding pay comparisons, it is observed that in actual practice wage comparisons are, in essence, a tool for preserving customary wage relationships (e.g., Belcher and Atchinson, 1975: 575). Moreover, it is widely recognized that, to make wage comparisons an effective tool in a pay policy aiming at pay fairness, much factual information is needed on the comparison referents used by employees, which employing organizations do not yet possess (e.g., pp. 589–600). Job evaluation suffers from a similar weakness. In particular there is a lack of factual information about the factors perceived by employees as relevant for rating the jobs (e.g., pp. 588–89). This and other judgmental processes involved in the procedure are open to differences in opinion, collective bargaining, the impact of traditions, and the existing wage structure. The resulting system is thus "a combination of tradition, employee acceptance, and customary relationships" (p. 576). As for the *potential* of job evaluation as a means of furthering an equitable pay system, Mahoney (1979a: 192) has aptly summarized it thus: "It [job evaluation] provides a procedure for the determination of just wage rates, but it does not provide a criterion of justice; rather, it can be applied with any criterion of justice." Regarding pay for performance, there is uncertainty that the measures employed are indeed effective for achieving the desired link between pay and performance. Doubts are expressed that the various input measures are indeed valid measures of individual productivity. Queries also arise over the various output and performance measures. The difficulties in implementation in regard to the latter are considered by some as downright prohibitive (e.g., Milkovich and Newman, 1987: Ch. 9).

The Beliefs Underlying Actual Practices

The belief that comparable wages and job evaluation and pay for performance can bring the employing organization somewhat closer to the target of pay fairness rests on the assumption of an exchange between the organization and the employee in which the latter is paid for his contributions to the former. It is further assumed that equity can be achieved on the one hand through matching the value of contributions with an appropriate wage (e.g., job evaluation and performance and productivity appraisal) and on the other through internal and external comparability, meaning that the employee is not deprived relative to comparable others inside and outside the employing organization. Indeed, comparability is another measure of worth since it reflects the employee's alternative value or what he could have received in a similar other job.

This view of fairness leads to the definition of certain pay-policy issues that do not fit the exchange formulation, being deemed as irrelevant to the issue of pay fairness. For example, the COLA—the cost of living allowance intended to prevent an erosion in the real value of wages—says Patten (1977) "seems to be more closely related theoretically to the meta-goals of adequacy and security in compensation than the notion of equity" (p. 182). Another example is the company's profitability or ability to pay. Belcher (1974: 488–90), for example, argues that "most employers regard profitability as an issue that is of no concern to employees and their unions." Employers also regard another matter—the purchasing power of wages in terms of attainable standards of living—as being of little concern to the issue of fair-pay policy: "A particular employer may not have any interest in the ethical duty to meet the requirements of a higher budget or level of living for his employees. He may believe that level of living is subjective and certainly does not reflect in any way the performance of an employee and market reality as well as do going wages" (Patten, 1977: 186).

The fact that certain issues tend to be considered by pay-policy makers as irrelevant to the issue of pay equity or pay fairness does not prevent the employees' representatives from expressing a contrary view: They believe that the employees' standard of living, the buying power of his wages, and the employer's profitability and ability to pay cannot be separated from the issue of pay fairness. They raise these issues at the negotiating table. As a result, the subject of pay fairness "spills over" into the arena of employer-employee power contests instead of being confined to the daily process of pay-policy making.

THE OPEN QUESTIONS

The above discussion suggests that there is widespread recognition among pay-policy makers that achieving a measure of pay fairness should be an important target of pay policy. While the means to achieve this goal are not perceived as readily available, there is widespread belief among pay-policy makers that certain practices, such as external- and internal-wage comparisons, job evaluation and job rating, and productivity and performance measurement can bring the employing organization closer to it. Employees' representatives share these beliefs to some extent, and take an active part in the process of implementation, which is pervaded by bargaining over specifics between the two parties. This cooperation no doubt provides the foundation for the acceptability of these practices among employees and enhances their effectiveness. On some issues, however, the two parties do not fully concur and conflicts over principles arise. These become a matter of power contests between them.

Policies aimed at achieving a measure of pay fairness are thus shaped in practice through a process of cooperation and conflict between the employing organization and the employees' representatives. Both sides, though close to the scene, are guided in their dealings by their own beliefs about pay fairness rather than by well-founded factual knowledge about the employees' pay-fairness notions. These notions, which in principle are supposed to guide the policies aiming at a measure of pay fairness, are in practice largely hidden from their eyes.

Still, the individual employee is not totally deprived of an opportunity to express himself. He has his own personal bargaining table: "Individual employees are 'bargaining' every day when they decide to remain with, quit, or reduce their contributions to an employer" (Patten, 1977: 13). But neither the employing organization nor the employees' representatives possess the factual data needed for a better understanding of what is happening at this table.

The present work is interested in the perceptions of pay fairness which the individual employee brings to his "bargaining table." The major aim is to improve the understanding of this subject and, if possible, to indicate the ensuing implications for a pay policy aiming at subjective pay fairness.

But before turning to this task it is important to note that not all researchers would agree that understanding subjective notions of fairness may necessarily further the pay-policy target of achieving a measure of subjective pay fairness. For example, some theorists argue that individuals are driven primarily by the desire to maximize their positive outcomes rather than by conceptions of justice and that they will follow externally imposed rules of justice only out of fear of sanctions (e.g., Walster, Walster, and Berscheid, 1978). This proposition negates the very existence of subjective notions of justice, and suggests that, in a world of limited resources, any attempt to achieve a "just" distribution is doomed to failure since no party will be satisfied with its share and will always contest the shares of its neighbors.

Another proposition raises doubts from another angle about the feasibility of achieving a measure of perceived pay fairness in employing organizations. It holds that subjective notions of justice are fundamentally idiosyncratic "Ultimately, equity is in the eye of the beholder" (Walster, Berscheid, and Walster, 1976: 4). Such a view suggests that few commonalities in perceptions are to be expected and that actually there are no rules to be discovered and followed by those aiming at perceived pay fairness.

These propositions however have strong rivals and opponents. For example, there are researchers who believe that people act according to *internalized* values of justice and that they have, generally, a basic need to believe that they live in a "just world" (e.g., Lerner, 1975). This suggests that individuals have clear and firm ideas about what is just and what is not and, moreover, that these ideas occupy a central place in their value system. From this perspective, justice in pay is an achievable and indeed *desired goal* of individuals, rather than an externally imposed constraint on individual behavior that is constantly threatened to be overthrown by the individual's self-interests.

The argument of idiosyncracy is also widely contested. As will later become clear, some researchers believe that notions of justice are universal (e.g., Jaques, 1970); others believe that they are widely shared by individuals in a given society (e.g., Adams, 1963a), or at least shared by larger groups in a society (e.g., Homans, 1974).

Obviously, it is not the pessimistic view that preoccupation with perceived pay fairness is futile that has led to the present work. The stand taken here is that at this stage, where several paradigms confront each other, the best way to promote a better understanding of the subject is to display the relevant theories and empirical research and to examine their implications. We turn now to this task. Chapters 2 and 3 discuss the prevalent theorizing on the subject; first the initial formulations and then more recent theoretical developments. Chapter 4, focusing on the questions emanating from this theorizing, is followed by three chapters (5, 6, 7) detailing what existing empirical research has to offer in answer to these questions. Chapters 8 and 9 treat the conclusions emanating from empirical research and their implications.

Part II   Theoretical Perspectives

2 The Initial Formulations

THE THEORY OF RELATIVE DEPRIVATION

The theory of relative deprivation originates in the writings of Stouffer and his colleagues reporting the results of one of the largest research projects on the American soldier in World War II (Stouffer, Suchman, et al., 1949; Stouffer, Lumsdaine, et al., 1949). In this study, several findings emerged that seemed paradoxical or contrary to conventional wisdom. For example, there were instances where those who had more of a valued outcome were less satisfied than those who were objectively in a worse position. The best known instance concerns attitudes toward promotion in the Military Police (MP) and the Air Corps: During World War II promotions were slow and piecemeal in the Military Police but widespread and rapid in the Air Corps. Yet Stouffer and his colleagues found that Air Corpsmen who were moving ahead relatively faster than MPs were considerably *less* satisfied and more frustrated over promotion than the MPs. The authors reasoned that the greater dissatisfaction and felt deprivation among the Air Corpsmen as compared to the MPs stemmed from the fact that in each case individuals were comparing themselves with others in their unit who had been promoted: In the Air Force, where promotion was rapid and widespread, such comparisons led to expectations and aspirations so high among the Air Corpsmen that even the generous promotion system seemed unsatisfactory. By contrast, the MPs who used the promotion system in their unit as a comparison standard did not anticipate rapid promotion and were content with what few advances they did achieve.

Another example is the finding of an unexpectedly small difference in the attitudes toward army life of soldiers stationed in the United States and noncombat troops overseas, despite a considerable difference in objective deprivation. Stouffer and his colleagues analyze the problem as follows:

In general, it is, of course, true that the overseas soldiers, relative to soldiers still at home, suffered a greater break with home ties and with many of the amenities of life in the United States . . . but it was also true that, relative to the combat soldiers the overseas soldier (in rear areas of an active theater) not in combat and not likely to get into combat suffered far less deprivation than the actual fighting man. (Stouffer, Suchman, et al., 1949: 172)

Again, the explanation offered by the authors for the attitudes among the non-combat overseas troops rests on inferences regarding the type of comparisons with fellow soldiers that individuals were making.

Formal Definitions and Models

Davis (1959) enumerates a total of 11 such instances of relative deprivation reasoning in the *American Soldier*. In an attempt to explain them, Stouffer and colleagues used the term *relative deprivation*. Yet as Merton and Kitt (1950) note, a formal definition of relative deprivation is lacking in the writings on the American soldier. The first such definition was advanced by Davis (1959); Its central concept is *social comparison*. Accoring to Davis, relative deprivation is experienced when an individual who lacks something desired compares himself with someone within his *own social group* who has it. When such comparison is made with an out-group member, the resulting attitude is "relative subordination." Davis is able to show that six basic assumptions made by him to formalize relative-deprivation notions fit with ten out of eleven uses of the principle by Stouffer and his colleagues. Moreover—as Pettigrew (1967) notes—Davis also derived additional hypotheses that are not obvious from the original statement of relative deprivation. For example, Davis (1959) hypothesized that, "If a given social category is correlated with objective deprivation, relative deprivation will be more frequent among the deprived in the *more* favored category" (p. 286). This hypothesis explains, for example, the findings of Stouffer and his colleagues showing that older and married soldiers—both belonging to social categories treated very liberally by the draft boards—felt relatively more deprived than younger and single men.

Runciman (1966), who studied attitudes toward social inequality among a probability sample of about 1,400 individuals in England and Wales, made some further theoretical contributions. He used the following sequence of questions as his major research vehicle: (1) "Do you think there are any other sorts of people doing noticeably better at the moment than you and your family?"; (2) (if the person had answered yes) "What sort of people do you think are doing noticeably better?"; and (3) "What do you feel about this, I mean, do you approve or disapprove of this?" (p. 208). The results tended to support the relative-deprivation theory. Specifically, they indicated a considerable discrepancy between objective inequality and relative deprivation and also revealed that "relative deprivation is low in both magnitude and frequency even among those who are close to the bottom of the hierarchy of economic class" (p. 208).

These paradoxes led Runciman to the following question: What is the relationship between the inequalities in a society and the feelings of acquiescence or resentment to which they give rise? Reflections on his own research findings and on the general fact that the unequal distribution of goods and opportunities rarely elicits discontent, either in the overprivileged or in the underprivileged, led Runciman to the proposition that a person

> is relatively deprived of X when (i) he does not have X, (ii) he sees some other person, which may include himself at some previous or expected time, as having X (whether or not this is or will be, in fact, the case), (iii) he wants X, and (iv) he sees it as feasible that he should have X. (p. 10)

In contrast to Runciman, Gurr (1970) was interested in the conditions that lead people to rebel against deprivation. He defined relative deprivation as

> a perceived discrepancy between . . . value expectations and . . . value capabilities [where] value expectations are the goods and conditions of life to which people believe they are rightfully entitled [and] value capabilities are the goods and conditions they think they are capable of attaining or maintaining, given [available] social means. (p. 13)

Williams (1975) argued that the three elements of *wanting, deserving,* and *expecting* (the feasibility element), though perhaps interconnected, should be regarded as *distinct* elements which when not fulfilled lead to distinct results:

1. To receive less than one *wants* (desires, needs) results in a sense of *deprivation*.
2. To receive less than one *expects* results in feelings of *disappointment*.
3. To receive less than is *mandated* by accepted social rules and values (that to which one is entitled) results in a sense of *injustice*. (p. 356)

As may be seen, Williams's definition of justice stresses the role of "accepted social rules" in defining justice, whereas deprivation is defined only in terms of wanting.

In 1976, Crosby proposed a model of relative deprivation that is more elaborate than its predecessors. According to this model, relative deprivation arises when people who lack some object or opportunity (X): (a) want X; (b) feel entitled to X; (c) perceive that someone possesses X; (d) think it feasible to attain X; (e) refuse personal responsibility for their current failure to possess X themselves (Crosby, 1976). If all five preconditions are not met, one of several different emotions results—disappointment, indignation, or jealousy.

Following a distinction made by Cook, Crosby, and Hennigan (1977) between past and future feasibility estimates (past feasibility, or past expectations, refer to a person's previous expectations about attaining some object or opportunity, while future expectations refer to a person's current expectations), Crosby formulated a revised model (Bernstein and Crosby, 1978). This revised model hypothesizes that felt deprivation occurs when past expectations are high while future expectations are low—other things being equal.

Critiques of the Theory

Martin and Murray (1983) note that no relative deprivation theorist has explicitly addressed and clarified the theory's assumptions about perceptual and cognitive processes. They argue that the theory fails to specify how prople process information about comparison with others, especially the dimensions used to establish similarity or dissimilarity with others, and how multiple dimensions are dealt with in this respect: "It is not known how people process information about radically dissimilar comparisons. There is a lack of clarity concerning the continuous and multidimensional nature of similarity" (p. 196).

Crosby and Gonzalez-Intal (1984) note that relative deprivation theorists have been "overly specific": "By focusing on situations in which people are aggrieved about their *own lack of x,* relative deprivation theorists have been blind to situations in which people are aggrieved about *someone else's possession of x*" (p. 149).

Walker and Pettigrew (1984) criticize relative deprivation theory for treating relative deprivation as a purely cognitive variable. In their view, a distinction between *cognitive* and *affective* components within the unitary concept of relative deprivation is essential for gaining important insights into the process and its consequences. The *cognitive* component is a belief reached through making a comparison. The *affective* component involves the centrality of the belief. The following example is given to illustrate the distinction:

> Suppose that B receives a better salary than A, even though they have the same experience and job. If A compares herself with B, A will arrive at the belief that she is deprived relative to B on the dimension of salary (the cognitive component). If neither equality or money is highly valued by A, she may attach scant affect to the belief. But if A places central importance on either equality or money, she may well attach intense affect to the belief (p. 308).

The affective component, the authors argue, may be important for understanding the behavioral effects of felt relative deprivation.

Another criticism of Walker and Pettigrew is that the relationship between relative and absolute deprivation has seldom been examined. They argue that absolute deprivation may be a determinant of relative deprivation, and that the two should be treated as intimately interrelated rather than mutually exclusive. Those states of absolute deprivation that maximize perceptions should be determined, and more attention should be paid to the question "why absolute deprivation often does not translate into relative deprivation" (p. 308).

Walker and Pettigrew (1984) also note that relative deprivation theory shares with other social evaluation theories the problem of failing to *predict* the referents individuals will use for comparison. Like Martin and Murray (1983), these authors also note the lack of attention to the dimensions used in referent selection. They note that the theory fails to explain why certain dimensions of the referent are selected for comparison and others not.

Some criticisms of Walker and Pettigrew (1984) are directed specifically toward certain theorists. They criticize Gurr (1970) and Crosby (1976, 1982) for the solipsistic nature of their theories, for emphasizing intra- and interindividual aspects of the process and neglecting intergroup processes.

Deutsch (1985) accused relative deprivation theorists of being "unconcerned with the many questions related to the social psychological determinants of the preferences for different distributive values (that is different rules of entitlement) or to the social psychological consequences of different distributive systems" (p. 110).

JAQUES' THEORY OF EQUITABLE PAYMENT

In his book *Equitable Payment,* first published in 1961, Jaques proposed a universal theory of "fair payment for work."[1] The theory is based on the findings of a research project by the author extending over several years and encompassing two thousand employees of the Glacier Metal Company (with which the author was associated in a social-analytic consulting capacity) and another thousand employees from five other firms: a heavy engineering firm, a food factory, a bank, a woodworking concern, and a chemical plant—all in the United Kingdom.

Two concepts constitute the backbone of the theory. One is the *felt-fair payment for work*—representing the wage or salary bracket perceived by the employees participating in the research to be fair for the work they were doing. The data relating to the felt-fair payment were obtained from the analyses conducted within a social-analytic relationship.[2]

The second concept is the level of work performed by the participants measured in terms of *timespan of discretion.* The timespan of discretion is defined as "the maximum period of time during which the use of discretion is authorized and expected, without review of that discretion by a superior" (Jaques, 1970: 21).

The author observes that a "totally unexpected" finding was a "regular connexion" between timespan of discretion of the employees and the sum of money which they claimed would constitute fair payment for their work. The author's analysis revealed that individuals in jobs whose range of level of work as measured in timespan was the same, tended in private to regard a very similar wage or salary as fair for the work they were doing—irrespective of their actual wage or salary, type of occupation, position in the hierarchy, and income tax paid.

Jaques calls the pattern of differential payment so derived the *equitable work-payment scale.*

The above finding, says Jaques, suggests the existence of an "unrecognized system of norms of fair payment for any given level of work, *unconscious* knowledge of these norms being *shared* among the population engaged in employment work" (1970: 146; emphases added).

These "intuitive norms," the author states, led him to the concept of equity in describing the scale of felt-fair differential payments. The term equity, he says, is used to express the notion of differentiated treatment of individuals, in accordance with the differential circumstances affecting them—in this case differential levels of work or responsibility they fulfill.

The equitable work-payment scale is described as having the following features, among others:

1. Payment refers to total emoluments (i.e., wage or salary plus any other fringe benefits such as use of car, assistance with purchase of home, etc.)

2. During the years of data collection, the standards of what constitutes equitable payment moved upward, conforming closely percentage-wise, to the wage index. Jaques argues that this finding is not surprising since "equity is concerned with the relative treatment, within any given economy, of individuals *compared with one another,* rather than with any absolute standard of living" (1970: 148; emphasis added).

3. The norms of equity are independent of the amount of income tax paid by individuals.

4. The norms of equity for all hourly- and nonhourly-rated workers are the same regardless of the length of their normal working week.

These shared norms of what constitutes fair pay for any given level of work, says Jaques, strongly influence a person's feeling about his actual pay: "A person's attitude toward the wage or salary packet paid for his work appears to be fundamentally influenced by the extent to which that bracket is consistent with what would be equitable for the range of level of work in his job, or deviates from equity either upwards or downwards" (1970: 153).

The Magnitude of Inequity and Its Impact on Perceived Fairness

According to Jaques, individuals react to conformity or nonconformity between their actual earnings and equitable payment in a characteristic manner, and the intensity of their reaction varies with the size of the discrepancy between the actual and equitable brackets. There are typical reactions in cases of under- and overpayment. The consistency in findings is such that it is possible to predict individual feelings about actual payment if data on the actual and perceived equitable payment are known, and conversely, a person's actual payment can be guessed if data on his perceived equitable payment and on his feelings about his actual payment are known.

The Origins and Economic Conditions of the Equity Norms

Like other theorists, Jaques seeks to answer questions that evoke our interest. For example, why are norms of equity experienced in terms of differential payments structures? The answer may lie in the division of labor: "Differential payment stems from the circumstances of men having to be brought together to produce something" (1970: 175). Because individuals differ in their capacities and not everyone can contribute equally to the final result, not everyone should share equally in the rewards: "There is a conception of each man reaping the just rewards of his own labour which is deepseated in the mind" (p. 175). Payment is essentially not substitutable with other satisfactions to be gained from work and its surroundings: "Payment is the practical and concrete means of expressing the evaluation and recognition of the relative value of a man's work—and in precise quantitative terms" (p. 176). Other psychological factors may be important too, but "if good psychological conditions of work are not matched by equity in pay, they are to a greater or lesser extent negated" (pp. 176–77).

Jaques assumes that the state of the economy affects perceptions of pay equity. For example, under subsistence economy he believes that the "notion of differential reward would be forgone, and would be supplanted by an economic egalitarian outlook" (p. 178). Nevertheless, in his view, an eqalitarian form of distribution is a "temporary and unstable form of distribution—a holding action until greater prosperity is achieved, rather than a form of distribution which fulfills in any lasting way a permanent human need" (p. 179).[3]

What are these needs? Why is it that fairness in a prosperous economy appears to be subservient to a man's being rewarded for his work differentially and in a manner which accords in some way with the level of work he undertakes? Here Jaques presents his main hypothesis to explain the shape of the equitable work-payment scale as follows:

> An equitable distribution of income in an abundant economy is that in which there is *a match* between the payment for any given level of work and the capacity for discriminating expenditure (and satisfaction consumption level) of an individual whose capacity is consistent with that level of work" (p. 189).

At the basis of this hypothesis is the postulate that "there is a direct correspondence between each person's level of capacity for discriminating expenditure [which is also the satisfaction consumption level] and his level of capacity in work" (p. 22). The optimum level of payment is hence that "which will provide a person whose capacity is just up to that work with an income which matches his capacity for discriminating expenditure and his level of satisfaction consumption" (p. 22).

How does the individual recognize his level of capacity and the equitable remuneration? This knowledge, says Jaques, is "built up from small increments of experience in which non-verbalized awareness and ideas—ideas-in-feeling— are repeatedly subject to the testing of reality and modified bit by bit until a moderately realistic set of internal standards is established" (p. 251).

Critiques of Jaques' Work

Jaques' work has not been received with much enthusiasm by other resear- chers interested in the subject. Some have shown a rather harsh attitude toward it (e.g., Beal, 1963; Vroom, 1964). Others, such as Opsahl and Dunnette (1966), have warned (in a milder tone) that its conclusions are highly tentative and must be regarded with caution. A thorough attempt to evaluate Jaques' work and its implications for compensation administration and research was made by Gordon (1969). Gordon's main criticism focuses on Jaques' methodology and especially on the methods employed in investigating the "felt-fair" pay concept. The use by Jaques, of such terms as "unrecognized system of norms," "unconscious awareness," and "unconscious knowledge" in describing his data creates the impression that "we cannot merely accept the straightforward verbal responses of a worker. Rather, the employee's initial conscious estimates must be modified in some respect through interaction with the interviewer in order to determine the interviewee's 'true,' unconscious compensation expectations" (p. 375).

There are no adequate published instructions for other investigators to recognize when an interviewee has reached the level of "unconscious awareness," says Gordon. This precludes replication and evaluation of the method. The potential of interviewer bias is great in the absence of clear established criteria for perceiving an interviewee's "system of unrecognized norms."

> Altogether then, the hypothesized relationships incorporated in the theory appear to be unverifiable because the theoretical constructs which they em- brace lack unambiguous operational definitions. In order to become func- tional, Jaques's system must be redefined in such a manner that the em- pirical constructs can be measured unambiguously and become amenable to intersubjective testability (p. 376).

While Jaques argues that "felt-fair" pay depends on a comparison with others rather than on the magnitude of pay itself, Gordon says that "the definition, iden- tity, and importance of the social referent and the pay-related dimension [of com- parison] are not presented explicitly in Jaques' theory of equity" (p. 381). In addition, Gordon notes, Jaques failed to report variances or any other measures of dispersion for the distribution of judgments of felt-fair pay but indicated only that there were but slight variations. In principle, rather large variations would be expected since other studies (e.g., Patchen, 1961; Andrews and Henry, 1963; Andrews, 1967) indicate that a number of factors influence the notion of equity.

The small variations found by Jaques, Gordon argues, must be due to his interviewing technique. If so, how does this technique operate? Does it account in any way for the various extraneous variables that have been shown to affect equity notions?

EXCHANGE THEORIES

In the early 1960s, three major works were published that constituted the first links in an impressive chain of research on justice in social exchange. The first of these is Homans' (1961, 1974) work on *distributive justice*. Next is Adams' (1963a, 1965) work on *equity theory* which, though using a somewhat different terminology, adopts Homans' basic ideas and attempts to elaborate on them. Blau's (1964) study on *fair exchange* is a third major link in the chain.

These works grew out of earlier research in social psychology and have essentially a similar perspective on justice in social exchange. This perspective is based first on the notion that social exchange is guided by the norm of contribution, specifying that rewards should be allocated in proportion to contributions made; and secondly, that for a person to regard his proportional rewards as fair he must perceive them as equal to the proportional rewards received by some comparison person(s). But as will become evident below, there are some significant differences between the theories. Following is a short description of each theory, its basic postulates and underpinning assumptions.

Homans' Theory of Distributive Justice

The central concept in Homans' work (1961, 1974) is distributive justice, which he defined as "justice in the distribution of rewards and costs between persons" (1974, p. 74). In presenting the problem, Homans used an example from one of his field studies, involving ledger clerks and cash posters in an accounting division (Homans, 1953). The two groups worked side by side but differed in their major tasks. The cash posters' task was to post customers' payments. This job is described by the author as the only "production" job in the accounting division that had to keep up-to-date on a daily basis. While the job had little variety, it allowed a great deal of movement between files. The ledger clerks' jobs involved everything necessary to keep the accounts up to date, except cash posting. They had a number of nonrepetitive clerical jobs requiring some thought but little physical mobility. All cash posters and ledger clerks were women. The regular line of promotion was from cash poster to ledger clerk; therefore ledger clerks were older and had more seniority in the company. Yet both groups received the same pay. Sometimes ledger clerks were transferred to cash posting temporarily—to keep the daily posting up.

In the interviews conducted during the research it became clear that the women performing the two jobs tended to compare them as more, or less rewarding or costly along a number of dimensions such as pay, seniority, chance for advancement, variety, and responsibility. They did not all rank the jobs similarly on every dimension but agreed on most rankings and shared most values. It also emerged that ledger clerks thought they were unjustly treated in comparison with cash posters: They felt that pay should not be equal since their jobs were more responsible. They also complained of being "put down on posting," which they saw as inferior in status and autonomy. The complaints, said Homans, are typical in industry and arouse the problem "of wage differentials—not of the absolute amount of wages but differences between groups in their wage rates" (Homans, 1974: 244). The problem of distributive justice, as Homans sees it, is one of relative differentials and not of absolute amounts.

Analytical Concepts and Definitions. Using the above example Homans developed his argumentation as follows. The dimensions of status along which the employees ranked the two jobs may be divided into three separate classes: (1) *reward* dimensions (i.e., what people got from a job—pay, variety, intrinsic interest, e.g.); (2) *cost* dimensions (i.e., what people gave to a job or what they gave up—responsibility, worry about making mistakes, peace of mind forgone); (3) besides these dimensions for ranking jobs there were dimensions for ranking people doing the job (e.g., sex, seniority). These are background characteristics in which some were "better" than others. Homans uses the term *investments* for these dimensions. Costs, investments, and rewards, says Homans, are not objective data but are as perceived by members of a group.

According to Homans, individuals cannot decide if the rewards they receive are fair unless they compare them with those received by another person: In the absence of an absolute standard a person must compare his reward with that of others and decide by the rule of distributive justice if he is receiving his due. And further: "If his investments and what he gives are taken as fixed and higher than or equal to those of another, but what he gets (his rewards) are equal or lower respectively he is a victim of distributive injustice." (1974: 248). Distributive justice will prevail when the following relationship between "person" and "other" exists:

$$\frac{P_1}{P_2} = \frac{R_1}{R_2}$$

where P_1 and P_2 are ego and alter and R_1 and R_2 are ego's and alter's rewards.

Homans' theory of distributive justice rests, as is evident, on the following assumptions: (1) that in social exchange people have subjective perceptions of costs, investments, and rewards; (2) that they evaluate (rank) these costs, investments and rewards and summarize somehow all the rewards, costs, and investments; and (3) that they compare their (summarized) costs and investments and their (summarized) rewards with those of others. If the ratios of investments/costs are equal to the ratios of rewards the person perceives a state of distributive justice.

Concerning the comparison with others, Homans believes that individuals are likely to compare themselves with those who are to some degree *close* or *similar*.

Homans perceives two reasons why comparisons will be with similar people. One is that, "One's own investments, contributions, rewards, must be at least similar enough to the other's to be ranked along the same dimension" (1974: 252). The second is that if the comparison person is similar at least in belonging to the same larger social unit, some means is likely to exist to change the comparer's rewards accordingly.

Homans goes on to argue that an individual who perceives himself as unjustly treated will display emotional behavior, reacting with anger and aggression. However, with the passage of time a given distribution of reward is likely to become perceived as just: "any distribution of reward, however unjust it may have appeared at one time, that does in fact persist long enough—but how long is that?—to become the expected thing will also become the just thing and cease to arouse resentment . . . whatever is, is always on the way to becoming right." (1974: 263).

The Scope of the Distributive Justice Principle. Homans expressed the belief, while admitting inadequate evidence, that adherence to the principle of distributive justice is not confined to one society or a particular historical age:

> Distributive justice is either explicitly stated or stands as an implicit major premise in the arguments and behavior of many men in many, and probably all, human societies. . . . The rule of distributive justice is a statement of what ought to be, and what people say ought to be is determined in the long run and with some lag by what they find in fact to be the case. (1974: 249-50)

However, says Homans, while people accept the same general rule of distributive justice they may not always agree on what is a fair distribution and may differ over what legitimately constitutes investment, contribution and reward and the ranking of persons and groups on these dimensions (1974: 250). Moreover, what is considered legitimate investments, contributions or rewards changes periodically in many societies; in fact, such agreement exists only for rather brief spans of time and among small groups of men. Concensus is indeed easier to achieve among persons who have acquired similar values through similar experience and similar backgrounds, but even here consensus is fragile (p. 251).

Adams' Theory of Inequity

Adams (1963a, 1965) refers explicitly to Homans's concept of distributive justice, as well as to the concept of relative deprivation of Stouffer and his colleagues (1949a and b). Like Homans, Adams presents his formulation in the form of an equation. The term used here is *equity*. According to Adams, equity exists when the following relationship prevails:

$$\frac{O_p}{I_p} = \frac{O_a}{I_a} \quad \text{where } p = \text{person, } a = \text{other, and } O = \Sigma oi, \, I = \Sigma ii$$

i.e., when the ratio of person's outcomes (O) to person's inputs (I) is equal to the ratio of another's outcomes to another's inputs. The major ingredients in Adams' formulation are *outcomes* (Homans' rewards), *inputs* (Homans' investments/costs) and the comparison with others. Like Homans, Adams postulates that inputs and outcomes are *as perceived* by the person. Regarding inputs, Adams emphasizes two distinct characteristics: *recognition* and *relevance*. The existence of an attribute in a possessor may be recognized or not. If the attribute is recognized and, in addition, perceived as relevant to the exchange it is an input. Problems of inequity arise, says Adams, only if the possessor of the attribute considers it relevant in the exchange. Adams uses an illustration from Crozier's (1964) study: In a government check-clearing agency, Paris-born clerks worked side by side with clerks who did identical work and received identical wages but were born outside Paris. The Parisians, who considered Parisian breeding as an input deserving monetary compensation, were dissatisfied with their wages. However, the management did indeed recognize the distinction between the two groups but did not consider it relevant to the issue of pay differentials.

According to Adams, "There exist *normative expectations* of what constitute 'fair' correlations between inputs and outcomes. The bases of the expectation are the correlations obtaining for a reference person or group" (1963a: 425; emphasis added). He believes that in a given society individuals tend to have similar views on what constitutes a fair or unfair input/outcome relation:

> To that extent that he [the individual] shares the same culture [with others], his psychological reaction will be similar to theirs. The larger the cultural group, the greater will be the number of individuals who perceive similarly and react similarly to a given set of relations between inputs and outcomes. . . .In a given society, even ours, there is usually enough invariance in fundamental beliefs and attitudes to make reasonably accurate general predictions. (p. 425).

We note here that Adams's view on the latter subject differs substantially from Homans's, a point we shall return to later.

Blau's Theory of Fair Exchange

While Blau (1964: Ch. 6) sees his concept of "fair exchange" as close to Homans's concept of distributive justice and tends to accept Homans's formulation basically, he makes some important contributions of his own. These lie mainly in his attempt to place the concept of fair exchange in the larger context of social expectations. Thus Blau, like Adams, contends that notions of fair exchange "are governed by *social norms* that define what fair rates of exchange are" (Blau, p. 145; emphasis added). In this respect he distinguishes between the *fair rate* and the *going rate* (i.e., the rate established in the course of exchange). The going rate is governed by the market forces of supply and demand. In contrast, the social norms governing conceptions of fair exchange "have their ultimate source in the society's need for this service and the investment required to supply it" (p. 155).

> The fair and joint rate both rest on social expectations, though of different kinds: The going rate . . . gives rise to expectations that certain returns will be received for certain services. Whereas these standards of expectation are not moral norms but merely anticipations that influence conduct, the normative expectations . . . are *moral* standards the violation of which evokes social disapproval (pp. 155–156; emphasis added).

In discussing the formation of expectations, Blau notes the crucial role of past social experiences and of comparison with others. Thus he contends that individuals acquire reference standards "partly as the result of the benefits they themselves have obtained in the past, and partly as the result of learning what others in comparable situations obtain" (p. 143).

The dynamics are as follows: (1) Past attainments influence future expectations: "[They] modify . . . expectations of what rewards can be realized and indeed what rewards need to be realized . . . and these altered expectations, in turn, affect the significance of future rewards" (p. 147); (2) Levels of aspiration (and expectations) are also influenced by the known standards of achievement in one's membership group and in other groups. Individuals are less likely to be satisfied with high rewards in a group where most others receive high rewards than in group where others receive fewer rewards. Aspirations tend to rise if a given standard of achievement prevails in an inferior group, and to fall if a given standard of achievement prevails in a superior group.

Summary and Discussion

All the exchange theories share a number of basic features.

1. The distributive principle governing notions of fair reward is held to be the contribution or equity principle, i.e., allocation should be proportional to the recipients' contributions to the profit to be allocated.
2. Each of the two basic components—rewards and contributions—are as perceived by the individual: rewards and contributions have to be first recognized as such and second considered as relevant to the exchange.
3. Rewards, as well as contributions, are multiple.
4. Judgments of fair reward involve a process of comparison with others.

But on other basic issues there is less agreement. Regarding individuals' notions about the relevancy of certain rewards and contributions, their origin and their durability, Homans (1974) suggests that they derive from similar values acquired through similar life experiences stemming from a similar social background. This leads to the twofold conclusion that wide social consensus on these matters is usually not to be expected, and that the notions themselves are likely to change rather frequently in response to changes in the social structure. Adams (1963), however, believes that the notions about relevant rewards and contributions are part and parcel of society's cultural heritage. This view, emphasizing the normative nature of the notions, suggests relatively long durability and a substantial measure of social consensus on these matters.

On individuals' notions about fair rates of exchange and their origins and durability, Homans again emphasizes their relatively low durability. He postulates a twofold dynamic: Notions about fair rates of exchange may change because of changed conceptions concerning the relevancy and weight of inputs or contributions. Changes in such notions may also occur because an input/outcome relationship once perceived as unfair may, in time, come to be perceived as fair since "whatever is, is always on the way to becoming right." Adams believes that notions of fair rates of exchange between inputs and outcomes are based on "the correlations obtaining for a reference person or group." In a sense, this latter postulate also suggests, like Homans's that "whatever is, is on the way to becoming right." Blau, however, draws a line between the "going rate"—Adams's "correlations" and Homans's "is"—and the perceived fair rate. He suggests that the normative expectations about fair exchange rates originate in society's need for the various services and the investments required to supply them. The two rates, (i.e., going and fair) might, on occasion, coincide in real life; yet in principle they are two different things that have different social origins.

Critiques of the Exchange Theories

The exchange theories, and most of all the equity version, have been severely criticized, to the point that doubts have been cast on their very foundations and scientific usefulness (e.g., Miner, 1984). A wide range of issues has been scrutinized, but several major foci are discernible. One concerns the comparison process: Although the comparison with others is central to all exchange theories, they are charged with being flawed regarding the selection and use of referents. For example, the proposition that referents are chosen from among similar people has been said to be very vague, since there may be many dimensions on which the comparer and the compared are similar or dissimilar (e.g., Martin, 1981; Cook and Parcel, 1977). Which of the manifold dimensions are relevant to the comparison? Is it one particular dimension or several dimensions, and what are they? How stable through time are the referents used? (e.g., Weick, 1966). Do individuals change their referents according to circumstances, and if they do—under what circumstances and what are the accompanying changes? (e.g., Austin, 1977).

Exchange theories have also been criticized for focusing exclusively on interindividual comparisons. Berger and colleagues (1972) asserted that interindividual comparisons are not really sufficient for a justice process. They argued that if an individual compares himself with another, he cannot determine if he is rewarded equitably, underrewarded or overrewarded. If, for example, P is paid $3.52 per hour and O is paid $4.33 per hour, does this mean that P is underpaid, or that P is equitably paid and O is overpaid? Or perhaps both are overpaid, or underpaid (both cases of collective injustice). An answer to these questions is possible only if P's and O's payment are compared to the pay *typical* for the work they are doing. For example, if P and O are mechanics, the typical hourly pay for mechanics should serve as a criterion. Generally, argue Berger and colleagues, focusing on interindividual comparisons obscures the justice process. First, some states that are just may be identified as unjust and vice versa. Second, collective injustice cannot be distinguished from individual injustice. Third, it is difficult to distinguish situations of overreward from those of underreward. Finally, situations in which P is unjustly rewarded cannot be distinguished from situations where O is unjustly rewarded.

Martin and Murray (1983) argued that the exclusive focus on interindividual comparisons is reductionist and eliminates consideration of higher levels of analysis. "Some theoretically important issues, such as the distinction between the powerful and the powerless, surface only when aggregates are directly or indirectly considered" (p. 178). The authors also claim that the emphasis on comparison with similar persons makes the discovery of large inequalities less likely.

Another major theoretical ingredient, the dimensions of evaluation, also comes under a variety of criticisms. One is that only vague outlines as to which inputs and outcomes will be perceived as relevant are provided (e.g., Deutsch, 1985). Another is that the theories fail to specify in detail the process by which relevancy is determined (e.g., Goodman and Friedman, 1971; Cook and Parcel, 1977). Moreover, inputs and outcomes may not be clearly distinguishable, may be interchangeable, or may be highly correlated (e.g., Weick, 1966; Cook and Parcel, 1977). A popular example in this context is responsibility. The question posed is whether responsibility is a reward, a cost, or both. If inputs and outcomes are indeed not clearly distinguished, a major condition underlying the assumption of additivity of inputs and outcomes—the independent perception of inputs and outcomes—is not fulfilled.

Another criticism has been that exchange theories are not capable of explaining well the significance of status characteristics included in their tentative lists of inputs. Such criticism was made by Berger, Zelditch, Anderson, and Cohen (1972), who stated: "Thus education and seniority might be thought of as effort expended to acquire high skill, but it is hard to see that age, sex, race or ethnicity can be looked at in the same way" (p. 126). Berger and colleagues also argued that the various formulations are not capable of accounting for the significance in justice perceptions of small reward differentials. The ledger clerks described by Homans are a case in point: "It seems that they [ledger clerks] ought to get just a few dollars more to show that their job is more important" (1961: 240). This symbolic aspect of reward differentials, the concern of the ledger clerks over a small pay differential that could symbolize their higher status vis-à-vis the cash posters, Berger and colleagues argue, has no place in the various exchange formulations.

Questions have also been raised concerning issues of information processing and information combination. None of the theories specify with sufficient detail and precision how the various inputs and outcomes proposed as relevant are combined to form a final justice evaluation (e.g., Goodman and Friedman, 1971; Austin, 1977).

All the exchange theories have been criticized for their monistic approach. They assume that the equity or contribution principle is the *sole* principle guiding the fairness evaluation of reward and that the other distribution principles such as equality, the equal distribution of rewards, or the distribution of rewards according to individual need are irrelevant (e.g., Lerner, 1975; Leventhal, 1976a; Cook and Parcel, 1977; Schwinger, 1980).

A related criticism is that exchange theories ignore completely the contextual factors of exchange relationships (e.g., Austin and Hatfield, 1980). Austin (1979: 133) uses the term *justicization* to indicate "a natural inclination to make sense of an act against the context in which it occurs." Thus, "in its broadest sense equity means that to be judged fair the matter in question must be seen as *appropriate for the context in which it occurs*" (Austin, p. 132; emphasis added).

Deutsch (1985) argued that exchange theories have neglected the interactional aspects of the exchange relationship and the negotiating or bargaining aspects involved in the participants' coming to a mutually acceptable definition of equity. Deutsch (1985) as well as others (e.g., Utne and Kidd, 1980) also argued that exchange theories have paid little attention to attribution processes. The basic argument is that causal attribution and the attribution of responsibility for a given reward distribution are central to understanding the conditions of perceived equity or inequity. Utne and Kidd (1980) argue in this context that usually individuals who are party to injustice "almost always have some information or at least speculate about *why* the inequity came about" (p. 67). Individuals often deal with the "discomfort of inequity" by seeking additional information on its causes. Specifically, the information sought is about the causes of inequity, its stability/ instability over time, its controllability and intentionality, and the degree of personal responsibility for its existence. Another line of criticism is the inattention of exchange theories to procedures that generate a given distribution of rewards (e.g., Leventhal, 1980).

THE STATUS VALUE THEORY

The status value theory formulated by Berger and his colleagues (1972; 1983) grew out of dissatisfaction with the exchange theories, as discussed above. Here we concentrate on the status value theory itself and its major components. The theory "is concerned with evaluations of worth, esteem or honor" (1972: 128). The formation of reward expectations is one of its major concerns: Reward expections reflect the status significance of rewards, not just their consummatory value. Status significance is defined as "honorific significance" (1972: 128). According to the theory, how rewards are distributed has status meaning for the individual and the implications for his esteem, self-esteem, and honor can be far-reaching. When reward distribution does not follow the expected pattern, people react strongly and feel outraged owing to the implications for their honor and esteem rather than the economic implications. The status value theorists argue that here status value theory is more successful than exchange theory in explaining the moral indignation of individuals facing a digression from an expected reward pattern. Say the authors: "but proportionality of rewards has neither the shared nor the moral character such expectations have in fact. The moral character of justice is one of its special peculiarities" (1972: 126). They further argue that exchange theorists have indeed pointed to the indignation of the underrewarded and the guilt of the overrewarded. "But the theory itself has treated anger and guilt as individual reactions to injustice, not as aspects of the moral character of the process" (126).

The theory has several basic components that enfold a niumber of key concepts. A major postulate is that an individual's status characteristics constitute a major basis for reward expectations. A *status characteristic*—a key concept in the theory—is defined as a characteristic of an actor that has two or more states that are differentially evaluated in terms of honor, esteem, or desirability, each of which is associated with distinct moral and performance expectations. Another key concept is *referential structure*; that is, "the socially validated beliefs that describe how the states of valued characteristics that individuals possess are associated with differences in reward levels" (Berger, et al., 1983: 133). A given referential structure is activated "when actors have developed expectations for rewards in a specific status situation on the basis of that structure" (p. 134). According to Berger and his colleagues, the concept of referential structure includes the following major ideas:

> First, referential structures describe *distribution principles*, that are thought to be true as a matter of social fact. . . . Second, they represent *socially shared beliefs* rather than idiosyncratic conceptions, and as such, they involve beliefs about *generalized actors* in some larger social context, as, for example, in the belief (again where held) that, in American society, the more highly educated are more highly rewarded. Third and most important, referential structures can serve as *generalized standards*, on the basis of which individuals come to develop expectations for rewards in specific situations. (p. 133; emphases added)

For a distributive process to unfold, the referential structure must have three fundamental properties (Berger, et al., 1972: 134–35). First, it must be unitary; that is, it must fulfill the condition that two objects that differ significantly in status value are not both asscociated with the same "generalized individual."

Second, it must be differentiated; that is, both the low and high states of a characteristic and the low and high states of a goal object must be contained in it. Third, the referential structure must be balanced because otherwise it is unstable.

Status value theorists, like the exchange theorists, recognize that multiple inputs are combined in arriving at judgments of fairness in reward allocation. Similarly, they also believe that comparisons with others are an important component in the process of evaluating the fairness of received rewards. In contrast to exchange theorists, they argue, however, as noted, that "local" comparisons where individuals compare themselves with other individuals cannot, in essence, supply an adequate standard of evaluation. Such a standard can be supplied only by "referential" comparisons, whereby individuals compare themselves with a "generalized other" such as an occupational group or a social class. Only referential comparisons can supply the criteria needed for distinguishing between justice and injustice, between over- and underreward, between individual and collective justice.

Critiques of the Status Value Theory

Cook and Parcel (1977) level a number of criticisms against status value theory. They argue that the theory is very limited in scope: It deals only with situations in which the status significance of goal objects or rewards, not their consummatory value, is paramount. This scope condition, they maintain, is unduly restrictive since it defines situations where distributive justice or equity considerations supersede the consummatory value of outcomes as outside the scope of the theory.

A further condition narrowing scope is the requirement that only one referential structure and one social characteristic (in the local system) serve as the basis for the justice evaluation. If more than one referential structure is activated and conflicting expectations ensue, how are these resolved? What determines which referential structure will be perceived as relevant to a given situation and how is the similarity of elements assessed? In fact, argue the authors, the similarity and dissimilarity relation between elements in the referential structure and elements in the local system are taken as given. In addition, they point out that the theory states that expectations in the local system about "what ought to be" form on the basis of beliefs about what is typically the case, but:

> Do normative expectations, however, emerge in the local system regardless of the specific 'content' of the referential structure? According to Brandt, 'similarities and differences should form the basis of action if it is to be just, but not all of them are relevant'; the question is 'which of them are just or unjust making?' (1962: 10). (Cook and Parcel, 1977: 80)

Markovsky (1985a) noted that many important concepts of the theory are primitive (undefined) or only denotatively defined (defined by example). . . . These include *goal object, characteristic, generalized individual, status value,* and *referential structure,* although the last was discussed at some length and quite explicitly characterized. . . . However, this characterization does not achieve the level of precision of the defined concepts. (p. 207)

He also noted that the theory cannot deal with degrees of departures from justice (p. 208) and that it does not recognize the relevance of local comparisons but only that of referential comparisons: "The authors of the theory imply that multiple actors are required in the local situation, in spite of the fact that this clearly need not be the case" (p. 209). Nor does the theory deal with collective injustice. Still, Markovsky commends the theory for being well formulated in terms of the assessment criteria, and for having constructed a conceptual system that is highly clear and parsimonious (pp. 209–10).

NOTES

1. A revised edition of Jaques' work which appeared in 1970 serves as the basis for the present review.

2. The major features of this social-analytic relationship are described as follows: (a) all discussions were carried out at the personal request of the member(s) concerned; (b) the discussions were confidential; (c) no executive action whatsoever was initiated by the researcher as a result of the discussions, their purpose being to help members clarify their own views; and (d) the researcher did not report on individual members to anyone else (Jaques, 1970: 145).

3. What is an abundant economy? Jaques hypothesizes that it is at a level close to those areas in the United States where affluence is widespread (1970: p. 191).

3 New Theoretical Refinements

The foregoing chapter has placed us at crossroads: The different paradigms suggest different solutions to the issue at hand. The picture is even further complicated in that the initial theories "skimmed" over many fundamental issues involved in the basic question. This chapter addresses the questions that have been left open and the attempts of theorists to deal with them. Most of these attempts have been made by researchers inspired by the original formulations—those following in the footsteps of the pioneers and trying to improve on them. But some have arisen as critiques of these, or have followed independent paths. Today, most of the work is still conducted within the confines of particular theoretical streams but the boundaries seem less firm than in the past. Over the years some researchers have ventured to cast their eyes at work done beyond the borders of their territory, some have been inspired by what they have seen, and some have even been tempted to try to build bridges between the streams.

Indeed, the work that has been done still bears the imprint of the original formulations and continues to display very different views about various aspects of the subject. But today, far more than in the past, one is aware that these separate streams also contain many elements that can complement each other, dealing with different facets of the problem rather than being variations on the same theme. This impression has led to the decision to ignore the dividing lines between the theories and present the more recent theoretical developments and empirical findings as if these lines did not exist. Instead of pursuing the thinking of specific theoretical streams or specific researchers the review will focus on the thinking revolving round the central elements of the issue under discussion. In our view these are: the norms of distribution guiding the fairness evaluation process, the standards of comparison used in it, and the dimensions of evaluation underlying it. At the end of the chapter we shall briefly return to the specific theoretical streams—to present some relatively recent attempts to compare and integrate a few of them.

Before proceeding, it is important to note that the work to be reviewed involves a great number of writings scattered throughout the literature. An attempt is made here to treat those propositions that in our view contain some fruitful ideas about issues left open by the initial formulations and to organize them in a way that will, as we see it, best reflect their potential contribution to the issue at hand.

THE UNDERLYING DISTRIBUTION RULES

The theories reviewed suggest that in evaluating a given reward, individuals are guided by some distribution norm or rule. For example, the exchange theories propose the equity or contribution rule, specifying the proportionality of rewards and contributions as the major guiding rule, whereas status value theory assigns this to rank or status. While the theories disagree on what the guiding rules or principles are, none has felt obliged to refer systematically to the rules that might, in principle, govern the justice process. Each presented its own particular version and "logic" without paying much attention to existing alternatives. In the 1970s, however, out of a critique of equity theory, a number of attempts were made to conceptualize, analyze, and present systematic lists of rules that might in principle apply. Deutsch (1975), for example, listed the following key values in the just treatment of people: effort, ability, need, investments or inputs, equality, accomplishments, equal opportunity, reciprocity, requirements of the common good, market supply and demand, and the maintenance of a specified minimum of outcomes. The number of principles or values listed by different authors varies: Reis (1984), for example, enumerated 17. Other authors referred to a much shorter list (e.g., Leventhal, 1976a). The *contribution* principle, specifying that rewards should be allocated according to contributions made, the *equality* principle, specifying that rewards should be allocated equally, and the *need* principle, specifying that rewards should be allocated according to needs, are considered the most fundamental and important distribution rules.

Different Rules for Different Conditions

The systematic analysis of distribution rules was generated by the idea that different distribution rules might apply under different conditions. A number of theoreticians formulated some propositions in line with this idea (e.g., Lerner, 1974; Deutsch, 1975, 1985; Sampson, 1975; Leventhal, 1976a). Leventhal (1976a), for example, observed that the *predictability* that any norm allows and the *benefits* associated with a particular norm may serve as important determinants of the particular norm adhered to. For instance, he proposed that the equity or the contribution rule will be used to enhance efficiency and maximize productivity since it is most appropriate for the achievement of such goals. Here, distribution may be directed at and tailored according to such subgoals as the efficient use of resouces, the control of group membership, and the encouragement of high performance and productivity. By contrast, the equality rule will be used where conflict avoidance and group harmony are of primary importance. This emphasis on the benefits associated with particular allocation norms focuses attention on the rational and instrumental aspects of allocbation norms. Indeed in Leventhal's view, allocators may be driven by justice and fairness motives as well as by rational-calculative motives related to the instrumental benefits associated with following a particular allocation norm.

Deutsch (1975, 1985) argued that where "economic productivity is a primary goal equity or contribution, rather than equality or need, will be the dominant principle of distributive justice" (1985: 38). Lerner and his colleagues (1976) suggested that the equity or contribution principle will predominate in situations characterized by "unit relationships" rather than by "identity relationships," and where individuals perceive others as "positions" rather than "persons." By contrast, parity or equality will predominate where identity relationships prevail and where others are perceived as persons rather than positions. Unit relationships are defined as relationships where people

> do not 'see' themselves in each other, but there is a perception of 'belonging to' similar to Heider's (1958) sense of the term. There is no emphatic connection but an awareness of a bond which links the participants. Unit relations most often appear where there is a strong perception of similarity and/or promotive interdependence (Lerner et al., 1976: 155).

The meaning of the term position "is similar to that of role behavior and status, in that considerations 'attached' to it are essentially independent of the individual occupant. . . . It is a relational concept and is often derived from our functions and place in a social organization" (p. 154).

Sampson (1975) argued that it is necessary to examine justice conceptions and the distribution rules applied in a historical, social, and psychological framework: "equity is neither natural, inevitable, or even functionally necessary to solving societal and interpersonal issues of distribution; that equality is an equally viable alternative; that the preference for equity over equality reflects *a particular historical and cultural pattern* which presently dominates Western civilization" (p. 61; emphases added).

Some researchers went a step further and suggested that situations may arise where various rules might be applied in *combination* or *sequentially* to determine the ultimate just or fair reward distribution (e.g., Leventhal 1976b; Cook and Yamagishi, 1983; Folger, 1984b). Others, however turned attention to the fact that incompatible or contradictory allocation principles may be a source of conflict. For example, Törnblom (1988) in a recent paper pointed out that such incompatibility may be the source of group-individual conflicts (when individual and group goals are incompatible); interindividual conflicts (when individuals have incompatible conceptions about allocation principles); or, intraindividual conflicts (when individuals perceive several incompatible principles as relevant). Lansberg (1984) proposed a contingency model which assesses the congruency between institutional, situational, and individual factors. Several authors addressed themselves to the possible sources of such conflicts, especially the group-individual conflict, and the ways these conflicts may be resolved (e.g., Simpson, 1976: 6; Leventhal, Karuza, and Fry, 1980: 182–83; Jasso, 1983: 186; Törnblom, 1988).

Obviously, the postulates proposing the relevance to the justice-evaluation process of a variety of distribution rules present a serious challenge to the monistic theories proposing a single distribution rule as the basis of such a process.

Equity theorists such as Walster and colleagues (1976, 1978) met the challenge to equity theory by reformulating this theory and extending the range of phenomena to which it is applicable. They extended it to explaining exploitative relationships, helping relationships, and intimate relationships. Each of these is seen essentially as an exchange relationship. The definition of inputs is extended too:

> In different settings people consider different inputs to be relevant. For example in industrial settings, businessmen assume that such hard assets as 'capital' or 'manual labor' entitle a man to reward. . . . In social settings, friends assume that social assets such as beauty or kindness entitle one to reward. (1978: 12)

The reformulation essentially reinterprets all justice principles as variations on the contribution principle. This is achieved through the reformulation of inputs; anything can be an input entitling one to reward: need, investment, or even "humanity". In this way, special rules such as need, contribution, or equality become redundant.

The attempt by Walster and colleagues (1976, 1978) to extend equity theory in this way was met with criticism by other authors (e.g., Sampson, 1980; Deutsch, 1985). For example, Deutsch (1986) argues: "This kind of ad hoc stretching of the term *input* and *outcome* makes them completely devoid of meaning" (p. 80). Austin and Hatfield (1980) also believe that other distribution principles such as equality or need should be treated as "markedly different from proportionality" (p. 50).

The Institutionalization of Justice Rules

The monistic theories by nature, do not generally deal extensively with the question of the institutionalization of the particular distribution rule proposed by them, as they view it as natural. Homans, for example, argued that "even if these rules were not taught to the young, they would discover it anew for themselves every generation" (1974: 249–50). Similar views are expressed by other exchange theorists as well as by Jaques (1970). But the postulate that different distribution rules may be relevant in different situations necessarily focuses attention on the process by which different norms come to be applied in different situations. Stolte (1987a) addressed this question.[1] He suggests that norms are institutionalized to encourage, sustain, or compel actions "which would not otherwise be undertaken," actions that are costly and not in the individual's immediate self-interest but are in the collectivity's interest. He further proposed that, once formed, norms are internalized through a process of socialization that occurs when persons "move in social careers across the life cycle through the complex exchange structural environment" (p. 200). While moving into and through normatively governed collectivities, individuals "are frequently socialized, and under certain conditions internalize various norms" (p. 201). These internalized norms are then activated in local exchange situations encountered subsequently by the individual at any given point of time.

THE STANDARDS OF COMPARISON

Comparison with others is a central element in all the initial formulations: All assume that justice evaluation processes are largely based on comparisons with relevant others. But all leave many open questions regarding this issue, its specific meanings and applications. In subsequent work several types of comparisons are distinguished, and propositions are made, concerning the process of comparison and its determinants. Together, these developments brought new theoretical depth to the subject, opened new avenues for empirical investigation, and supplied new and more refined analytical tools with which to carry out this investigation.

Types of Comparisons

Concerning types of comparisons, several distinctions were made as follows. *Local Versus Referential Comparisons.* As indicated earlier, these twin concepts have been introduced by status value theorists criticizing the exchange theories for their conceptualization of comparisons. According to these theorists (e.g., Zelditch, Berger, Anderson, and Cohen, 1970) a distinction needs to be made between local comparisons and referential comparisons. A local comparison is one with another individual or with other individuals, while a referential comparison is one with a general social type. These authors argue that local comparisons cannot really produce a distributive justice process since such comparisons do not contain a stable external reference point, which, they assert, is a necessary condition for a process of distributive justice. This condition can be fulfilled only by referential comparisons—comparisons with a general social type.

Törnblom (1977a, 1977b, 1982) developed a typology of equity comparisons in which he introduces referential comparisons in addition to local comparisons. He asserts that the major types of equity comparisons are comparisons between Person and Other, as mediated by the comparison of each with the Reference Person.

Austin (1977) notes that local and referential comparisons "occupy opposing extremes on a proximity or 'closeness continuum' " (p. 290). Referential comparisons, in contrast to local comparisons, are by definition removed from any given situation. Local comparisons, Austin notes, may also vary in how close they are to a relationship, and may be subdivided into *partner* comparisons (e.g., colleague, spouse, neighbor) and *third party* comparisons (e.g., employer, mutual friend). These distinctions seem important in the employment situation where employees interact with an employer (third party) and with other employees (partners/third party) and where other more remote groups of "generalized others" may easily become salient for the individual employee because of the tendency of employing organizations to standardize their dealings with individuals and to categorize them into groups when dealing with them.

Comparisons with Similars or Dissimilars. Another important theoretical addition is the distinction between similars and dissimilars as comparison referents. Runciman (1966), a major contributor to relative-deprivation theory, distinguished between *egoistic deprivation,*—a feeling of deprivation that occurs when an individual feels deprived vis-à-vis similars (i.e., fellow in-group members) and *fraternal deprivation*—a feeling of deprivation that occurs when an individual feels that his/her membership group is deprived vis-à-vis another nonmembership group. Vanneman and Pettigrew (1972) defined fraternal deprivation as comparisons with other out-group members rather than comparisons between groups. Martin and Murray (1983) offered a reformulation of both concepts:

> Egoistic deprivation should be redefined as based upon a comparison to an individual or a group that is similar on the dimensions considered relevant to the comparison by the subject. Fraternal deprivation should be redefined as based upon comparisons to an individual or a group that has higher outcomes and at least one dissimilar input that is considered relevant to the comparison by the subject. (p. 195)

Martin (1981) postulated that egoistic and fraternal deprivation are not mutually exclusive and that both types can be felt simultaneously:

> The choice of a similar or dissimilar comparative referent reflects a difference in the concern of the comparer. The first type of deprivation is labelled egoistic because the comparer is concerned about his or her own welfare. Fraternal deprivation has a broader base of concern; if the cause of the deprivation were removed, all the members of the disadvantaged group would benefit. Thus, egoistic deprivation reflects a concern about one's *own status*, while fraternal deprivation stems from a concern about the status of one's *membership group*. (p. 61; emphases added)

Yet, cautions Martin, researchers have not obtained data concerning these postulated differences in the concerns of the comparer. Hence, egoistic and fraternal deprivation are defined in terms of the similarity of the comparative referents rather than in terms of differences in the concerns of the comparer.

Comparisons to Abstract Standards, System or Self. Among both relative deprivation theorists and equity theorists there are those who argue that the comparison with others is not the only route to determining deservingness or inequity. This is a significant change from the early formulation. For example, Pritchard (1969) in his review of equity theory postulated the existence of "internal standards." These derive from "past experience in exchange relationships and the knowledge of the 'market value' of various outputs" (p. 205-06).

Gurr (1970), a relative deprivation theorist, argued that "an individual's point of reference may be . . . an abstract ideal, or the standards articulated by a leader as well as a reference group" (p. 25).

Goodman (1974, 1976) argued that, in evaluating the fairness of his pay, the individual may compare himself with others but also use the system or himself as referent. In *system* referents, the focus is on the exchange between the employer and the employee. When joining the organization individuals enter into an implicit or explicit contract with the organization about inducements (outcomes) provided by the organization and contributions (inputs) made by the individual. This contract provides the basic source of system referents: The input/outcome ratios promised by the contract can be compared to the actual input:outcome ratio. But

> even more powerful as referents are the normative expectations about the pay system that are learned over time and reinforced by various forms of communication and sanctions. For example, if a new employee was led to expect an automatic raise with promotion but did not receive it, feelings of inequity would result (Goodman, 1974: 173).

Self referents refer to input/outcome ratios unique to the individual but different from that individual's current input/outcome ratio. Self-referents may derive from comparisons involving input/outcome ratios of the individual in the past or in the future. They may also derive from conceptions of self-worth. For example, an individual may develop an ideal input/outcome ratio related to his conception of an acceptable standard of living or he may develop an internal standard of self-worth in terms of pay. These may then be compared with the present input/outcome ratio (Goodman, 1976: 109). Austin (1977) maintains that:

> To the extent that self-comparisons are anchored to an identifiable past relationship and accompanying social referents . . . they constitute equity comparisons and should affect equity *and* satisfaction. . . . However, when individuals appraise current outcomes in terms of what they expect or think they "deserve" in an unconditional sense *this is not an equity comparison* and the outcome should affect only satisfaction. (p. 295)

Also, Austin (1977) argues that self-comparisons are only vaguely conceptualized and are hence not well understood. This is reflected in the various labels utilized in connection with self-comparisons such as "internal standards," "comparison levels," "expectancy comparisons," and "self-comparisons." We shall encounter some of these labels in the sections reporting the results of empirical research.[2]

The Role of Temporal and Aggregate Aspects in Comparison

What, if any, are the effects of temporal changes in reward levels and of the aggregate pattern of reward distribution on felt fairness? Exchange theorists have shown little interest in this question. But relative deprivation theorists and others have treated it fairly extensively.

One of the earlier attempts to deal with the issue of temporal changes in reward levels was made by Davies (1962). Contrary to the classic versions of relative deprivation theory (Stouffer et al., 1949a and b; Davis, 1959), Davies suggested that temporal comparisons and not only interpersonal comparisons may be an important determinant of the feeling of relative deprivation. He postulated that a long period of rising prosperity followed by a levelling off, and then short rapid drop (an inverted J-curve), should have strong attitudinal effects. Because of the long history of increasing prosperity, people should have high expectations. If these expectations have been violated by the sharp drop in prosperity, high rates of discontent and bitter dissatisfaction are to be expected. Davies supported his thesis by evidence from the United States in 1842, Russia in 1917, and Egypt in 1952, where, he argued, an inverted J-curve was associated with an escalation of class conflict and rebellion.[3]

Gurr (1970) suggested that temporal changes in expectations or capabilities, if unbalanced, may lead to feelings of relative deprivation: *Aspirational deprivation* is a condition where capabilities remain relatively constant while expectations increase. In *decremental deprivation* the opposite happens: Expectations remain relatively constant while capabilities decrease. In *progressive deprivation* there is a change in both parameters: Expectations increase while capabilities decrease.

Williams (1975) also presented some interesting hypotheses about the effects of temporal changes in rewards, expectations, and aspirations, which he derived from existing empirical research:

1. When a majority of a population experiences increase in real income over a substantial period, the expected levels, aspirations, and feelings that the achieved levels are appropriate and deserved are also likely to increase.

2. Of the three consequences (aspirations, expectations, and norms), aspirations will increase most, expectations next, and normative levels of claims or rights will change least.

3. Increases in incomes and other rewards are likely to be more quickly accepted as normal and warranted than are decreases, and greater social opposition usually will be generated by rapid decreases.

4. Declines in rewards are likely to be least resisted when they are experienced over a long period, do not cause the actual level to fall below a normative minimal level, and when they are generally shared throughout a community or society.

5. Changes in individual gratification levels are most likely to lead to changes in expectations and aspirations when shared with many similar others.

6. Claims to increased reward can be produced by prior changes in some other category of right or privilege.

Some equity theorists have criticized the theory for presenting a static view of the equity process and for ignoring the time dimension (e.g., Carrell and Ditrich, 1978; Mowday, 1979; Vecchio, 1982; Cosier and Dalton, 1983). Cosier and Dalton (1983) have argued that "no design taken at a single point with set levels of inequity can account for an individual's motivation to reduce tension. The notion of time and repeated inequity is central to understanding behavior in such cases." (p. 316). These authors have attempted to build a model that is based on a reformulation of equity theory that includes the time dimension and that specifically illustrates the time-lagged effect of prior inequity. In this model, "time periods reflect changes in either outcomes and inputs that cause comparisons and equity in a given situation. . . . *Any event that triggers a comparison defines the beginning of a new time period.* The model assumes, however, that the prior experienced inequity is not forgotten." (p. 313; emphases added). The model thus posits that the motivational strength to reduce inequity is a function of current inequity and previous motivational strength to reduce inequity (p. 314).

Some researchers focused on the *magnitude of intergroup reward differentials* and their effect on felt relative deprivation. A major argument presented in this context is that a pattern of reward distribution in which relatively large inequalities exist between groups is relatively more likely to lead to feelings of fraternal deprivation since, under these conditions, the disadvantaged are more likely to compare themselves upwardly with the advantaged and feel relatively deprived than under conditions of small inequalities (e.g., Pettigrew, 1967; Martin, 1981).

A major attempt to explore mathematically the relationship between the existing distribution of rewards and feelings of equitability or deprivation was made by Jasso (1980) in her *New Theory of Distributive Justice.* Indeed, establishing a link between individual evaluations (the justice evaluation function) and properties of the aggregate (aggregate phenomena premised on distributional parameters) is the central feature of Jasso's theory. The establishment of this link makes possible a derivation of statements about individual justice judgments based on the assumptions about aggregate phenomena and vice versa. The "fully mathematized" theory builds on the empirically based justice evaluation function (Jasso, 1978) proposing that the justice evaluation varies as the logarithm of the ratio of the actual share of a good to the perceived just share:

$$\text{justice evaluation} = \ln \frac{actual\ share}{just\ share}$$

The sense of justice is represented by the full real-number line, with zero representing perfect justice, the positive segment representing unjust overreward, and the negative segment representing unjust underreward. Jasso introduces two simplifying restrictions called the Primitive Alternatives, which are intended to simplify the mathematization and the task of testing the theory. One such restriction is that "the Just term is equality."[4] The second restriction is that Social Aggregates in the Primitive model are characterized by consensus of the goods of value. These two restrictions allow Jasso "to move swiftly from knowledge about the distribution(s) of the good(s) of value to the distribution of justice evaluations." Two approaches are utilized in the analysis. One is to ask—given such-and-such an observed frequency distribution of the reward, what does the distribution of justice evaluations look like? What are the observed values of the parameters of interest? This approach, says Jasso, is particularly useful when studying Social Aggregates of small size N. Several conclusions are derived from the model. Of special interest to the present discussion is the conclusion that "the sense of injustice of the underreward sort has no bounds."[5] A similar prediction is made in relation to the overreward extreme value insofar as quantity-goods are concerned.

The second approach consists of utilizing classical probability procedures to answer the following questions: If the distribution of the goods of value has such-and-such density function, then (given the Primitive Restrictions) what is the density function of the expected distribution of justice evaluations? What are the expected values of the parameters of interest? Two cases of quantity goods (e.g., pay or earnings) are explored: 1. the case of a Pareto-distributed good; 2. the case of a lognormal distribution.[6]

In summarizing her analysis, Jasso (1980) notes that:

> the perspective embodied here suggests that there are many forms of inequality (not merely many measures of inequality) and that each form of inequality affects a different aspect of social life. . . . Whatever parameter of the distribution of justice evaluations one is interested in minimizing (that is, whatever form of inequality one is interested in minimizing)—whether it be the magnitude of unjust underreward experienced by the 'bottom' person . . . or the mean experience of justice or injustice . . . or any other—if all the curves under review belong to the same distributional family, then there is but one uniform counsel: for distributions of justice that arise from Pareto-distributed goods, the curve with the higher Pareto's constant is the curve with the minimum values on all parameters of interest (that is, minimum values on all forms of inequality); for distributions of justice evaluations that arise from Lognormally distributed goods, the curve with the smaller value of the shape parameter c is the curve with the minimum values on all parameters of interest. (p. 27)

Gartrell (1985) proposes that fairness evaluations of pay differentials in a wage structure may be better represented by block models rather than by Jasso's model which is anchored on the average wage. Block models, in contrast, "partition positions in the wage structure into sets of blocks if their members experience unfairness in relation to other positions and, in turn, are viewed by members of other positions in a similar way" (p. 79). Gartrell supports his argument by an analysis of the fairness evaluations of pay differentials by a sample of blue-collar workers.

Mark (1980) and Brickman, Folger, Goode, and Schul (1981) also discuss the relevancy of some parameters of the aggregate reward distribution on justice judgments. Mark (1980) suggests some evaluation criteria that are likely to be fairly common in this context. These are the *social minimum* criterion, specifying a level below which no one should fall; the *ceiling* criterion, specifying the level beyond which none may rise; and the *range* criterion, specifying the socially acceptable gap between the scale ends.

Some further theoretical developments in exploring the relationship between aggregate levels of reward distribution and individual-level justice evaluations were made by Markovsky (1985b) in his paper *Toward a Multilevel Distributive Justice Theory*. Markovsky defines the injustice experience (IE) as a function of comparison unit (CU) and justice indifference (JI):

$$IE'_{xx} = \log_{JI} xx' [CU'_{xx}]$$

The comparison unit (CU) is defined as the ratio of actual reward (R_x) to a reward standard (R'_x):

$$CU'_{xx} = (R_x)/(R'_x)$$

and justice indifference (JI) is defined as "the inverse of the degree to which justice is desired for a given comparison unit."[7]

Justice indifference (JI) "is determined by and negatively related to three factors: (1) the extent to which the justice evaluator *identifies* with x, the subject of the evaluation, (2) the extent to which x' is seen as a *valid referent,* and (3) the *quality* and *reliability* of R and I information" (1985b, p. 828).

Markovsky presents a number of derivations and hypotheses from his theory. For example, he hypothesized that individual incongruence will be greater under conditions of high indifference to group incongruence (low identification with the group), whereas under conditions of high identification with the group, concern with individual incongruence will be less than concern with group incongruence.

The potential influence of JI (and its determinants) on injustice experience (IE) is a new theoretical element not considered in previous theories. The concept of *anchors* contained in the theory is also interesting. Markovsky introduces this concept in dealing with situations in which the ordinality of the rewards and investments compared and evaluated is known to the evaluator but not their exact magnitude. In this case, the minimum and maximum conceivable levels of the ordinally scaled rewards and investments—owing to the relative ease with which they may be discriminated from other points on the scale—may serve as "end-anchors" in the evaluation process. It is proposed that the weights attached to the two end-anchors may differ but are restricted so that they sum to one: "In the context of a justice judgment, the 'weights' are given by the relative salience of the anchors. It many work settings, for example, the minimum conceivable wage is much more explicit than the maximum conceivable wage, and so . . . the minimum will receive more emphasis in a pay evaluation" (1985b: 829). In a later paper (Markovsky, 1988), the author specifies some of the scope conditions under which anchoring should occur, as follows: 1. the judgment is indeterminate; 2. an anchor exists; 3. anchors are salient. He also suggests that anchors may have an *assimilation effect* (when a judgment is biased toward an anchor) or a *contrast effect* (when a judgment is biased away from an anchor). The author argues that justice theories have generally ignored anchoring and situations with only ordinal information. In his view, however, these are most important:

> Anchors cause perceptual shifts by altering the background against which focal stimuli are judged . . . Thus anchors have extremely important con-sequences for the likelihood and strength of justice restoring responses. In addition, even though a distribution of rewards remains fixed through time, the apparent fairness of specific reward levels can be affected by changes in socially constructed frames of reference. Because such frames are sub-ject to purposeful manipulation it is important to determine their role in justice evaluations. (1988: 213)

A series of five experimental studies conducted by the author (Markovsky, 1988) demonstrate that anchoring effects "occur in predictable ways in evaluations of just rewards and degrees of injustice" (p. 222), and exemplify the profound im-pact such anchors may have on justice evaluations.

The Determinants of Comparisons

The distinction between several types of comparison raises a critical question: What determines the type of comparisons made? For example, what determines the choice of others as comparisons and what the use of abstract standards, self- or system comparisons? Several writers address this question.

Williams (1975) specified some of the conditions applying to the use of com-parisons with others as standards of deservingness:

> Since it is implied that deprivation refers to states defined as desirable by the relevant social actors, relative deprivation can be measured by reference

to *consensual norms* of desirability. When such clear norms exist, collectivities are uniquely defined, and intergroup references are easily made.

When social norms are lacking, are ambiguous or vague, or are multiple and contradictory, social comparisons become highly variable and uncertain (1975: 357; emphasis added).

Other researchers have considered the conditions under which comparisons with others are more likely to be used than other standards. For example, Weick (1966) postulated that "persons would rely on comparison persons and try to adjust their ratios toward equality with them largely when it is difficult to gauge task accomplishment. When concrete measures were available, persons would have less recourse to social standard" (p. 429). This postulate is based on Festinger's (1954) statement of comparison theory. Festinger distinguished between evaluations based on objective data (physical reality) and those based on social consensus (social reality), and hypothesized that persons prefer objective standards and turn to social comparisons only when objective data are ambiguous.

Similar propositions were made by Pettigrew (1967) and Lerner and Miller (1978). Pettigrew suggested that internal standards are replaced by comparisons where evaluators are uncertain about how to evaluate an attribute. Lerner and colleagues (1976) argued that, "where the requirements of physical or social reality are vague . . . we turn to others." (p. 148).

A number of propositions were made regarding the choice of specific persons or groups for comparison. As was indicated in Chapter 2, exchange theorists propose that referents will be chosen from among similars, mainly those receiving similar rewards, those engaged in a similar task or those with similar inputs. Indeed, a major thesis in reference group theory is the *similarity thesis*. In an early formulation, Merton and Kitt (1950) suggested that "some similarity in status attributes between the individual and the reference group must be perceived or imagined in order for the comparison to occur at all" (p. 61). Merton (1957) also argued that individuals compare themselves with others with whom they are in "actual association, in sustained social relations." This is the *proximity thesis*. Turner (1955) hypothesized that only those groups which are relevant to a particular aspect of self-appraisal will be taken as points of comparison. Festinger (1954) did not study the choice of comparison directly, but on the basis of a large number of studies concerning influence, attraction and rejection, communication, and level of aspiration within groups, he formulated a number of hypotheses constituting "a theory of social comparison processes." Among these is the hypothesis that "given a range of possible persons for comparison, someone close to one's own ability or opinion will be chosen for comparison" (p. 167). Festinger also hypothesized that the more attractive a group is to a member, the more important that group will be as a comparison group for him.

Merton and Kitt (1950) proposed that an orientation to a nonmembership group may serve the twin functions of aiding one's rise into that group and of easing one's adjustment after becoming part of it. They termed this function of reference-group behavior as *anticipatory socialization.* Here Weick's (1966) suggestion that mobility and mobility aspirations should be incorporated into a theory dealing with the antecedents and consequences of injustice in human exchanges seems relevant. Specifically, Weick proposes that "a person who aspires to a higher position probably will pay more attention to ratios of persons in the desired group than to those of his own group, and therefore will be more interested in establishing equity with supervisors than with the coworkers" (p. 427). Weick argues further that such comparison might put the comparer in a position of coworker inequity since in identifying himself with management the comparer will see his own situation as one of low inputs and high outcomes, the mirror image of the coworker. If promotion is quite rapid within the firm, the person would have to tolerate the discomfort of coworker inequity for a relatively short period of time. As more time is required for promotion, the person would confront the dilemma of deciding who the relevant comparison person was—the coworker or the employer manager.

Merton and Kitt (1950) postulated that the range of groups taken as effective bases of comparison will be closely connectd with the legitimacy ascribed to the prevailing social structure: In a rigidly stratified system, individuals within each stratum will be less likely to take the situation of the other strata as a context for appraisal of their own lot. Lipset and Trow (1957) noted, however, that large employment organizations, such as government, may supply frames of comparative reference that may become independent of the institutional framework that generated them.

Another major determinant of comparison, according to some researchers, is the *magnitude of intergroup differentials.* It is postulated that relatively large intergroup differentials are likely to lead to feelings of fraternal deprivation (e.g., Pettigrew, 1967; Martin, 1981).

Gartrell (1983) postulated that an "upward drive" is likely to occur in pay comparisons as a result of a "hedonic treadmill" effect: As people adapt to a given level of compensation, satisfaction with that level fades and is replaced by a new level of striving (Brickman and Campbell, 1971).

Some authors postulated that the choice of referents may also be guided by *instrumental considerations* such as "self-enhancement" or "self-depreciation" and "ego-protection" (e.g., Austin, 1977). Austin (1977) speculated that advantageous comparisons (e.g., comparisons that highlight the importance of one's inputs) are utilized "to maintain a desired level of outcomes." In contrast, disadvantageous comparisons (e.g., comparisons that highlight the meagerness of one's outcomes), are made to rectify a perceived injustice or to achieve a high level of outcome (ibid., p. 292). Goodman (1974) postulated that individuals always make those comparisons that fulfil their needs.[8] Levine and Moreland (1987) introduced the term comparison motive to deal with this determinant of comparison.

Gartrell (1983) argued that where comparisons are used instrumentally, computational ease and accuracy of information are important in determining the choice of referents. He thus expanded an earlier postulate of Goodman (1974) suggesting the accuracy of input/outcome information and the computational ease of various ratios as factors affecting the choice of comparison referents. Gartrell (1983) adds that from this perspective similar referents may fulfil the function of providing the most useful evaluative information:

> Because differences in job content are more difficult to assess than pay differences (since they lack the ready metric by which pay is measured), the most useful equity evaluations involve referents whose job content is as similar as possible to the evaluator's. Moreover, evaluators likely are more familiar with similar jobs and more confident in evaluations which involve them. (pp. 138–39)

By contrast, "comparison with social positions considerably different from one's own may produce 'rank balancing' (Cook, 1975) in which ill-defined inputs are inferred from outcomes or vice-versa" (p. 139).

Homans (1974) pointed to another factor that might affect the direction of comparisons, postulating that disadvantageous comparisons will be made only when there is a realistic chance that equity will be restored:

> A man does not go on forever making comparisons that show him to be unjustly treated, if he can do nothing about it. . . . Accordingly, he is particularly likely to complain about unjust treatment relatively to others that are similar to him at least in belonging to some larger social unit, for only in such a unit is there likely to be some superior power, some mechanism, capable of changing his rewards relative to others. (p. 253)

Lipset and Trow (1957) hypothesized that the social structure may serve as a determinant of comparison choices. For example, they hypothesized that "individuals or groups who are subordinate to the same authority are more likely to use each other as reference groups" (p. 396).

Austin (1977) focused attention on some other dimensions of the social context; the nature of social relationships between the comparer and the others. He postulated that depriving comparisons are most likely to occur in permanent and cooperative relationships and when individuals believe that they have been previously overrewarded.

Levine and Moreland (1987) postulated two general determinants of comparison choice. The first is the salience of a particular person or group. " 'Salience' depends on the availability of information regarding the target's standing on dimensions relevant to the comparison" (p. 112). Goodman (1976) postulated that the availability of information will be a function of structural and individual factors such as an individual's role characteristics (e.g., level in organization, position in communication network) and individual characteristics (e.g., level of aspiration). The second major determinant is attractiveness of the target as a source of comparison information. "Attractiveness depends on the source's motive for seeking comparison information and the target's assumed instrumentality in satisfying this motive'' (Levine and Moreland, 1987: 112).

THE EVALUATION DIMENSIONS

All exchange theories as well as status value theory assume that the potentially relevant dimensions of evaluation are manifold. Some theoreticians distinguish between several types of evaluation dimensions. Homans, for example, distinguished, as indicated, between *costs*, namely, what people give to a job, and *investments*, namely, the job incumbents' background characteristics that are used in evaluating the rewards they deserve. He (1974: 247) also argued that ''there are costs and costs.'' For example, a job that involves high costs in responsibility accepted, skill expected, anxiety borne, and peace of mind forgone is an important job that entails great reward potential. High costs of this kind are congruent with high investments and rewards. On the other hand, a job that involves high costs in ''mere dirt or monotonous drudgery'' is usually not important and does not entail great reward potential since the capacity to perform it is probably not rare. High costs of this kind are congruent with low investments and rewards.

Berger, Fisek, Norman, and Wagner (1983) distinguished between three types of referential structures according to types of characteristics evaluated:

> *Categorical referential* structures are ones in which the valued characteristics associated with different reward levels are typically broad social categories . . . such as sex, race, educational attainment and age. These structures primarily involve criteria of 'who you are' in determining the distribution of rewards. *Ability referential structures,* by contrast, are ones in which the valued characteristics associated with different reward levels. . . . These structures relate rewards primarily to 'criteria of what can you do' or 'what are your capacities' in this task situation. Finally, in *performance-outcome referential structures,* rewards ae associated with actual performances and achievements in the immediate situation. . . . In performance outcome structures, rewards are primarily to criteria of 'what have you done' or 'what have you actually accomplished' in this immediate situation. (p. 134)

Indeed this later work of the status value theorists extends the scope of the theory to include situations where reward ranks are positively associated with ability and performance criteria and clarifies how multiple inputs or investments, and hence multiple referential structures, operate. It shows how statuses become relevant to differential abilities or task outcomes and how they combine to determine positions in the prestige hierarchy. It also provides clearer insight into the reverse process whereby inferences are made about abilities and performances from reward levels achieved by individuals.

The Ambiguity of Inputs and Outcomes

In discussing some of the problems associated with equity theory, Weick (1966) points to a problem concerning the dimensions of evaluation: the potential ambiguity of input and outcome. He argues that in everyday work situations many behaviors can be assigned to either side of the ratio, namely, the inputs or the outcomes. For example, when a worker sees that his comparison person sweats profusely while he works, he could view this behavior either as an indication of hard work and an investment of much effort (i.e., a high input), or as an indication of considerable discomfort from the job (i.e., a low outcome). The result of such ambiguities may be that "persons perceive ambiguous work behavior in whatever form will create equity" (pp. 419–20). And if so, "in a work situation in which there are several ambiguous work behaviors, it might be difficult for inequities to develop. Possible inequity could be met by frequent reinterpretation of ambiguous work behavior so as to preserve equity" (pp. 420–21).

The Integration of Dimensions

Given that there are indeed several types of dimensions of evaluation and given that each type consists of a number of dimensions, the question arises as to how dimensions are combined to arrive at an evaluation of just rewards. The dominant assumption was that this process involves the combining of the weighted sums of relevant inputs and outcomes according to a simple additive function. However, more recently, the validity of this view was questioned by a number of theorists. For example, Adams and Freedman (1976) speculated that inputs may be integrated at a roughly linear rate, while outcomes may diminish in utility. Farkas and Anderson (1979) argued that different information-integration models apply, depending upon the degree of similarity of the inputs to be integrated in the process of evaluation. They proposed two models: In the input integration model, applied when inputs are similar, all relevant stimulus information is combined to arrive at a single input score; in the equity integration model, applied when imputs are dissimilar, separate outcome estimates are derived from each single input value and then combined to arrive at a final equity judgment.

Cook and Yamagishi (1983) postulated that the way in which various dimensions are weighted as well as which distribution rule is applied depends upon the type of inputs to be integrated as well as the nature of rewards to be allocated. Specifically, it is proposed that the equity rule will be applied where there are multiple inputs such as contributions and personal attributes, and where the rewards depend on contributions. In such a situation, greater weight will be attached to contributions than to personal attributes. Where rewards are fixed, "the relationship between inputs . . . and 'fixed rewards' or outcomes is . . . somewhat arbitrary and thus likely to be culturally or situationally determined on the basis of 'agreed upon' norms of allocation or specific contractual agreements" (p. 105), the basic assumption being that cultural beliefs focus on the relevance of various inputs as well as on the appropriate distribution rule.

ATTEMPTS TO COMPARE AND INTEGRATE THEORETICAL PERSPECTIVES

Among the more recent theoretical developments are also attempts to systematically compare and integrate some of the major theoretical perspectives. Such attempts are relatively new and deserve special attention for their constructive approach of theory building.

Relative Deprivation and Equity Theory

Most efforts to systematically compare and integrate theoretical perspectives have focused on these two most popular theories. Exchange theorists such as Homans and Adams expressed the belief that relative deprivation theory is akin to their own theories. Homans (1974), for example, asserted that relative deprivation is the same as distributive injustice. Adams (1965: 268) claim to have integrated in his theory of inequity "two major concepts relating to the perceptions of justice and injustice," namely, the concept of relative deprivation and of distributive justice. Similarly, Pettigrew (1967: 266), in a review of social evaluation theory, argued that " 'an unfair exchange' and 'injustice' are essentially a recasting of relative deprivation."[9] Wheeler and Zuckerman (1977: 353–54), too, expressed the belief that relative deprivation and inequity are not different constructs. In their view, "relative deprivation is a state experienced by the victim of inequity."

Cook, Crosby, and Hennigan (1977) attempted to systematically compare the two theories. The authors considered these theories as similar in components and presumed consequences and their major aim was to pinpoint the differences between the two. Table 3.1 presents the results of this comparison.

The authors concluded that the only difference between the two theories is that feasibility is mentioned by relative deprivation theorists but not by equity theorists. They also maintained that "if studies were to show that feasibility makes no difference in mediating anger-related responses, than the construct of inequity would be more parsimonious than relative deprivation for explaining the same findings" (p. 315).

But recent reviews seem to disagree with the views emphasizing the similarity or even identity of relative deprivation and equity theory. Crosby and Gonzalez-Intal (1984) as well as Martin (1981) note some significant differences between the two in respect of justice distribution rules or justice norms. Crosby and Gonzalez-Intal argue that, in contrast to the exchange theory, relative deprivation theory does not postulate particular standards for the experience of relative deprivation.

Martin (1981), in an attempt to compare the two theories—mainly with the aim of showing the advantages of intergrating them—found some important similarities

Table 3.1
Conditions Contributing to Perceptions of Injustice from Relative Deprivation and Inequity

| | Components of relative deprivation | | | | Factors channeling responses | |
	Not have	*Want*	*Social comparison*	*Feasibility*	*Entitlement*	*Personal responsibility*
Relative deprivation	nec	nec-pos	nec-any similar other	nec-at some time high	nec-pos	nec-neg
Inequity	nec	nec-pos associated with an exchange	nec-other	—	nec-pos	nec-neg

Note: nec = necessary for anger-related responses; pos = positive relationship between variable and responses; neg = negative relationship between variable and responses.

Source: Adapted from Cook et al. (1977), p. 315.

but also some significant dissimilarities. According to Martin, both theories lean on the same basic model. This proposes a four-stage process: "(1) rewards are distributed in a particular pattern which causes (2) certain comparisons to be made. Those comparisons cause (3) a feeling of deprivation which in turn causes (4) a particular behavioral reaction" (p. 59). While the basic model is similar, there are significant contrasts between the theories: One such contrast, according to Martin, relates to the treatment of comparison processes. In Martin's view,

> equity's treatment of comparison processes is both narrow and complex. It is narrow in its focus on individuals. . . . This narrow focus on the individual minimizes the roles that groups and social systems play. On the other hand, equity theory is complex in that the comparer and the comparative referent are conceptualized as multidimensional entities. Both can vary on a theoretically unrestricted number of input and outcome dimensions. (p. 95)

On the other hand, relative deprivation theory recognizes that comparative referents can be groups as well as individuals. An integrative model should include both groups and individuals, similar and dissimilar comparisons. It should also recognize the possibility that the preference for types of referents can change, and so the time interval over which comparisons are studied should be considered.

Another contrast, according to Martin, is the significantly lesser attention of relative deprivation theory to inputs. Martin (1981: 97) argues that relative deprivation theorists "have devoted less attention to inputs which might be used to justify a given reward distribution." In a schematic presentation and comparison of the two theories, the basic proposition of relative deprivation theory is presented as one where outcomes are compared with outcomes (outcomes:outcomes) in contrast with the basic proposition of equity theory, which is presented as one where comparisons are made between the ratios of inputs to outcomes

$$\frac{(inputs}{(outcomes} : \frac{inputs)}{outcomes)}$$

Martin also argues that relative deprivation focuses on *aggregate* aspects of reward distribution and on *changes* in outcomes which reduce or exacerbate the discontent. "A model which integrates these two theories should consider both changes in inputs and outcomes at both the individual and aggregate levels" (pp. 97–98).

A treatise by Folger (1984b) suggests that the differences between exchange theories and relative deprivation theory may be deeper than suggested above. He distinguishes between two basic orientations in justice concerns. One type of orientation he calls a *distributive-pattern orientation*. This reflects concern with the shape and character of the distribution of outcomes considered as a whole, that is, the overall pattern of distribution, and looks for its conformity with what seems good, proper, and fair. The other type of orientation he calls an *exchange orientation*. This reflects a concern with two-way transfers and looks for their equivalence. In contrast to the exchange orientation, the distributive-pattern orientation "pays attention only to outcomes (i.e., to their distribution) and does not deal with inputs (in the sense of contributions to an exchange). Furthermore, a distributive-pattern orientation need not involve symmetry or balance" (p. 11). This distinction between orientations calls in question the possibility of integrating relative deprivation theory, which is typified as being concerned with fairness in aggregate aspects of reward distribution, with exchange theories, which are typified as being concerned with fairness in exchange.

Status Value Theory and Exchange and Relative Deprivation Theories

Crosby and Gonzalez-Intal (1984), in discussing their version of relative deprivation theory, argue that the concerns of status value theory are "closest to our own concern." As they see it, status value and exchange theories differ mainly in two respects. One is that exchange theories emphasize local comparisons, in contrast to the status value theory stating that referential comparisons and not local comparisons are at the heart of people's feelings of injustice. The other major difference concerns meanings: Status value theory, in contrast to exchange theories, proposes that the status value of rewards, that is, their symbolic value, and not their exchange value is at the center of justice processes.

Crosby and Gonzales-Intal (1984) also see some major differences between status value theory and their version of relative deprivation theory. First, they assert that their interpretation of outcomes and inputs is not limited to the status values of these. Second, they do not regard referential comparisons as comprising all justice comparisons: "Instead, we think that in determining justice and deservingness people sometimes use local comparisons alone; they sometimes use referential comparisons alone; and sometimes they use both types of comparisons. Furthermore, we think that at times people may not even use social comparisons but instead judge the fairness of outcomes on the basis of abstract ideals or societal dictates" (p. 159). Third, unlike status value theorists, they view agency, that is, the person or people creating the negatively valued situation, as an important aspect of felt injustice.

NOTES

1. See also Montada (1980) on the dispute between the development and socialization perspectives.

2. The reader may also wish to consult Masters and Keil (1987) for an attempt to analyze the 'anatomy' of comparison processes and develop a taxonomy of factors relevant to these processes including the types of information that may be involved and parameters of the comparison process itself.

3. Miller, Bolce, and Halligan (1977) criticized Davies' work on the following grounds: (1) for an imprecise definition of the J-curve; for example, Davies did not specify how long or how precipitously prosperity must fall before revolution will occur; (2) for the fact that the explanation offered is post hoc and is hence less convincing than a predictive research design would have been; (3) positing a model consisting of individual-level variables but inconsistently testing this model with highly aggregated data.

4. The rationale for this assumption is that "most thinkers on distributive justice agree that the only just division of a fixed pie is an equal one."

5. The discussion of the mathematical operations underlying these conclusions is omitted here.

6. The following parameters are examined: the overall arithmetic mean of the distribution of justice evaluations, the upper and lower limits, the proportions in various segments, the arithmetic means of the various segments, and the Gini's mean difference.

7. CU according to the author may also be defined as:

$$CUxy = (Rx/Ry)\ (Ix/Iy)$$

Where Rx and Ry represent one's own and one's referent's rewards respectively, and Ix and Iy represent one's own and one's referent inputs respectively.

8. See Greenberg and Cohen (1982b) for an expanded treatise on the instrumental versus normative approach to justice evaluations.

9. Pettigrew, however, goes on to say that " 'a fair exchange' and 'distributive justice' are not . . . equivalent to 'relative gratification' but to the neutral comparison level" (1967: 266).

4 Major Controversies and Open Questions

The overall picture emerging from the foregoing review of prevalent theory is highly complex and leaves many open questions. The opposing paradigms dominating the field and seeking a solution obviously contribute to the complication. But there are also many other issues to be explored. The way is obviously by empirical research, which is indispensable for providing the evidence that could settle the many disagreements among theorists, but which is also crucial for testing the specific propositions they have advanced and for clarifying the questions they have neglected. The purpose of this chapter is to highlight the major issues in this task and present the questions that arise in relation to each. These will be discussed under the major headings set forth in Chapter 3.

THE UNDERLYING DISTRIBUTION NORMS

Several important questions arise in regard to the distribution norms underlying pay-fairness evaluations. But before turning to these, it should be noted that not all theorists believe that the fairness evaluation of rewards is basically guided by internalized social norms adhered to by individuals. For example, Walster, Berscheid, and Walster (1976) believe that "man is selfish" and that individuals strive first and foremost to maximize their outcomes and moreover, given the opportunity to achieve this goal by behaving inequitably they will do so: "So long as individuals perceive that they can maximize their outcomes by behaving equitably, they will do so. Should they perceive that they can maximize their outcomes by behaving inequitably, they will do so" (p. 5). Nevertheless, these authors recognize that social norms are important for the regulation of social life and that consequently "societies develop norms of equity and teach them to their members" (p. 4) and punish persons who digress from these norms. As a result of the punitive measures accompanying nonconformity to equity norms, "individuals should quickly come to associate 'participating in an inequitable relationship' with punishment. As a consequence of the inevitable socialization experiences, we propose that . . . when individuals find themselves participating in inequitable relationships, they become distressed" (p. 6). Deutsch (1985: 27–28) observes that the latter proposition is inconsistent with the statement that man is selfish and is primarily concerned with maximizing his rewards, and that it "builds 'morality' into the postulated amoral man" (p. 27). While we fully agree with this critique, the basic question raised by Walster, Berscheid, and Walster's (1976) proposition remains: Are individuals selfish? Do they strive to maximize their rewards or will they be satisfied with rewards that satisfy an internal norm of fairness? The dispute is not if "people have other motives besides the justice motive, and sometimes these other motives give rise to feelings and behavior that are in contradiction to those that would arise purely from equity considerations" as Deutsch (1985: 27) argues, but rather if people have justice motives at all! Essentially, it is the perennial question of human morality: Do people assimilate and internalize the social norms surrounding them or do they comply with them only for fear of the sanctions backing them? Obviously, internal motives are difficult to investigate and no ready-made means to settle the question are yet available. The position taken here tends to side with those believing that social norms in this sphere, like any other social sphere, have a more profound influence on individuals than the mere fear of sanctions accompanying them.

Given that people do indeed base their reward evaluations on certain internal norms of justice, the next question following is: What are these norms? The various theories presented suggest different answers. Some theories emphasize one single principle, such as the exchange theories proposing the equity or contribution principle as the major and, indeed, sole guide to the fairness evaluations of individuals; or the status value theory, which contends that status value and ranking is the basic guiding principle.

The above monistic approaches are contested by the theories proposing that the distribution rules considered as normatively just may vary from situation to situation. Finally, a number of theorists even argue that the process of reward evaluation may be guided by several rules in combination.

These different views leave the question of the distribution rules governing pay-fairness evaluation wide open and in search of a solution. At first glance, the exchange formulation seems to have more appeal then the others: After all, what can be more reasonable than to assume that in the economic sphere individuals expect to be rewarded according to their productive contributions (e.g., Folger, 1984b). This assumption becomes even more attractive when one considers the arguments of those theoreticians proposing that, in contexts where productive goals predominate, equity will be the dominant principle (e.g., Deutsch, 1975; Leventhal, 1976). On second thoughts, however, other theoretical arguments are not easily dismissed and seem fairly plausible too, especially when one takes a closer look at some of the arguments underpinning fair-pay claims and at the immediate and wider employment context.

The proposition of status value theory, for example, is hard to ignore and even has much to recommend it when consideration is given to the arguments underpinning certain fair-pay claims. One example is the heavy emphasis on an occupation's "social standing" that appear in many instances of fair-pay claims made by occupational groups (e.g., physicians, judges, high-ranking politicians, academics). One can hardly avoid the impression that these emphases on an occupation's social standing are related to the social prestige image of the occupation rather than its inputs and investments, as the exchange theories would argue.

Another relevant instance is the fair-pay claims made by hierarchical position incumbents. Careful scrutiny of the argumentation involved in these claims shows how difficult it is to decide if they are based on the "bundles" of duties carried by the position incumbents or on their organizational status and "social standing" (e.g., Barnard, 1952).

Another common case of fair-pay claims raises questions about the relevancy in pay-fairness evaluations of other distribution principles. We refer to the often-heard complaint of employees that their wages are not fair since they do not allow a decent standard of living. Indeed, neither the exchange theories nor the status value theory recognize need as an underlying principle in pay-fairness evaluations and neither recognizes the relevance of the consummatory value of pay to the process. But are these really as irrelevant as these theories suggest? The above example casts doubts on this approach and suggests quite strongly that this question is worthwhile of being put to empirical test.

The argument of some theorists that the distribution rules considered as just may vary according to certain contextual factors should also not be easily dismissed. After all, employment contexts exhibit great variability in task structure, social structure, and predominant goals—all considered by the proponents of these theories as directly relevant to the subject. For example, some contexts involve team work and much mutual dependency and cooperation, while others do not; in some contexts, friendly relationships develop and social cohesiveness is high while in others these elements are lacking; in some instances, harmony and conflict avoidance are of paramount importance while in others competitiveness is greatly valued; some employing organizations have very lean resources and place great emphasis on their efficient use while others are less concerned with this issue. So, why assume a priori that these and other contextual variances are irrelevant to the process and ignore the possibility that they may determine the distribution rules governing pay-fairness evaluations, as some theorists would argue?

Consideration should also be given to other variations in the employment context: those stemming from the socio-cultural setting surrounding the employing organization. The question here is whether the wider socio-cultural context, not just the particular employment context, affects in any way the distribution norms applied in pay-fairness evaluation. Do these, in fact, vary in different cultures, as argued by some theorists (e.g., Sampson, 1975; 1980) or are they universal as others hold (e.g., Homans, 1974; Jacques, 1970)? Some theorists believe that social norms that govern economic exchanges "spill over" into other life spheres (e.g., Deutsch, 1975; Sampson, 1975). But the question may also be reversed. Given that different cultures have different central value systems, do these in any way appear also in the norms governing the justness evaluations of economic rewards? For example, what happens in socio-cultural contexts emphasizing norms of equality? Do these "spill over" into the context of pay-fairness evaluation or not? And if they do, how exactly? Is the contribution norm de-emphasized in favor of the equality norm? Is there a lower tolerance for large wage differentials? Or is there an enhanced tendency to consider the "needs" of individuals?

The arguments relating to the possible effects of the immediate employment context and the wider socio-cultural context lead directly to another proposition which contends that several distribution principles may govern combinedly the reward-evaluation process. When considering the complexity of real life situations this proposition becomes difficult to dismiss out of hand. For example, the immediate employment context may expose employees to a variety of different and perhaps even opposing cues. So may the wider socio-economic context. For instance, while today's Western societies do indeed emphasize economic rationality and efficiency in resource allocation, their core value system also contains egalitarian and humanitarian values that exert no little pressure on the economic system, including the spheres of wages (e.g., demands for more wage equaliza-tion and responsiveness to individual needs regardless of productive contribu-tions). How are these complex and often opposing cues emanating from the im-mediate employment context and the wider socio-cultural context met? Would it be too far fetched to assume that a possible solution lies in the combined ap-plication of several distribution rules as some theorists would argue, or perhaps in the choice of a solution that seems, under the circumstances, least offending as others propose? This question, like all others preceding it, cannot be answered without relevant empirical evidence.

STANDARDS OF COMPARISON

As noted, all the major theories reviewed propose that social comparisons con-stitute a major and essential ingredient in the fairness evaluation of rewards. Yet all of them have been criticized for failing to elaborate on this issue and for leav-ing many open questions. A leading question here is if reward evaluations *always* involve a process of comparison with others. This may be asked in light of the statements that individuals may use an internal normative standard, an abstract ideal, themselves (in the past or in the future), or the system as referents. But are internal standards, self-comparisons, or system comparisons in fact used as standards of comparison in pay-fairness evaluation? If they are, do they serve as substitutes for social comparison or do they complement social comparisons in some way? If the former, under what conditions do individuals tend to com-pare themselves with others and under what conditions do they tend to base their evaluations on internal norms, self-comparisons, or system comparisons? If the latter, what functions do such referents as internal standards, self- or system fulfil, as opposed to social comparisons?

The nature of the social comparisons made is another question. As noted, recent reviews indicate that theories differ substantially on this. Exchange theories have been typified as emphasizing similar comparisons and as focusing mainly on interindividual comparisons. Status value theory, however, argues that interindividual comparisons are of little consequence to the process. Relative deprivation theory, for its part, has been typified as recognizing the possibility that referents may be similar or dissimilar, groups or individuals. Again, the propositions and the arguments for them all make sense; and so, again, it falls to empirical research to clarify the issues involved. The questions here are: Do individuals tend mainly to compare themselves with similars or dissimilars; in other words, are comparisons mainly of the egoistic type or the fraternal type? Do individuals tend to compare themselves mainly with other individuals or with certain groups of individuals; in other words, are comparisons mainly of the local or the referential type? If no dominant pattern exists, what factors (if any) explain the existing variations? But perhaps, individuals generally make more than one comparison. Perhaps they compare simultaneously to similars as well as dissimilars, individuals as well as groups. In this later case, how is the simultaneous use of multiple comparisons explained? Is it that each type of comparison fulfils a different need, as some theorists argue?

A no-less-important question is the role of the employing organization in the process. Do individuals evaluating the fairness of their pay tend mainly to compare themselves with others within the organization, or conversely, with others outside it? A challenging proposition in this context is the notion that large employment organizations may supply frames of comparative reference that are independent of the surrounding institutional setting. This thesis, together with the social proximity thesis and the proposition that comparisons will tend to be made with those subordinate to the same authority, suggests that the employing organization may fulfil a most crucial role in the process of comparison. Is this indeed so? If no uniform pattern exists, what determines the varying tendencies?

Assuming that comparisons with others do indeed occupy a central place in the process of pay-fairness evaluations, how is the information about other referents acquired? What factors affect this process and what are its effects on the process of comparison?

Relative deprivation theory focused attention on one aspect of comparison largely ignored by other theories, namely that the aggregate level and overall pattern of reward distribution might fulfil an important role in the process of evaluation. This proposition is based on the assumption that individuals may use nonmembership groups as comparison referents and implies that the evaluation process may include a number of parameters that relate to the overall configuration of the reward distribution, such as the magnitude of intergroup differentials, the magnitude of the overall range (highest/lowest extremes of the scale), and the average level of reward. Individuals may compare their membership group with other groups and assess the justness of existing differentials; they may take the range of the entire scale as a referent, for example, compare themselves with the highest and/or lowest point in the scale, and assess the justness of their rewards on this basis; and they may take the average level of reward as a point of reference. Moreover, it is proposed that changes over time in the overall pattern and in their relative position within it may become important ingredients in the process of reward-fairness evaluation of individuals and groups.

There are a number of questions here. First, are the above propositions empirically supported? Do the overall reward configuration and specific elements within it serve indeed as points of reference in the process of reward-fairness evaluation? Second, what exactly are the specific elements serving as referents—the magnitude of intergroup differentials; the upper or lower extremes of the scale; or the average; or several/all of these simultaneously? Third, what function does each element fulfil in the process of evaluation? If there are any factors that affect differentially the tendency to choose any of these elements as referents, what are they and how do they work? Fourth, do changes in the overall pattern of reward distribution and in the individual's or his membership group's position within it affect the process of evaluation, and how exactly?

The questions presented here clearly involve much that is unknown about the determinants of comparisons. Indeed, a major task of empirical research is to test the many specific propositions about these determinants. A number of propositions suggest that social comparisons are more likely under certain conditions and less likely under others, and need to be tested. Specifically, social comparisons are deemed more likely when consensual norms of desirability exist and when objective standards of comparison are lacking or vague, or when there is doubt about how certain attributes/inputs should be evaluated. Other propositions concern the factors that affect the choice of specific referents. These include the similarity and relevancy theses, the social proximity thesis, the institutional framework thesis, the instrumental or comparison motives thesis, the anticipatory socialization thesis, and the salience and attractiveness theses, as well as all their derivatives. Obviously the empirical investigation of these propositions is of paramount importance for understanding the process of comparison. All the more, considering that these propositions often contain contradictory elements or elements that somewhat diminish from the importance of comparisons such as Homans' thesis proposing that "a man does not go on forever making comparisons that show him to be unjustly treated if he can do nothing about it." This is indeed a very challenging proposition with which not all would agree (e.g., Martin, 1981).

THE EVALUATION DIMENSIONS

Not all the theories reviewed place equal emphasis on the dimensions that might be used in evaluating the justness of a given reward distribution. As already noted, for example, relative deprivation theory tends to emphasize the comparison of outcomes and devotes little attention to the inputs or investments, or other dimensions that might be used to evaluate a given reward distribution. On the other hand, the theories that refer explicitly to such dimensions do not agree as to what they are. Jacques (1970), for example, claims, on the ground of his findings, that in essence there is only one universal dimension of evaluation. Exchange theorists such as Homans (1974), Adams (1963a, 1965), and Blau (1964) postulate the existence of multiple dimensions, all of which, moreover, must be perceived as relevant productive contributions or, in Homans' terms, as inputs or investments. But the exchange theorists are divided in their views as to the *sources* of conceptions of what the relevant productive contributions are as well as to the degree of social consensus on these dimensions. As indicated, Adams (1963a, 1965) believes that these conceptions are anchored in a society's central value system and are *consensually* held by its members; Homans (1961, 1974), on the other hand, believes that they vary from one social subgroup to another and expects little social consensus and perhaps also little stability in these conceptions. Blau's (1964) position is that the relevancy and weight of evaluation dimensions are contingent upon their perceived importance to society. This implies again a substantial measure of social consensus on and stability in the perceived relevant dimensions.

Yet a different position on the underlying dimensions of evaluation is taken by status value theorists. Berger and colleagues' (1972) position is that external status characteristics, i.e., characteristics "significant in the larger community or society of which the organization is a part," constitute a major element in the pay-evaluation process. These authors argue that in practice such status characteristics carry substantial weight in the structuring of organizational status systems and that wage structures in organizations are highly interwoven with the organizational status system, and through it with the external status structure (Zelditch Berger, and Cohen 1966).

The fundamental disagreements about the nature of the relevant evaluation dimensions and the degree of social consensus and permanency that may be expected regarding them—as well as the belief by most theorists that there are multiple dimensions of evaluation but who offer only tentative lists of what these might be—suggest all that empirical research in this area is of utmost importance for furthering our understanding of the subject. Such research should be able to settle the debates over the nature of the dimensions involved and over the issues of social consensus and permanency in prevalent conceptions, as well as indicate specifically which dimensions are involved and what their respective weights are.

Another issue also requires empirical research. Theorists have pointed out that a certain ambiguity in evaluation dimensions is possible: some dimensions may be perceived as inputs as well as outcomes. This proposition needs to be substantiated by empirical research. First, it is necessary to establish if it has any empirical support. If so, the specific dimensions that bear this characteristic must be pinpointed. Thirdly, it seems important to investigate the sources of this ambiguity. Finally, the conditions under which a dimension is considered an outcome—or an input—has to be revealed.

The final evaluation depends not only on the nature of the evaluation dimensions but also on the way they are integrated. Various propositions have been advanced on this: Not all agree with each another and not all address themselves to the same aspects. These, too, present a number of open questions that need to be clarified through empirical research.

SUMMARY

The above discussion suggests that prevalent theoretical thinking places a heavy burden on, or alternatively presents a great challenge to, empirical research. This challenge is not easy to meet and no quick solutions should be expected or hoped for. In the following three chapters (chpts. 5, 6 and 7) we review what is available so far. The studies reviewed in each section will usually be in chronological order. Each such study will be described in greater detail when it is first mentioned; subsequent references to it will, as a rule, lean on this description or, if necessary, supply some additional information that seems important in the particular context discussed. An overview and summary of the main findings and a discussion of the conclusions emanating from them and of their implications are presented in subsequent chapters.

Part III Empirical Research on Some Major Elements

5 The Underlying Distribution Norms

Most of the empirical studies that can shed some light on the distribution norms underlying pay-fairness evaluations were guided by particular theories and aimed at testing some of the propositions deriving from them. These studies are typically experimental and may be broadly divided into two major categories. One of these includes studies aimed at investigating the *reactions* of individuals to a given reward allocation in task performance situations. The underlying assumption in these studies is that the individuals' reactions will reflect their perceptions about the fairness of the given reward allocation. Specific hypotheses about the expected reactions, derived from the underlying theory, are usually (but not always) formulated and tested. In a few cases the framework is more "open": Reactions to a given reward allocation are investigated with the intention of learning something about underlying perceptions of fairness rather than testing specific hypotheses derived from theory.

The second category includes the studies investigating the patterns of *reward allocation* preferred by individuals in task performance situations. The basic assumption in these studies is that these preferences will reflect the distribution rules perceived as appropriate in the situation investigated. Here too, quite often, specific hypotheses deriving from the guiding theory are tested. Some studies, however, make no attempt to predict the resultant preferences.

Most of the studies in the first category were carried out by the adherents of equity theory. In contrast, most of the studies in the second category were conducted by researchers inspired by the idea that the distribution norms followed by individuals might vary according to circumstances. Besides these relatively large bodies of study, there are a few open-ended field studies.

The following review starts with the studies conducted in the wake of equity theory and continues with the studies inspired by the theories proposing that the distribution norms followed by individuals may vary according to circumstances. Finally the few open-ended field studies will be reviewed.

REACTIONS TO GIVEN REWARDS:
TESTING THE EXCHANGE FORMULATION

Experimental Research

Not all exchange theories have equally stimulated empirical research. Most of the relevant empirical studies were inspired by Adam's (1963a, 1965) equity theory and were carried out in experimental settings. The studies were designed to test predictions about reactions to perceived inequities and began shortly after the appearance of Adam's initial theory. Extensive past reviews of this line of research (e.g., Lawler, 1968a; Pritchard, 1969; Goodman and Friedman, 1971; Adams and Freedman, 1976) obviate the need for detailed descriptions of these studies. Here, only a concise picture of basic methodologies, major conclusions, and overall critical evaluations is presented.

Most studies focus on one of Adam's basic propositions of inequity resolution; that individuals perceiving an inequity in outcomes will change their inputs to achieve a balance between them and available outcomes. Outcomes are typically defined operationally as payment for a task while inputs are typically defined as performance levels measured in terms of quantity or quality, or both.

The studies may be subdivided into those investigating reactions to underpayment and those investigating reactions to overpayment.

1. Reactions to Underpayment. The major guiding hypothesis here is that individuals perceiving themselves as underpaid decrease their inputs to achieve an input/outcome balance.

• Under a system of *hourly rates*, where pay is based on time at work, the prediction is that underpaid individuals will be relatively less productive (in terms of quantities produced) than equitably paid individuals.

• Under a system of *piece rates*, where payment is based on quantity produced, the prediction is that underpaid individuals will produce greater quantities but lower qualities as compared to equitably paid individuals.

2. Reactions to Overpayment. The basic hypothesis is that individuals perceiving themselves as overpaid increase their inputs to achieve an input/outcome balance.

• Under a system of *hourly rates* the prediction is that overpaid individuals will be relatively more productive than equitably paid individuals.

• Under a system of *piece rates* the prediction is that overpaid individuals will produce output of better quality than equitably paid individuals.

The basic research design for testing the above hypotheses emulates an employment situation: The researcher poses as employer and advertises for part-time employment. The "hired" subjects (typically students) are informed by their "employer" about their tasks and their pay. The description of the pay rates is made in a way intended to induce in the subjects the belief that they are paid equitably or, alternatively, inequitably (over- or underpaid). After the necessary job training, subjects perform the assigned task for a short period of time. The quantity and quality of work performed, as well as pay-equity attitudes, are then measured.

Reviews of these studies (e.g., Pritchard, 1969; Goodman and Friedman, 1971; Adams and Freedman, 1976; Greenberg, 1982) conclude that, generally hypotheses have been confirmed in the *hourly underpaid* situation (e.g., Evan and Simmons, 1959; Pritchard, Dunnette, and Sorensen, 1972) and in the *underpaid piece-rate* situation (e.g., Andrews, 1967; Lawler and O'Gara, 1967). But some reviewers (e.g., Goodman and Friedman, 1971) note that more studies are needed to provide full confirmation of the hypotheses.

The overpayment studies—both hourly and piece-rate—are relatively more abundant than the underpayment studies. Some of the *hourly overpayment* studies tended to confirm the basic hypothesis (e.g., Adams and Rosenbaum, 1962; Goodman and Friedman, 1969; Pritchard et al., 1972). Other studies produced equivocal results (Friedman and Goodman, 1967; Lawler, 1968b; Wiener, 1970), while some studies did not support the hypothesis (e.g., Valenzi and Andrews, 1971; Evan and Simmons, 1969; Anderson and Shelly, 1970). Goodman and Friedman (1971) note in their critical review that the major distinguishing characteristic of the supporting studies was the method of overpayment induction. In the supporting studies this method was based on challenging the work qualifications of subjects and making them believe that their pay was more than they deserved for their qualifications. This method of overpayment induction has been criticized (e.g., Lawler 1968a; Pritchard, 1969) on the grounds that the subjects may have been perceiving devalued "self-esteem" rather than inequity, as intended. And if so, the argument continues, the higher productivity in the investigations using this method of overpayment may be the result of an attempt to demonstrate higher than attributed qualifications rather than an attempt to redress a perceived inequity. This argument finds support in a number of studies showing that feelings of self-qualification can affect performance variation in equity experiments (e.g., Andrews and Valenzi, 1970; Evans and Molinari, 1970; Wiener, 1970; Wilke and Steur, 1972).

Commenting on the studies demonstrating that feelings of self-qualification can affect performance variations, Goodman and Friedman (1971) argued that it is difficult to extrapolate from these studies to those supporting the main hypothesis. They argued that, whereas experiments have demonstrated that reactions to devalued self-esteem can affect performance, it has not been empirically demonstrated that such reactions account for more productive variance than feelings of inequity in studies supporting the hypothesis. Goodman and Friedman (1971) in their review as well as Greenberg (1982) in a later review conclude that overpayment effect is "*not* limited to settings in which the overpayment induction is confounded with threats of self-esteem" (Greenberg, 1982: 394). Both reviews cite Pritchard, Dunnette, and Sorensen's (1972) study[1] as a prominent example. In this study the authors induced an overpayment situation by a different method—by telling subjects that an error in advertisement had occurred. Nevertheless, they found that overpaid subjects were, as expected, more productive than equitably paid subjects. This example, and others (e.g., Andrews, 1967; Garland, 1973) led Greenberg (1982) to conclude in his review that "overpayment effects are relatively *reliable* across a *variety* of induction procedures" (ibid., p. 494: emphasis added).

Some of the supporting hourly overpayment studies were criticized on other grounds as well. For example, one of the first studies—that of Adams and Rosenbaum (1962)—cited by Adams (1963a) as an outstanding example supporting his basic theory was criticized for leaving the length of future employment ambiguous and undefined, and therefore opening the way for feelings of job insecurity among their subjects. Job security, it was argued (e.g., Lawler, 1968b; Pritchard, 1969) reduces the efficacy of the equity explanation: overpaid unqualified subjects may be assumed to produce more not in order to reduce inequity but rather to buy job security and enhance their chances for continued employment.

Empirical support relating to the piece-rate overpaid situation is considered "relatively straightforward" by Goodman and Friedman (1971). As expected, a number of studies (e.g., Adams and Rosenbaum, 1962; Adams and Jacobsen, 1964; Goodman and Friedman, 1969) reported lower quantity and higher quality in this situation. Still, in evaluating these studies the authors point to some problems that raise doubts about whether the data did indeed support some of the assumptions underlying the hypothesis. For example, since the subjects were usually completely inexperienced with piece-rate payment systems it is doubtful that they initially felt overpaid or conceptualized overpayment on unit basis. Nevertheless,

> although the data did not support some of the mechanisms underlying the piece-rate hypothesis, the findings could be interpreted in the inequity framework. That is, overpaid subjects did experience inequity after an initial performance period and differentially emphasized quantity or quality outputs—whichever seemed more successful in resolving inequity. The problem with most piece-rate studies is that the perceived instrumentality of quantity or quality outputs was a function of artifacts in the induction and task rather than intrinsic characteristics of the payment system as suggested by Adams (Goodman and Friedman, 1971: 276).

In their summarizing overview, Goodman and Friedman (1971) place the *underpaid piece-rate* studies under the heading of studies that have clear empirical support; under the heading of studies that have tentative empirical support they include the underpaid hourly, overpaid piece-rate, and overpaid hourly studies.

Other Experimental Studies. Some experiments, inspired by equity theory instead of focusing on the effect of over- or underpayment on output quantity or output quality, investigated other dependent variables. For example, the proposition that equitable payment helps to maintain *effective group membership* was examined in laboratory studies conducted by Valenzi and Andrews (1971) and

Schmitt and Marwell (1972). In the Valenzi and Andrews (1971) study, subjects were hired at an hourly pay rate for clerical work. After working for one session, subjects' pay was decreased (underpaid group), increased (overpaid group), or left the same (control group). The findings indicated that 27 percent of the underpaid group subjects quit, while no subjects quit in the other two (overpaid and control) groups. In the Schmitt and Marwell (1972) experiment, subjects worked on cooperative or individual tasks. Rewards for cooperative tasks were greater, favorably inequitable, as compared with individual work. The experimentally created inequities were small, moderate, or large. The results indicated that, with withdrawal as the only alternative to inequity, a significant proportion of subjects chose to forgo the greater rewards and withdraw from the inequitable situation. Moreover, withdrawal from cooperation was an increasing function of inequity.

Weinstein and Holzbach (1973) investigated the effect of *mode of reward distribution* on member's productivity. They found that in task groups where reward allocation was differential—based on members' productivity—overall productivity was higher than in task groups where reward allocation was equal.

In an interesting recent experimental study, Sheehan (1988) found support for the hypothesis, based on equity theory, that employees who believe that their colleagues quit because of dissatisfaction with an aspect of their job or because of the availability of a better job will react negatively to their own job.

Field Research

The effect of perceived inequities on *performance* has also been examined in some field studies. Lord and Hohenfeld (1979) conducted an archival study on 23 major-league baseball players who for contractual reasons were paid lower salaries in one season (1976) than in the previous season (1975). It was hypothesized that these players would perceive themselves as underpaid relative to their payment in the previous year and would react with lowered performance. This hypothesis was supported by the data obtained: The players' lowered performance in the next season was indicated by reduction in batting averages, home runs, and runs batted in. A similar research conducted by Duchon and Jago (1981) failed to reproduce Lord and Hohenfeld's (1979) results. Duchon and Jago suggested that the discrepancy in results was due to the different surrounding circumstances: Lord and Hohenfeld's study was carried out on a sample of players that were facing much uncertainty concerning future contracts since this was the first season that free agency was widely used in baseball. By contrast, their own study included subsequent seasons when players were already aware of the possibility of obtaining multi-million dollar contracts which gave them an expectation of successful contract negotiation. These expectations, the authors claim, explain the players' different reactions to perceived pay inequities: "Looking toward the end of the season for their opportunity to restore inequity they exhibited no decline in performance" (Duchon and Jago, p. 73). Also, in subsequent years there was the awareness among players that a poor performance might lower their market value and thus decrease their chance for a good contract. The different surrounding conditions, conclude the authors, "make both our data and those of Lord and Hohenfeld (1979) interpretable in terms of equity theory and, therefore, compatible with each other" (p. 32).

There are also some field studies that have investigated the relationship between perceived inequities and *employee turnover*. Telly, French, and Scott (1971), in an investigation among hourly employees in high- and low-turnover shops in a large manufacturing company, found that turnover correlated positively with perceived overall inequity. Separate analyses for each outcome revealed, however, that perceived inequities regarding pay, security, and advancement were not significantly related to turnover. The authors suggested that these findings may be due to the fact that these aspects were typically tightly controlled by union contracts: "Union contracts, or, of course, other constraining structures . . . may minimize certain types of perceived inequities" (p. 171).

Finn and Lee (1972), in their investigation based on a sample of 170 professional and scientific personnel in Federal Public Health service, found that the subsample of employees perceiving their salary as inequitable had a higher propensity to quit their job than those in the subsample perceiving their salary as equitable.

Dittrich and Carrell (1979), in a study based on a sample of about 160 clerical employees in 20 departments of a large metropolitan office, found that employee perceptions of equity were related to *absenteeism*, which in turn was found to be related to *turnover*. From among the five dimensions of equitable treatment measured, the one displaying the strongest relationship was pay level. Perceived equity of pay level (compared externally with employees in other organizations) also affected turnover through direct comparison of inputs and outcomes; "a comparison which can lead to job change decisions" (p. 38).

Farrell and Rusbult (1981) investigated the relationship between *job satisfaction, job commitment* and *turnover*, and perceived reward and cost values. The study included an experiment simulating a work setting, and a cross-sectional field survey of about 160 industrial employees in the United States. The results of the experimental study indicated that perceived high-reward value was positively related to job satisfaction and commitment and negatively to turnover, whereas the opposite relationships obtained in regard to perceived high-cost value. The results of the field study were similar in regard to job satisfaction and commitment. While data about turnover rates were not available in this study, its findings indicated that intent to turnover is significantly related to organizational commitment and attachment (low intent–high commitment/attachment).

In a recent study based on a sample of 360 employees in a public health agency in the United States, Ziemak (1988) found that pay equity and pay satisfaction were related to important attitudinal outcomes like *intentions to turnover* and *commitment* but not to actual turnover and absenteeism.

THE PREVALENCE OF THE CONTRIBUTION
PRINCIPLE IN REWARD ALLOCATIONS

A series of experimental studies investigating *reward allocation* patterns and expecting these patterns to follow the contribution or equity norm was inspired by Leventhal's (1976a) proposition that the norm of equity will be maintained in task-oriented groups since it is instrumental in fostering high levels of task performance.[2]

These studies typically employ a reward-allocation paradigm having several basic variants. In one variant, subjects are required to fulfil a task that they are led to believe they are performing with a partner for monetary awards. The experimenter supplies participants with (fictitious) information about their and their "partners" inputs. After task completion, rewards are allocated on an underpaid, equitably paid, and overpaid basis. Subjects are then allowed to reallocate the rewards, thus providing a test for the theory. In another variant, instead of being allowed to reallocate rewards, subjects are supplied with an amount of money and asked to distribute it after their task completion as they see fit.

In a third variant, the allocator of the reward is an *outsider* not participating in the task group and its rewards. He is given a description of a work situation and is provided with the same information about total achievements, individual contributions, and size of reward. He is then asked to propose a plan of his own for allocating the reward.

A number of experiments (e.g., Leventhal, Allen, and Kemelgor, 1969a; Lane, Messe and Phillips, 1971; Mikula, 1974) support the equity theory proposition that rewards earned will be allocated by subjects in accordance with each member's contribution. For example, in studies where subjects were allowed to reallocate rewards as they saw fit, the findings indicated that overpaid subjects reduced their share of outcomes, underpaid subjects increased their share, and equitably paid subjects did not change their share. In another study Leventhal and colleagues (1969b) demonstrated that equity theory is more successful in explaining the above findings than alternative theoretical explanations. In this experiment, some of the subjects were told that the partner allocated reward intentionally, whereas others were told that he did it casually. The results indicated that subjects overrewarded intentionally decreased their share of reward more than those overrewarded by chance. All underrewarded subjects increased their rewards to the same extent.

A specific experiment testing reward allocations as a function of duration and quantity of performance was performed by Leventhal and Michaels (1969). The results indicated that with amount of work constant, subjects who worked longer took less reward than subjects who worked for shorter duration. When amount of work and duration were equal for each partner, subject divided reward equally (i.e., followed the contribution principle).

Lane and Messe (1971) conducted two experiments whose findings were similar to those of Leventhal and Michaels (1969) above. In the first, subjects performed a task with partner and distributed rewards equally to selves and partner when both had equal inputs. In the second, where subjects' inputs were varied systematically, allocations tended to be based on relative inputs. The authors concluded that both experiments indicate that persons conform to a norm of equity when allocating rewards in task groups.

In an experimental study among American and Colombian subjects, Marin (1981) utilized a vignette situation that described reward distributions among individuals who had performed an unspecified task in an experiment. Payments were variously described as based on contributors' performance or as equal. Subjects were required to rate the fairness of the payment and to estimate how they themselves would have allocated the reward. The findings indicated a clear preference by subjects of both nationalities for the contribution rule both in ratings of fairness and when asked how they would have divided the reward.

THE EFFECT OF CONTEXTUAL FACTORS ON REWARD ALLOCATIONS: A TEST FOR VARYING DISTRIBUTION RULES

A relatively large number of studies were guided by the thesis that different distribution rules may apply in different circumstances. Most of these studies are experimental and most employ varying forms of the reward-allocation paradigm. They focus on such factors as the nature of prevalent social relationships, the goals to be achieved, the scarcity or abundance of resources, and the nature of contributions made, as major determinants of the distribution principles adhered to (e.g., Deutsch, 1975; Leventhal, 1976b; Lerner, Miller, and Holmes, 1976; Mikula and Schwinger, 1978). The studies are reviewed in chronological order and according to major variables investigated.

The Nature of Social Relationships

Reward-allocation studies in this sphere focused mainly on some aspects of group-member interactions and interpersonal attitudes, and on the longevity of their relationships.

Patterns of Interaction. A number of studies were guided by the hypothesis that member *competition* or a lack of *task interdependencies* will be associated with a tendency to prefer the contribution rule, whereas cooperative relationships will be associated with a tendency to prefer the equality rule. Most relevant studies support the basic hypothesis. For example, Valentine (1971) found that with experimental instructions emphasizing group members' interdependence, subjects with superior performance tended to reduce their own shares of reward and divide rewards equally.

Lerner (1974) in an experiment with children found that both superior and inferior performers tended to move toward equal allocations when their work group was defined as a "team"; however, when the group members were called "coworkers" rather than "team members" allocation patterns followed the equity principle more closely.

Schwinger (1980: 110–13), in a study similar to Lerner's but based on adult subjects, found that superior performers tended indeed to divide rewards equally in the "team" condition and equitably in the "individual work" condition. However, the inferior performers tended to follow the contribution rule in both experimental conditions. A possible explanation for the discrepant findings of Lerner's (1974) and Schwinger's (1980) studies regarding inferior performers is that Lerner's six-year-old inferior performers in the teamwork condition were not aware of or could not resist behaving selfishly, whereas the adult inferior performers in the teamwork condition in Schwinger's experiment were able to restrain themselves and divide rewards according to contributions though it was to their disadvantage.

Schwinger's study had also an additional, interesting, experimental element. Given the chance to negotiate the distribution rule to be followed, subjects tended to follow the same principles: In all instances of teamwork, equality was the agreed principle; in the individual-work situation the tendency was to prefer the contribution principle.

In a recent study, Törnblom and Jonsson (1985) found that female subjects judging the fairness of contribution and equality in the distribution of rewards under conditions of cooperation and competition, tended to consider contribution as more just in competitive situations and equality as more just in cooperative situations.

Bierhoff (Bierhoff, Buck, and Klein 1986: 169–78) also examined judgments about reward allocators in a series of experiments varying social context (team/nonteam), contribution fulfilment (high/low), and equality fulfilment (high/low). The results indicated that subjects tended generally to evaluate the allocators following the equality rule more positively, and that a manipulation of the contribution rule made a difference only in the nonteam condition, when allocators following the contribution rule were evaluated more positively.

Why should a team work situation invoke the equality principle (at least among high performers)? One explanation offered is conflict avoidance: Teamwork, which is by definition a cooperative undertaking, cannot be sustained under conditions of interpersonal conflict. But such conflict is likely to occur when joint contributions to a common goal are emphasized but rewards are not equally divided. Support for this kind of explanation may be found in a number of studies. Shapiro (1975) found that superior performers who divided rewards equally expected relatively more favorable evaluations from their peers than superior performers who took more for themselves. Leventhal, Michaels, and Sanford (1972) found that subjects who were instructed to prevent conflict tended to reduce the reward differentials between the superior and inferior performers, whereas subjects who were expressly told to disregard the possibility of conflict tended to follow the contribution principle.

Direct evidence that a reward distribution policy that compresses interindividual differences is chosen in order to increase group harmony and decrease group conflict, was found by Leventhal, Michaels, and Sanford (1972). These authors found that subjects tended to rate large pay differentials between the best and worst performers as more likely to generate intragroup conflict and hostility than small differentials. They also found a perfect rank-order correlation between the estimated likelihood of conflict and the perceived difference between the satisfaction of high and low performers. Obviously, large differences in satisfaction provide fertile ground for disharmony and conflict.

In a second study—where subjects were supplied with different information about the personality traits of the best performers ("unselfish and slow to anger"; "selfish and quick to anger"; no information)—the findings indicated that the perceived impact of an equal reward distribution on intragroup conflict depended on the personality of the best performers: When these were described as unselfish and slow to anger, subjects tended to believe that an equal distribution of rewards was less likely to cause conflict than any other division of reward. Such a belief was held by only a minority of subjects where the best performers were described as selfish and quick to anger. The authors suggest that these findings indicate that equal distributions will be preferred to moderate ineqality when group members have a cooperative and relaxed attitude toward each other.

A study by Marin (1981) produced results in line with those emanating from Leventhal and Michaels' (1972) study. In this study it was found that equal allocators are perceived as relatively more concerned with conflict avoidance, promoting friendliness, and trying to maintain good relations than allocators following the contribution rule.

Interpersonal Attitudes. Several studies addressed to the hypothesis that, in contexts where *friendly relationships* prevail or are emphasized, where subjects perceive *similarities* between themselves and others, or where *person-* rather than *role-salience* prevails, the equality principle will be preferred over the equity principle. Generally, the findings of these studies tend to support the basic hypothesis. For example, in one such study conducted among soldiers belonging to the same unit, Mikula and Schwinger (1973) formed dyads on basis of previously administered sociometric tests while varying the affective relations between dyad members. The findings indicated that allocators who made larger contributions to the attained reward chose the equality principle more often in the positive situation, i.e., where the partner was liked, than in the condition where the partner was not liked. The findings also indicated that when partners were requested to *agree* on the final allocation, in the positive condition the tendency was to follow the equality principle; whereas in the negative condition, the equality and contribution principles were used about equally.

The findings of later studies fall in line with the above findings. For example, in an experiment conducted by Curtis (1979) subjects were previously led to like or dislike the partner. The results of the study indicated that subjects who liked the other tended to divide rewards equally, whereas the others tended to follow the contribution rule. The results also indicated that subjects with negative attitudes towards the partner allocated a significantly greater amount to themselves than did subjects with positive attitudes toward the partner.

In an experimental study conducted by Larwood, Levine, Shaw, and Hurwitz (1979) subjects, participating in pairs, had the opportunity to become acquainted with one another. As predicted, the findings indicated that when allocating rewards after task performance subjects tended to apply the contribution principle when their partner out-performed them. In contrast, when they themselves excelled they tended to divide rewards equally.

Austin (1980) studied the reward allocation patterns of roommates and strangers under conditions of either low or high performance. He found, as expected, that roommates tended to overlook differences in merit and chose to distribute rewards equally, whereas strangers tended to choose an equal distribution when they performed poorly and followed the contributions principle when they excelled.

Lamm and Schwinger (1980) investigated the effect of interpersonal relationships on need considerations. They asked a sample of subjects to indicate how they would allocate a sum of money between team members who had contributed equally to attain this money. The team members were described alternately as close friends or superficial acquaintances who differed in their needs. The findings indicated that a sizable proportion of the subjects tended to favor the needier person regardless of the interpersonal relationships of the team members. Still, need consideration tended to be greater when teammates were described as close friends than when they were described as superficial acquaintances. The findings also indicated that need consideration was hardly affected by whether the needier person was responsible for his/her distress or not.

Bossong (1983), in a study conducted in Germany, found that subjects asked to determine the just allocation in fictitious situations in which two persons with different contributions earned a common salary, tended relatively more to follow the contribution rule when the interaction between the task performers was described as businesslike than when it was described as friendly.

Debuscherre and van Avermaet (1984) distinguished between two contexts in their experiment. In one, the relationship between members was described as harmonious and long lasting, while in the other the importance of performance maximization was emphasized and no future interaction was expected. The findings indicated that subjects in the first condition tended relatively more than their colleagues to follow the equality principle in allocating rewards.

Leung and Park (1986) investigated the fairness judgments of allocations, the judgment of allocators, and the pattern of hypothetical allocations in a study presenting to subjects scenarios of a working situation occurring either in a neighborhood or business context. In each case, the authors also investigated the subjects' perceptions of the importance of two goals: productivity and friendship. The findings indicated that the equity rule was rated as fairer in the business context, whereas the equality rule was rated as fairer in the neighborhood context. They also indicated that the subjects tended to allocate a higher share of the total reward to the high performers in the business situation than to their colleagues in the neighborhood situation. In the business situation, an allocator using the equity rule was judged as higher on social competence than one using the equality rule. The opposite occurred in the neighborhood situation. Significant correlations were found between perceived interactional goals and perceived preferences for distribution rules: A perceived goal of productivity produced a positive correlation with the fairness rating of equity and with the share allocated to high performers. In contrast, a perceived goal of friendship produced a positive correlation with the fairness rating of equality, and a negative correlation with the share allocated to high performers. These later findings confirm that the perception of interactional goals mediates individuals' choice of distribution rules.

The effect of *similarity* perceptions was studied by Greenberg (1978a). In this study, subjects were led to believe that they performed better on a task than a similar, dissimilar, or unknown opponent. The findings indicated that when dividing a reward after the task, subjects kept a relatively higher portion of the reward when the opponent was dissimilar. In contrast, even though their contributions were greater, subjects divided rewards equally when their opponents were similar.

Mikula (1974) likewise found that subjects of the same nationality residing in a foreign country and feeling drawn together by virtue of their common status as aliens tended to reduce their own share of rewards and divide rewards equally when their performances were superior to those of others; as well, they took smaller proportions of the reward for themselves when their performances were relatively inferior.

The effect of *ingroup-outgroup* categorization on distributive rule application was studied by Messe, Hymes, and MacCoun (1986). The authors hypothesized that, in task-oriented work situations, the norm of equity will predominate but its influence will be moderated by group-categorization processes. Subject playing the role of supervisor had to allocate pay to two "workers" who were alternately characterized an outgroup member or an ingroup member. As expected, the findings indicated that subjects were more equitable in their reward allocations when the worker was an ingroup member than when he was an outgroup member.

Carles and Carver (1979), investigated the effects of *person salience* versus *role salience* on reward allocations. Their hypothesis that person salience will be associated with a tendency to allocate rewards equally while role salience will be associated with a tendency to follow the contribution principle, found support among female subjects but not among male subjects. Contrary to expectations, males tended to allocate themselves more of the group's earnings in the person-salient condition than they did in the role-salient condition or the control condition. Further analyses revealed that these results may be due to the way males perceived their cosubjects. White females tended, as expected, to perceive their cosubjects as competitors in the role-salient condition, males, unexpectedly, tended to perceive their cosubjects as competitors in the person-salient condition: "This unanticipated perceptual-cognitive transformation," suggest the authors, "influenced even male subjects' allocations in a perfectly intelligible fashion" (p. 2077).

The Longevity of Relationships. A number of studies have explored the thesis that an actual or anticipated long-term relationship will result in the choice of the equality principle rather than the contribution principle in the allocation of rewards. These studies tend to support this thesis. Shapiro (1975) found that high contributors divided rewards equally when future interaction was expected but followed the contribution principle when no such interaction was expected. By contrast, low contributors tended to follow the contribution principle regardless of their expectations of future interactions. The findings also indicated that in both cases allocators expected to be evaluated favorably by their partners. Von Grumbkow, Deen, Steensman, and Wilke (1976), in an experiment manipulating performance levels and future interaction with task performers, found that subjects expecting future interaction with the task performers tended relatively more to follow the equality rule and allocate relatively higher rewards to the low performers than subjects not expecting future interaction with reward recipients.

Austin and McGinn (1977) found that the contribution principle was preferred when interaction with the high-input worker was expected, whereas when interaction with the inferior performer was anticipated the equality principle was preferred. Sagan, Pondel, and Andrisin (1981) found that when future interaction was expected, subjects of both sexes tended to allocate rewards equally, whereas when no future interaction was expected, men tended to allocate rewards according to contributions while women tended to divide rewards equally. The authors argued that these findings are explicable by the higher threshold in males for eliciting an equality norm. For them, "a clear expectation of future interaction" was required to become person-oriented and favor equality.

The Goals Pursued

A series of studies have focused on the thesis proposing that group goals may affect group members' preferences for a given distribution rule. The goals studied were conflict avoidance, maximizing production and motivating high performance, membership control, and attaining or improving efficiency in resource allocation and utilization. Some of the relevant studies have been described earlier. To avoid duplication we will mention these studies only briefly.

Conflict Avoidance. The studies relating to this issue were reviewed earlier. They indicate that when avoiding conflict is a principal goal, the tendency is to follow the equality rule (e.g., Leventhal, Michaels, and Sanford, 1972).

Increasing Production and Efficiency and Motivating Performance. Leventhal and Whiteside (1973) found that subjects who were instructed to encourage performance tended to allocate relatively higher rewards to task performers with lower aptitude, as compared with subjects instructed to reward fairly.

Similar findings emerged from Greenberg and Leventhal's (1976) study. These findings indicated that in some instances subjects who were instructed to encourage performance even violated the equity norm by giving poor performers higher rewards than they gave to high performers. Questionnaire data indicated that subjects did indeed believe that raising the rewards of low performers was an effective method for eliciting improved performance.

Stake (1983) found that when expected to follow an abstract fairness norm, subjects tended to make allocations according to productivity (i.e., number of work units produced). In contrast, when expected to maximize productivity they tended to make allocations in line with the capability of workers (i.e., units produced per hour). When the goal was to promote good relationships, subjects tended—as expected—to make equal allocations.

The findings also indicated that under conditions of low ambiguity in deservingness subjects tended to be more consistent in allocations across conditions than in conditions of high ambiguity. The author argues that this suggests that motives have more effect on allocations when the relative deservingness of recipients is ambiguous than when it is clear.

Membership Control. The thesis that group membership considerations may affect the preferred mode of reward allocation was tested in a number of studies. For example, Baskett (1973) found that subjects who were required to evaluate a candidate for a post in a large company, besides tending to favor the high-performing individuals also tended to recommend higher salaries for such individuals whom they wished to encourage to join the company.

Landau and Leventhal (1976) investigated the effect of a variety of membership goals on reward allocations. Subjects were asked to make judgments about the size of salary increases for employees who had received a job offer from another company that was either highly or moderately attractive. Conditions were varied in regard to the principal pay-policy instruction: In the selective condition subjects were instructed to retain high performers and weed out low performers. In the unselective condition they were instructed to encourage all employees to stay on. In the unspecified control condition subjects were instructed to bestow raises as they saw fit. The findings indicated that in all policy conditions subjects gave higher raises to productive than to nonproductive employees. They also indicated that in all policy conditions subjects tended to give productive employees counteroffers that exceeded the outside offer. Finally the findings indicated that when allowed to follow their own discretion, male subjects behaved as if they wanted to get rid of the low performers. Female subjects behaved as if they wanted to retain them.

Two recent studies conducted by Rusbult and colleagues (1988, 1990) also focused on the effect of employee mobility on reward allocations, like the Landau and Leventhal study, but also investigated how these allocations are affected by reward availability and labor availability. The findings indicated that subjects acting as baseball team managers (the 1988 study) and as chairman of a large physics department (the 1990 study), tended generally to allocate higher rewards to the more competent and productive members, and tended to allocate higher rewards to the competent mobile members as compared to their less mobile counterparts. This latter tendency was more pronounced under conditions of low reward availability and low labor availability. In the 1990 study it was found, in addition, that the tendency to favor competent mobile individuals is greater when allocators are led to believe that instrumental group goals (e.g., productivity, productive capacity) are most important, as compared to when social-emotional group goals (e.g., morale) predominate.

Efficient Resource Allocation. A few studies investigated the thesis that the preferred mode of reward allocation is influenced by considerations of efficient resource allocation. The studies generally support the thesis. Pondy and Birnberg (1969) found that subjects playing the role of a chief budget officer were generally readier to allocate resources to unit managers whose past efficiency in resource allocation was greater.

In another study, Leventhal, Weiss, and Butrick (1973) manipulated subjects' concern about preventing waste: Some subjects were led to believe that the resources they were supposed to allocate would deteriorate if not used promptly. These subjects tended relatively more than their colleagues to allocate resources to those who were likely to use them frequently.

Resource Scarcity or Abundance

Does the abundance or scarcity of resources have any effect on allocation choices? And if so, what are the effects? Not many studies have addressed this question. The few that have, indicate that scarcity and abundance of resources may indeed affect allocation choices. In their study, Lane and Messe (1972) manipulated the amount of reward available to those supposed to distribute it. The manipulation of reward was relative to a fair "internal standard" of the distributors. The findings indicated that the equity principle was applied only when rewards were sufficient (i.e., commensurate with the internal standard of fair pay). When the amount of reward was greater or smaller than this, subjects allocated more to themselves . Coon, Lane, and Lichtman (1974) obtained similar results in their research with children.

In a recent study, Hegtvedt (1987), like Lane and Messe (1972), manipulated the scarcity or abundance of resources. In addition, she manipulated the performance levels of the participants and used a three-person team design instead of dyads. The author argued that the nondyadic context alters the zero-sum nature of the distribution, enhancing concern for the group and making the "defense" of self-interested behavior more difficult since more members are affected. The results tended to confirm this thesis. They indicated that, as expected, in conditions of reward scarcity, performance level is positively related to a preference for equality and negatively related to a preference for equity. In contrast, when rewards were sufficient, the reverse, self-interested trends emerged. Average performers, however, tended to prefer equality under both scarcity and abundance conditions. The author argues that when rewards are scarce, allocators following self-interest may be perceived by others as acting unfairly and irresponsibly, that is, against social norms of fairness and responsibility to others—a perception costly to themselves. As a result, "an allocator may minimize perceived costs by acting responsibly to others and distributing rewards in a way that benefits others." And further, "even though average performers appear to have no self-interested distribution-rule preference, consideration of perceived rewards and costs may be useful in understanding their behavior. For example, if the rewards and costs associated with an equal and equitable distribution are the same, average performers might opt for equality" (Hegtvedt, pp. 202–03).

Resource scarcity was also manipulated by Rusbult and colleagues (1988, 1990) in their recent studies investigating the effect of employee mobility on resource allocations. They found that the tendency to allocate higher rewards to mobile and competent members is more pronounced when resources are relatively scarce than when they are relatively abundant.

In a study by Greenberg (1979a), subjects were asked to rate the perceived fairness of each of three pricing schemes for a scarce resource (oil) and an abundant resource (coal). The findings indicated that for the scarce resource an increasing sliding scale was considered most fair, and a decreasing sliding scale as least fair. By contrast, the flat rate was considered most fair for the abundant resource. These findings indicate that efficiency in resource allocation and the preservation of resources is a predominant consideration under conditions of resource scarcity but not under conditions of resource abundance. In the latter case, equality is preferred. Greenberg (1981) notes that some caution about the above findings is in order: Subjects in the above research were college students who probably did not have to pay utility bills and may therefore have been freer to recommend more "idealistic" policies than those who might be directly affected by these policies.

The Nature of Inputs

Several studies investigated the effect of the nature of inputs or contributions on the preferred distribution rules. For example, Mikula and Uray (1973) manipulated a *performance maxima* while keeping the (fictitious) performance feedback constant. The findings indicated that subjects with relatively large contributions tended to apply the contribution principle more frequently where their partner's contribution, as measured against the performance maxima, was close to that maxima. Subjects with relatively small contributions, however, tended to follow the contribution principle under all circumstances.

A series of other studies addressed a different question: What happens when individuals are not fully responsible for the results produced? What distribution rules are considered just when causality is partly or wholly determined "externally"? In a study by Leventhal and Michaels (1971), subjects had to judge how rewards should be administered for performance in high jumping. The authors found that with performance constant, persons whose height and training enhanced their jumping were rated less deserving than those whose height and training did not help them. The findings also indicated that individuals with high effort were considered more deserving than those with low effort. The results suggest that personal responsibility for outcomes, displayed, for example, in amount of effort invested, is given greater weight in reward distribution than external factors.

A study that directly manipulated the "locus of control" variable was conducted by Cohen (1974). Some of the subjects were led to believe that they had complete control over the joint performances required of them, while others were told that their joint performances were primarily a function of their having been assigned to relatively easy or difficult task conditions. The prediction that reward distributions would reflect the perceived causal locus of control was supported only under lax environmental constraints; that is, under a low criterion of group success where the costs of abandoning the contribution rule were not too high. Under more stringent conditions, high performers received more rewards and the pattern of reward distributions was quite close to that in the control groups. The author interpreted these findings as evidence for the predominance, in group allocation decisions, of performance (termed mastery) considerations over locus of control considerations.

In a similar experiment, Uray (1976) found that when manipulated conditions suggested person-related internal causes (differences in effort), there was a tendency to use the equity principle. However, when differences in performance were attributable to external factors (differences in task difficulty), high-performance allocators tended to use the equality principle while low-performance allocators tended to decide on allocations lying midway between strict adherence to the contributions rule and strict adherence to the equality rule.

Larwood, Levine, and Shaw (1979) manipulated the nature of the task on which subjects were engaged (task requiring skills vs. task based on luck) and performance feedback (above/below specified norm). The findings confirmed the hypothesis that the contribution principle would be used more often in the skilled than in the chance task, and that contribution-rule users would be less likely than equality-rule users to attribute the performance outcome to luck. The findings also supported the hypothesis that subjects using the contribution principle would cite inputs on which participants might vary as reasons for their reward allocation. These subjects found inputs such as ability and score to be more important than did subjects who tended to apply the equality principle; the latter found cooperation relatively more important. Time and effort emerged as overlapping between equity and equality users. The authors concluded that "performance-related individual inputs such as score and ability are associated with the objective use of equity, while less relevant inputs such a cooperation lead to objective equality" (p. 60).

Greenberg (1980c) found that subjects dividing rewards between themselves and a competitor following task performance tended to make allocations according to contributions when they were responsible for their performance. When not responsible, they tended to follow the equality rule.

Witting, Marks, and Jones (1981) conducted an experiment where subjects of both sexes participated in tasks in which success was set at either luck or effort. All subjects received feedback that they contributed higher input than their partner and had been chosen to allocate a group reward between themselves and partner. The findings indicated that subjects of both sexes allocated more to themselves when they attributed their success to effort than to luck.

Schwinger, Kayser, and Mueller (1981) found that inequalities in effort and performance led to unequal allocations. Differences in effort led to unequal allocations even when the workers performed equally well. The data on the fairness judgments of allocations also indicated that unequal allocations were judged as more just when workers differed in effort and/or performances than when they did not.

Situational Ambiguity and Computational Complexity

What happens when there is situational ambiguity; for example, when the situational demands or the goals to be attained enter into conflict as to the distribution rules to be applied? Will there be a tendency to use one rule exclusively or to reconcile the opposing situational demands by compromise between the rules? A recent study by Debusschere and Van Avermaet (1984) addressed the important question. They note that theorists do not agree on the solutions: Some argue that to avoid cognitive dissonance the tendency will be to follow one rule exclusively (e.g., Meeker, 1971; Shapiro, 1975), whereas others argue that individuals will find it difficult to ignore certain aspects of the situation and will therefore try to compromise (e.g., Leventhal, 1976a, 1976b). Following analysis of 30 previous studies, the authors suggested that situational ambiguity is a major determinant of compromise. Specifically, the analysis indicated a significant negative correlation between strength of situation orientation and the tendency to compromise between distribution rules. But there were some exceptions. In one of the studies analyzed, there was a lack of compromise in a seemingly ambiguous situation. The authors suggested that computational complexity may have hindered compromise. They hypothesized that compromising between relevant rules will occur only where the allocational computation is fairly simple. In their own study, they sought to investigate the effect of both variables—ambiguity and complexity. Complexity was manipulated by supplying more/less complex information on performance. Ambiguity was manipulated by devising a clear equity- or equality-oriented situation or by devising a situation which lay in between these two situations. Contrary to expectation, the authors found no interaction between situational ambiguity and complexity. Instead, they found that compromising tended to decrease with complexity. Moreover, in rule-unambiguous situations complexity did not affect relative preferences for equity or equality, whereas in ambiguous conditions complexity was found to be positively associated with preference for the equality rule. The authors concluded that greater computational complexity has a double effect: It decreases the amount of compromising and induces a preference for equality over equity allocations, if situational demands for equity are not too strong. They suggest that these effects are expressions of the same tendency: to switch to computationally easier allocations as allocation computations become more complex. Thus, equal allocations are much easier since contributions can be completely ignored and the only requirement is a simple division of rewards according to number of recipients.

Organizational Position

Does an employee's organizational position in any way influence his preferences about pay-allocation patterns? A field study conducted by Lansberg (1984) suggests that it may. The study was conducted on 70 employees in clerical, middle-management, and upper-management positions in one department of a research and development laboratory in the United States. Participants were required to choose "the fairest way" of dividing a lump sum among employees. The results indicated a preference among the managers for allocations based on contributions. However, middle- and upper-level managers differed in their views as to which specific mode was preferable: Upper-level managers tended to view an all-organization performance criterion as fairest, whereas middle-level managers perceived allocations based on the individuals' contributions to their unit's performance as fairest. Clericals did not differentiate between equity and equality, and tended to perceive both as fair. The authors suggest that the differing views of the managerial echelons reflect the fact that each level prefers the mode that best reflects its respective contributions. The fact that among clericals the equality rule was viewed as fair and as relevant as the contribution rule, the authors suggest, is related to the fact that unlike the managers, this group experienced group solidarity and cooperation vis-à-vis one another that would tend to induce perceptions of equality.

Tradition

What, if any, is the effect of tradition on the preferred mode of reward allocation? A field study by Larwood and Blackmore (1977) suggests that a traditional mode of reward distribution tends also to become the preferred mode. Specifically, these findings indicated that salaried employees, whose pay is not directly linked to performance, preferred the equality principle while hourly employees and commission receivers, whose wages are based on contributions such as time and productivity, preferred the contribution principle. Data from background questions revealed that commission personnel, more than others, thought of themselves in competitive terms. They also felt, more than others, that their pay was directly keyed to their "doing a good job."

To rule out the possibility of alternative explanations, the authors conducted two additional studies. One aimed to prove that preferences are not fixed and, hence, the results in the first study cannot be attributed to selective recruitment or self-selection biases. This study manipulated the nature of the settings to which subjects (students) were exposed. The findings indicated that the preferences regarding distribution principles varied according to the setting to which they were exposed: Where this setting was a gambling establishment, the preferred distribution principle was winner-take-all (WTA); where it was a banking institution, the preferred principle was contribution; and where the setting was a socialist youth group, the rule preferred was equality. These findings, the authors argue, indicate that preferences are not fixed but vary according to institutional circumstances.

In an additional study by the authors, settings associated with normative exchanges were deliberately selected to further test the original findings. Participants were bankers, who "might normatively be expected to prefer the equity exchange"; union members, who "might produce a bias for equality"; and unemployed, who "are normatively expected to prefer WTA to a greater extent than bankers or union members, since they have less to lose in any such exchange." The main hypothesis was that participants would "favor the exchanges associated with their method of pay" rather than exchanges dictated by the nature of their respective settings. Specifically, it was expected that the greatest equality preference would be found among the salaried bankers and the strongest WTA preference would be found among the union members competing at a union's hiring hall for a day's work. The unemployed, preferring to work rather than receive welfare, were expected to embrace the equity norm. The findings fully confirmed these hypotheses.

An effect of tradition was also obtained by Dornstein (1990a) in a field study aimed at investigating the perceived fairness of various pay-incentive plans among four groups of employees ($N = 165$) in an industrial organization. The findings of this study indicated, among others, that individuals who have been exposed to a particular type of pay-incentive plan (e.g., individual incentives/group incentives/organization-wide productivity incentives) tended to consider this system fairer than the others.

THE WIDER SOCIOCULTURAL CONTEXT

Some theorists suggest, as indicated, that the distribution rules applied in judging the fairness of pay may vary from culture to culture. Is there an empirical support for this proposition? And if so, what exactly are the effects of the sociocultural context? The empirical studies in this case are not sufficient for answering these questions: They are relatively few, mostly experimental, of limited scope, and are not well-founded theoretically. All these limitations, and especially the latter, make it difficult to derive any firm conclusions from these studies. Still, a review of these studies can illuminate the intricacy of the problems involved in researching this area and can perhaps also presage answers to a few major questions.

The review follows the order already established, starting with studies testing propositions arising from equity theory and continuing with studies of reward allocation inspired by theories emphasizing the multiplicity of distribution rules.

Studies in the Wake of Equity Theory

Equity theory did not generate many cross-cultural studies. One of the exceptions aiming directly at the question at hand is the study conducted by Weick, Bougon, and Maruyama (1976). Specifically, the study aimed at investigating the effect of different socio-cultural contexts on preferences of forms of equity. A basic postulate was that equity "is also an issue involving definition of inputs, outcomes and the desirable contingencies between these elements" (ibid., p. 63). The study was conducted in the Netherlands and employed a method used in an earlier study by Weick and Nesset (1968). Subjects were presented with pairs of hypothetical work situations and asked to assume that they were one of the two actors in each situation described. They were then instructed to select that situation in which they would feel most comfortable and to mark which of eleven adjustments they would make for their least-preferred alternative to make it more comfortable for themselves. The alternatives in each pair contained different forms of equity: own-equity, where one's inputs were proportionate to one's outcomes; other-equity, where one's coworker's inputs were proportionate to his outcomes; and comparison-equity where one's input/outcome ratio was equal to one's coworker's input/outcome ratio. The authors compared the findings from the Netherlands with those obtained earlier in the United States. It was found, among other things, that the Dutch subjects preferred high inputs for self regardless of the outcomes while the American subjects preferred high outcomes for self, regardless of the inputs. The authors argued that the Dutch results are explainable by certain specific features of the sociocultural context in that country. Two of these are the Calvinistic heritage and the prominence of the value of benevolence in the Dutch. The authors assert:

> If one rephrases Calvinism in equity language the doctrine reads: 'high inputs are good, outcomes are irrelevant—they come later.' To say that Calvinism is a current influential determinant of the Netherlands' equity context is unwarranted, but to say that it is part of Dutch heritage and that the doctrine is consistent in emphasis with a separation of inputs from outcomes is reasonable. It might also be noted that benevolence, a prominent Dutch characteristic, can be rephrased in equity language as situation of high input . . . with little expectation of matching outcomes. (Weick, Bougon and Maruyama, 1976: 36–37)

A third relevant feature is the traditional mode of wage/salary administration. Here the authors note that

> the Dutch situation works against a person perceiving that inputs and outcomes are related. . . . Hourly rates and piece-rate wages are rare . . . as are wages paid on a weekly basis. The importance of this pattern . . . is that it works against a person thinking in terms of specific inputs for which specific outcomes are realized. (p. 36)

Studies Investigating Reward Allocations

A number of experimental studies employed the reward-allocation paradigm to examine, on a cross-cultural or more precisely cross-national basis, the distribution rules preferred by individuals in reward allocations. Some of these studies, comparing mainly individuals from a variety of Western countries, exhibit little cross-cultural variance. Among the first of these studies were two conducted by Pepitone and colleagues (Pepitone et al., 1967; Pepitone et al., 1970). These studies involved a "prisoner's dilemma game" in which rewards are determined by the combinations of the joint choices of two colours, red and green, of the two partners in the game. It was pointed out that green is a "competitive" choice in that it could maximize the subject's own rewards and minimize his partner's rewards; red, on the other hand, is a "cooperative" choice in that it could provide a modest reward to both players equally. "Partners' " choices were preprogrammed and manipulated so as to make subjects believe that if they wished they could maximize the available rewards. Subjects were "tested" for their abilities and received experimentally manipulated "feedback" about these abilities. In one study (Pepitone et al., 1967) involving U.S., French, and Italian undergraduates, it was found that French and U.S. "high-ability" subjects tended to maximize their rewards by making relatively more competitive choices as compared with "low-ability" subjects. These findings were explained by an equity-seeking tendency on the part of the U.S. and French subjects: "S's compete for rewards . . . in accordance with what they think they are worth" (ibid., p. 151). The results obtained for the Italians were, however, ambiguous and could not be interpreted in a similar fashion.

A like ambiguity in regard to Italian subjects emerged in the second study (Pepitone et al., 1970) involving U.S. and Italian subjects. Here, a slight procedural change was introduced: "High-ability" subjects received from the experimenter a monetary reward that was proclaimed to be based on the "aptitude test" results (equity condition). Monetary rewards were also distributed to other subjects, in other groups, on an arbitrary basis—without reference to test scores (inequity condition). The results indicated that in the inequity condition subjects of both nationalities made fewer gain-maximizing choices than their partners that is, attempted to restore equity. In the equity condition, U.S. subjects maintained apparent test-related reward inequalities. However, Italian subjects who did not receive the award (those with low-ability test scores), awarded themselves more than those receiving the awards. These results may be interpreted as reflecting a preference, among Italians, for the equality principle over the equity or contribution principle. The authors claimed, however, that this interpretation may not apply since the ability manipulation in Italy may not have been successful. This reservation calls in question the conclusions that may be drawn from the Pepitone and colleagues' (1967, 1970) studies about the basic orientation of the Italian subjects.

An experimental study by Mikula (1974) comparing the reward-allocation patterns of Austrian and American students indicated "no ethnically caused differences in the reward allocation'' (p. 435). The findings indicated that generally low performers tended to follow the equity rule, while high performers tended to follow the equality rule.

An experimental study by Kahn, Lamm, and Nelson (1977) testing the attitudes of American and German subjects toward allocators in a fictitious scenario revealed, among American subjects of both sexes, a strong preference for high-input *equal* allocators and for low-input *equitable* allocators. Among the German subjects, however, the results indicated a "weaker, less consistent pattern." The results indicated that the German subjects indeed believed that *others* would like the generous allocator (i.e., the allocator with high inputs and equal distribution) but they *themselves* did not consistently prefer the generous allocator. The authors maintain that this may be due to the tendency to "equate generosity with a lack of potency." This explanation is supported by data showing among the German subjects studied a positive correlation between potency and evaluation of the allocator (negative correlations were obtained for the American subjects).

The findings of Feather and O'Driscoll (1980), who investigated Australian subjects' evaluations of allocators and allocations, were very similar to those obtained by Kahn, Lamm, and Nelson (1977) regarding the American subjects. The subjects in Feather and O'Driscoll's study tended to perceive the high-input equal allocators in more positive terms, liked them more, and tended to view their allocation as fairer, as compared with the high-input equitable allocators. All these differences were reversed for the low-input equal allocators: these were less liked and their allocations were perceived as less fair compared with the low-input equitable allocators.

Similar findings were obtained by Feather (1983) in another study with Australian subjects. Specifically, subjects in this study displayed a more positive attitude toward a high-input equal allocator and to a low-input equitable allocator than toward a high-input equitable allocator or a low-input equal allocator. Marin (1981), in a study with Colombian and American subjects, found that subjects of both nationalities judged the allocations by the contribution principle as fairer than those by the equality principle and preferred the contribution principle over the equality principle when asked to choose. Similarly, the allocators applying the contribution rule were perceived to be fairer than those applying equality rule.

The Effect of Situational Factors on Reward Allocations. The picture emerging from another set of cross-cultural studies employing the reward allocation paradigm is one of somewhat greater inter-cultural variety than the one emanating from the studies reviewed above. In contrast to the latter, these studies focus on the effect of a variety of contextual factors on reward allocations, and also include individuals of other than Western origin. One of the earlier studies in this line is a study conducted by Aral and Sunar (1977) among Turkish and American subjects focusing on the effects of *direct exchange* as against *mediated interaction* (i.e., people interacting as members of a system and affecting, by their action, the system as well as themselves). These authors found, as predicted, that equity was preferred for mediated situations while equality/reciprocity was preferred for direct exchanges. They also found that (for mediated situations), Turkish subjects preferred equity relatively more than Americans. Among the Americans, attitudes were somewhat ambiguous: While they decisively approved of equality, they neither approved inequity nor favored a strict application of the equity rule. The authors suggest that this ambiguity reflects a duality between equity and equality in the American value system.

Murphy-Berman and colleagues (1984), in an experimental study among Indian and American students, found that American subjects tended relatively more to favor contribution or equality when allocating a bonus between two hypothetical employees, whereas Indian subjects tended to favor need. The authors suggest that this tendency among Indians is due to greater Indian cultural emphasis on *collectivistic values*, whereas the United States is essentially an *individualistic* society that emphasizes independence and self-sufficiency. The tendency found in both nationalities to favor the needy when money cutbacks rather than rewards are involved is explained by the fact that when there is a positive resource to allocate, "people may think of it as a reward and want to use it to reinforce productive work," whereas when resources must be reduced, " protecting the needy rather than rewarding the meritorious . . . becomes the dominant motive" (p. 1271).

Mann, Radford, and Kanagawa (1985) also made an attempt to compare the effects of a collectivist culture (Japan) and those of an individualist culture (Australia) on the allocation decisions of children. They found, as expected, that the Japanese tended to favor a decision that would allow equal chances of winning a reward to contesting groups whereas the Australian children tended to favor a decision that would give greater chances to their own group.

Siegal and Schwalb (1985) examined adolescents' reward allocations according to *family need* among Japanese and Australian boys. Their findings indicated that in both samples high need was rewarded significantly more than low need, except when workers' ability was high but their effort and productivity were stated as low. When outcome was presented as high, Japanese subjects with increasing age allocated more to workers with high family needs than their Australian counterparts. The authors note that these differences reflect differences in philosophies of economic justice between the two countries: Management in the Western countries tends to consider work and family as separate and independent, whereas in Japan the family is "taught to serve as a prototype for identification and loyalty concerning one's workplace" (ibid., p. 322). The indication of a tendency among the Japanese subjects to allocate relatively more to low-ability workers reflects, according to the authors, cultural differences in the concept of ability. The authors argue that in Japan, in contrast to Western cultures, ability tends to be considered something that can be improved through learning rather than as a fixed trait and that under the egalitarian ideology prevailing in the Japanese school, children may be less willing to penalize lack of ability.

Marin (1985), in a study with American and Indonesian subjects, found that subjects, irrespective of nationality and *level of friendship* between allocator and recipient, tended to prefer an equitable over an egalitarian allocator. The former allocation was also perceived as fairer, in both nationalities, than the latter. Subjects of both nationalities also more often chose an equitable distribution when asked to distribute rewards. Indonesians however reported the need to consider the recipient's need, effort, and luck to a greater extent than Americans.

Kashima, Siegal, Tanaka, and Isaka (1988) in an experimental study among Japanese and Australian subjects used a vignette method in which teams of two workers employed by a company were described. The descriptions included variations on worker's *need* (e.g., age, indebtedness) and contribution to the team task. Subjects were required to judge the fairness of a bonus allocation policy, alternately described as based on contributions or equality. The findings indicated that, overall, the contribution principle was considered fairer than equality. Still, the Japanese subjects tended to judge contribution as less fair and equality as less unfair than the Australian subjects. A significant interaction between culture, rule (contribution, equality) and need (age, indebtedness) became evident: The Japanese perceived equality to be fairer and contribution to be less fair than Australians when the lesser contributor is older. On the other hand, the Australians perceived contribution to be less fair and equality fairer when the lesser contributor had a justifiable debt than when he had no debt or an unjustifiable debt, whereas the Japanese emerged as indifferent to the debt manipulations. This finding, the authors suggest, indicates that while in both cultures need, as expected, affects the justice evaluation of the distribution rule applied, the conception of need varies from one culture to another. In Japan, age is a major determinant of need while in Australia indebtedness, not age, affects the perceptions of need. Despite the effect of need on the justice evaluation of distribution rules, equity remains the preferred principle among subjects from both countries—evidence of the "robustness of universalism" in the distributive justice principles. More such evidence stems from the finding of the same research that relatively few were willing to change their judgments about the rules applied even when told that there was general consensus for such change. Referring to the findings of Mann, Radford, and Kanagawa (1985), which suggest that Japanese prefer the equality rule in reward allocations (a finding that contrasts with their own results) the authors comment that the difference may be due to the different context situations—a classroom as compared with a work setting. They say: "It is plausible that, in industrialized societies, the equity rule is accepted as just in the work environment, and other rules may be regarded as just in the classroom setting" (ibid., p. 62). Supporting evidence for this argument is found in Tindale and Davis' (1985) study, which indicated that subjects (American) tended relatively more to take into consideration need when dividing scholarships than when allocating rewards in a work situation.

Leung and colleagues (Bond, Leung and Wan, 1982; Leung and Bond, 1982; Leung and Bond, 1984) studied the impact of cultural collectivism on another variable: reward allocations to *in-group* and *out-group* members. Collectivism is typified as involving a heightened distinction between in-groups and out-groups;

a concern for harmony in in-group situations; and a willingness to sacrifice for in-group members. The studies were carried out among Chinese subjects, assumed to have basically a collectivistic orientation, and American subjects, assumed to have basically an individualistic orientation. The findings indicated that in in-group situations Chinese subjects tended to be more egalitarian in reward allocation than American subjects (Bond, Leung and Wan, 1982; Leung and Bond, 1982). In the out-group situation, the Chinese subjects tended to follow the equity norm more closely than the American subjects; this also occurred when the subjects' input was low regardless of in-group/out-group context. The higher emphasis on the equity norm in the out-group situation by the Chinese as compared to the American subjects is explained thus:

> In individualistic cultures, members are socialized to treat groups as transient and contractual engagements may be more important. Persons can join a variety of groups and strangers are regarded as potential group members. Thus, social skills and friendliness become necessary in interacting with strangers so that potential future interactions can be facilitated. Collectivists on the other hand, are more concerned with harmonious interactions with existing group members, and may view strangers as having a low potential for becoming group members. (Leung and Bond, 1984: 795).

Leung and Park (1986) investigated, among American and Korean subjects, the hypothesis that the contribution rule is likely to be used in situations emphasizing *competition* and *productivity*, whereas the equality rule is likely to be used in situations emphasizing group *harmony* and *solidarity*. The results indicated, as expected, that in a situation in which productivity was emphasized, subjects judged the contribution rule as fairer, used this rule more often, and judged the allocator using this rule as more competent and less unfriendly. Conversely, when harmony was emphasized, subjects used the equality rule more often, judged it fairer and regarded the allocator using this rule as higher in competence and more friendly. Korean subjects even tended to differentiate more than American subjects between the two situations in their evaluations of the allocator. The findings of this study also indicated that when subjects perceived the goal of productivity as most important, they tended to judge the contribution rule as fairer than the equality rule, whereas the opposite relationship obtained when they perceived the goal of group harmony as most important.

Other Relevant Studies. Apart from the studies utilizing the reward allocation paradigm there are also a few other experimental studies that provide some data relevant to the question at hand. These studies focus on the relationship between type of resource allocated (e.g., money, status, love, service, etc.), institutional context (e.g., economic, welfare, social relationships) and preferred distribution rules. Here, only the results obtained for the economic context will be discussed. A fuller review may be found in Törnblom and Foa (1983). These authors compared the results of several studies based on subjects in Sweden, the United States, and Germany (Foa and Stein, 1980; Kayser, Feeley and Lamm, 1982; and two then unpublished studies by Törnblom and Jonsson, and by Schwinger and Nährer (1983) described by the authors). The results indicated, among other things, that the Swedish subjects preferred equality for all contexts including the economic; the American subjects preferred equality and contribution for the economic context. (Does this reflect a similar ambiguity to that found by Aral and Sunar (1977) in the research cited above?) The German subjects in one sample preferred need (Schwinger and Nährer, 1983) while in the other two samples they preferred equality (Kayser, Feeley and Lamm, 1982).

In a study by Törnblom, Jonsson, and Foa (1985), investigating the relationship between type of resource allocated and preferred distribution rules with American and Swedish subjects, it was found that "Swedes preferred equality more than Americans, who preferred equity more than Swedes" (p. 51). The preference order for Swedes was uniform for all resources while the order varied with resource class for Americans. Americans preferred equity for the allocation of money. This study contains a wealth of other data which is not discussed here but the concluding remarks are important for the issue at hand:

In this study we have found evidence that cultural factors and resource class are related to preferences for rules to govern the distribution of resources in many and intricate ways. . . . If our findings are valid, they alert us to potential conflicts in cross national encounters. . . . The application of an inappropriate distribution rule in the allocation of resources is likely to cause feelings of injustice. This is, for example, likely to prevent smooth interaction among individuals and groups. (p. 74).

THE EFFECT OF PERSONAL CHARACTERISTICS

Studies attempting to investigate the effect of personal characteristics or individual predispositions have been concerned mainly with the effect of certain value orientations: mainly a Protestant ethic orientation and the influence of sex. Most of these studies, like those investigating the effect of situational factors, are experimental and employ the reward allocation paradigm.

The Effects of a Protestant Ethic Orientation

Sampson (1980) argued that a preference of equity over equality is inherent in a Protestant ethic philosophy, whose guiding motto is "you shall receive in proportion to what you give" (p. 296). This and similar arguments presumably inspired studies attempting to investigate the impact of a Protestant ethic orientation on distribution-rule preferences. These studies were aided by a PE (Protestant ethic) scale developed by Mirels and Garrett (1971) that evaluates the degree of adherence to the ideas of industriousness, asceticism, and individuality. In their review of the relevant studies, Major and Deaux (1982) note that they do indeed tend to confirm the hypothesis that persons with high PE favor the equity rule in the distribution of rewards more than persons with low PE. This applies to studies conducted by Garrett and colleagues (Garrett, 1973; Garrett and Bloom, 1975) and two studies conducted by Greenberg (1978b:, 1979b).

One study by Greenberg (1979b) is worth describing in more detail since it focused not only on the association between a PE orientation and reward allocation patterns but also on some of the underlying considerations. The results of one experiment manipulating performance quantity and duration indicated that people with high PE tended to take both quantity and duration into account in allocating rewards. In contrast, those with low PE tended to disregard differences in quantity and to pay in accordance with duration only. The second experiment aimed at examining the possibility that a high PE orientation is associated with concern about the nature of bases for differential contribution (i.e., whether these bases are internal or external to the contributor). As expected, the results indicated that people with high PE believed that it would be fair to pay workers in proportion to their performance *when performance differences were attributed to internal factors*; those with low PE, as expected, believed that it would be unfair to do so. Conversely, people with high PE believed, as expected, that it is unfair to base rewards on externally based factors; but those with low PE, supposedly less sensitive to the nature of performance bases, as expected, believed relatively more than subjects with high PE that reward based on such factors is fair.

The findings of an experimental study conducted by Feather and O'Driscoll (1980) among Australian subjects are consistent with those of the above studies in the United States, and provide cross-cultural support for the PE thesis. Specifically, the findings in this study indicated that subjects with relative strong PE and achievement-oriented values such as a sense of accomplishment and being ambitious tended to prefer an equitable allocator over an equal allocator in a team-task performance situation. Conversely, subjects low on such values tended to prefer an equal allocator.

But the findings of another study conducted in Australia by Feather (1983) did not conform with the foregoing studies. This research investigated the judgments of subjects of vignette allocators that distributed a reward equally or according to contributions to their partners in a task. The findings indicated that subjects' reactions to the allocation and the allocator were unrelated to values of the PE scale.

In a recent experimental study, Stake (1983) aimed at investigating further the effects of a PE orientation. Two of the variables manipulated were the degree to which reward recipients could control inputs and the degree of clarity in their relative deservingness. The findings indicated that the PE orientation was unrelated to reward allocations in the low-ambiguity situation. In the high-ambiguity situation, however, people with low PE made a greater distinction between workers than did those with high PE. The latter, as expected, gave greater weight to the input under the recipients' control whereas low PE subjects were more influenced by the input over which recipients had no control.

Sex Differences

In their extensive literature review on this subject, Major and Deaux (1982) note that sex is the "individual differences variable that has received the most attention in justice research" (p. 46). In summarizing the pertinent findings the authors note that

> sex differences in reward distribution occur primarily when the allocator is also a recipient of his or her allocats. That is, women and men typically allocate rewards similarly to others but differently to themselves. In general, women allocate less reward to themselves . . . particularly . . . when women's inputs are greater than their partners. In this situation, women appear to follow a norm of equality, whereas men appear to follow a norm of equity. (p. 51)

These patterns were observable in a number of studies (e.g., Leventhal and Anderson, 1970; Leventhal and Lane, 1970; Lane and Messe, 1971; Wahba, 1972; Katz and Messe, 1973; Mikula, 1974).

Major and Deaux (1982) note a number of situational factors that may moderate these patterns. One such factor is coworker(s) sex. Studies (e.g., Callahan-Levy and Messe, 1979; Kahn, Nelson, and Gaeddert, 1980) suggest that both sexes assume that women believe it is more appropriate to be generous toward women than toward men and that women prefer a more equal reward between themselves and others. Another factor of relevance is the sex-linkage of the task. Research evidence suggests that in situations involving opposite-sex tasks, i.e., tasks that are considered as typically fulfilled by a sex opposite to the allocator's, women tend to follow equality while men tend to follow equity (e.g., Reis and Jackson, 1981). A third situational factor noted by Major and Deaux (1982) is salience of self-presentational concerns. Research evidence suggests that in public situations women prefer equality whereas in private situations they prefer equity (Kidder, Belletterie, and Cohn, 1977). Kidder and colleagues (1977) suggest that these differences are due to the fact that women follow the traditional role expectations in the public situation, but feel "released" from them in the private situation. An investigation by Major and Adams (1984) tends to confirm this thesis.

Several explanations have been offered for the consistent findings indicating that women tend to allocate to themselves smaller amounts of reward than they do to others. Reviews of this literature (e.g., Major and Deaux, 1982; Major, 1987a; 1987b) suggest that the most frequent explanations are:

1. Women prefer equality over equity (e.g., Leventhal, 1976a). This explanation, note Major and Deaux (1982), is usually offered on a post-hoc basis and is not fully consistent with empirical findings indicating that in many instances women do not follow the equality rule.

2. Women tend to choose other women, or themselves, as comparison referents, and since women typically earn less than men, women would have a lower standard of fairness (e.g., Chesler and Goodman, 1976; Major, 1987a; 1987b).

3. Women, as compared with men, attach more importance to interpersonal relationships (e.g., Callahn-Levy and Messe, 1979; Kahn, O'Leary, Krulewitz, and Lamm, 1980), are more communal (e.g., Watts, Messe, and Vallacher, 1982), are more status neutralizing, and attach less importance to money (e.g., Kahn, 1972; Crosby, 1982). Consistent with these priorities, women tend to allocate rewards in a more egalitarian manner than men. In her recent review, Major (1987b) notes that this explanation, emphasizing differences in the value orientations of the sexes, is the most popular and enduring.

4. Women whose sex-role socialization about work-pay links differs from that of men, perceive less of a correlation between their work and pay. As a result and to their own disadvantage, their pay-fairness judgments are likely to be affected by various situational factors such as interpersonal or impression management factors (Callahn-Levy and Messe, 1979).

5. Women devalue their work-related inputs (e.g., Major and Deaux, 1982: 66).

Subsequent studies have attempted to test these various theses. The different value-orientation thesis was put to the test in several experimental studies. One by Watts, Messe, and Vallacher (1982) focused on *agency* versus *communion*. Their findings indicated that females, as expected, were on average more communal whereas males were on average more agentic. Moreover, high-agentic subjects tended, as expected, to allocate a higher percentage of rewards to themselves than did low-agentic subjects. The findings also indicated that high-communion subjects actually paid themselves less than they thought was fair. But most important for the question at hand is the indication that when males and females were equated within each level of agency and communion, a significant main effect of sex of allocator emerged: females, as compared with males, tended to allocate a smaller proportion of the reward to themselves. This latter finding suggests that personal agency versus communion orientation cannot fully explain the differences found in past studies in the reward-allocation behavior of men and women.

A study by Major and Adams (1983) tested other portions of the value-orientation hypothesis, and the findings tended to refute the interpersonal orientation thesis. When level of interpersonal orientation was equated, women were still found to allocate more rewards to their partners than men. The findings also negate the self-presentational explanation: Both men and women allocated rewards more equally when allocations were public than when they were private, and when future interaction was expected than when it was not.

Thesis 2 above, stating that the differences between the sexes are anchored in the differential standards of comparison they apply in the assessment of personal entitlement, tends however to find support in a series of recent studies conducted by Major and colleagues.[3] One study conducted by Major and Konar (1984) focused on the pay expectations of females and males and the determinants of these expectations, and was based on a sample of management students. The findings of this study indicate that the females have lower career entry and career peak pay expectations than men, and that objective factors such as career paths chosen (women chose lower-paying specializations) or different value orientations (women tended to value money less and placed a higher value on the interest of their work) explain only part of the differences in expectations. The major explanatory factor that emerged was the subjective perceptions of women about the earnings of similar others: Women thought others in their field earn less than men thought they do. These findings tend to support the comparison standards thesis stating that women tend to use relatively lower comparison standards than men.

In another recent experimental study, Major, McFarlin, and Gagnon (1984) investigated the effect of internal *standards* versus *external* comparisons on the sexes' reward allocation behavior. One experiment manipulated the availability of external comparisons (available/not available) and the nature of external comparisons (men and women paid equally; men paid more or less than women). The findings indicated that where external comparisons were unavailable, women tended to award themselves considerably less than men. In contrast, where external comparisons were available, women, like men, tended to award themselves about equal amounts; both sexes tended to choose the average amount taken by others (men and women alike) as the fair standard. These findings indicate that women are guided by *lower internal* standards when external comparisons are unavailable, but tend to follow external standards when these are available.

The findings of the first experiment also indicated that

> both men and women in the absent condition believed that other females would pay themselves significantly less than would other males. Furthermore, women's and men's self-pay in the absence of social comparison information correlated highly with what they thought same-sex, but not opposite-sex, others would pay themselves. This suggests that in the absence of salient comparison others, men and women may base their judgments of what is fair pay for their work on internalized beliefs about the pay of others of their own sex. (pp. 1104–5)

Two other experimental studies conducted by Major and colleagues investigated more directly the effect of social comparisons (i.e., comparisons with others) on perceptions of personal entitlement among men and women. One study by Major and Forcey (1985) examined women's and men's comparison preferences when evaluating the fairness of their pay. Male and female subjects were randomly assigned to jobs described as masculine, feminine, or sex neutral. They were also described as being of comparable difficulty and requiring about the same abilities. After working on the job and privately receiving identical pay, subjects were required to rank order their preferences for knowing the average pay of "different groups of people who have worked on the three jobs." The findings indicated that the majority of subjects tended to prefer same-sex comparisons over combined-sex comparisons. The only group which diverged somewhat from this pattern were those assigned to a work group described as dominated by the other sex. In this case, the findings indicated a more even distribution between same-sex, cross-sex, and sex-neutral first choices.

A second study conducted by Major and Testa (1989) was designed to investigate the proposition that similarity biases in comparisons can lead to different pay standards and consequently to different judgments of entitlement when some (e.g., women) receive different pay rates than others (e.g., men). In this study, male and female subjects worked on one of two (identical) sex-neutral tasks and were privately paid an identical rate. They were then given the opportunity to choose one person out of eight (two males and two females from each task group) whose pay they would like to know. The pay for males and females in the two task groups was experimentally manipulated, without the subjects' knowledge, so that in one case the pay for females was lower than that for males, whereas in the other case this was reversed. As expected, the findings indicated a strong similarity bias: The great majority of selections were of the same-sex/same-job type. They also indicated that subjects assigned to tasks with higher payment for their own sex tended to believe that the prevalent rate was higher and that they personally were entitled to a higher pay than those with lower payment for their sex.

The findings of some recent studies by other authors support the findings and conclusions of Major and colleagues. One such study on sex differences in pay expectations (Summers, 1988), required business students in a U.S. university to state their expectations for the range of starting salaries for graduates in their own major, and the salary levels which would make them feel overrewarded and underrewarded. The findings indicated that, as expected women, as compared to men, expected salaries at the lower end of starting salaries and had higher tolerance for underpayment. But there were also some unexpected results: At the higher end of starting salaries women expected higher salaries and had lower tolerance for underpayment than men. The author suggests that these findings reflect the fact that recruiters had been aggressively recruiting the "best" females, as a result of which actual starting salaries for women "stars" had risen. These higher salary offers apparently served as standards of comparison for the higher-end expectations.

Other studies provide additional evidence for the existence of lower internalized pay norms for women—norms shared by women and men. One such experimental study, conducted by Messe, Hymes, and MacCoun (1986) asked male and female subjects playing the role of supervisors in three different industrial/business contexts to allocate pay to two temporary workers whose sex was experimentally manipulated. The subjects were informed that for the same time spent at the job, one worker had substantially outperformed the other. The findings indicated that payment tended to reflect performance differences; that is, subjects tended to follow the contribution rule. They also indicated a marked sex bias: An examination of the average pay allocations according to worker sex and worker performance level revealed that the highest average payment was obtained by the high-performing male/low-performing male dyads and the lowest average payment score was obtained for the parallel female dyads. The average payment score for the mixed dyads were intermediate and reflected the same biases: The pay for the high performing male/low performing female dyad was higher than the pay for the opposite mixed dyad (male low performer/female high performer). Given that the worker's actual output, as well as the supervisors' perceptions of that output were constant across conditions, these findings indicate a systematic bias in favor of males: They systematically received a higher share.

Rotter (1987) investigated the salary recommendations of male and female subjects assigned the role of supervisor to vignette "bookkeepers" whose job performance was described identically and whose sex, age, marital status, and tenure were described differently. The findings indicated that though the female bookkeepers tended to be judged as having higher work commitment and holding jobs of greater importance and higher status than their male peers, they were assigned lower salaries. These findings suggest again the existence of lower pay norms for women among both sexes, norms that cannot be explained by nature of inputs, relative status, or occupation.

In their study on judgments of appropriate occupational pay, Mahoney and Blake (1987) similarly obtained findings suggesting lower social pay-norms for female occupations. In this study, conducted on a sample of students at a U.S. university, participants were required to judge the "appropriate" pay for 20 occupations. The occupations selected were reasonably familiar and represented a range of earnings, sexual stereotypes, and proportion of male employees. The study aimed at investigating the influence of job characteristics including femininity of the occupation in the determination of appropriate compensation. The findings indicated that the sex characterizations of occupations influenced the judgments of appropriate compensation independently of the other, work characteristics. The perceived masculinity of an occupation was found to be weighted positively by both female and male participants in making judgments about appropriate compensation. The findings further indicated that sex characterizations did not influence perceptions of the work characteristics of occupations.

Altogether, the above studies support the thesis that the tendency of women to allocate relatively less rewards to themselves stems from a lower sense of personal entitlement in regard to pay, which is in turn affected by the comparison standards utilized by women: They internalize the lower pay norms for women and tend to have lower internal standards as a result. Women also tend to compare themselves to other women, who usually earn less than men, and consequently tend to have lower social comparison standards.

Other recent studies investigated other aspects possibly associated with the different reward allocation behavior of women and men. Major, McFarlin and Gagnon (1984), for example, examined the actual and estimated performances of women and men working under "private" and "public" situations. Subjects worked for a fixed amount of pay with the instruction to do as much work as they thought fair for the sum paid. No external comparisons were available. The findings of this experiment indicated that: (a) in both private and public conditions women's time input, quantity and quality of work performed, and efficiency considerably surpassed the men's; (b) women revealed themselves as more susceptible to impression-management considerations: they, but not the male subjects, worked for a longer time in the public situation; (c) women did not differ from men in their performance evaluations, attributions, or satisfactions, even though their performances were superior by objective standards. Taken together these results suggest that women's sense of personal entitlement with respect to pay is lower than men's; that impression-management goals are more likely to influence the input/outcome ratios of women than of men; that women undervalue or men overvalue their respective work inputs.

Two recent experimental studies suggest that females put less emphasis on contributions than males. A study conducted in Germany by Bierhoff and Renda (reported in Bierhoff, Buck, and Klein 1986) indicates that males tended to be more positive in their evaluations of a female allocator when she followed the contribution rule than when she followed the equality rule; for females a much smaller difference was found. The authors suggest that it "seems reasonable to conclude that males emphasize the evaluative difference between high equity and low equity more than females" (p. 172).

Support for the thesis that males differ from females in their emphasis on contribution is also found in a study by Reis (1984). Reis attempted to establish the dimensionality of justice evaluations using a list of 17 justice motives (statements) that might be used in justice evaluations. He asked his subjects "to make judgments on how similar these statements are in determining what is fair in an employment situation" (ibid., p. 43). The findings indicate that males tended to use one of the three dimensions that emerged in a multidimensional scaling more than women. The positive pole of this dimension depicted, among others, such rules as "proportionality" whereas the negative pole depicted, among others such rules as "help others without expecting return benefits" and "need." Since this study employed a very different methodology from Bierhoff and Renda's, it lessens the suspicion that the latters' results are due to certain methodological biases, such as judgments involving female allocators only, or that evaluations of allocators may reflect to a greater extent attitudes, values, or sex role orientations than actual allocations (Major and Adams, 1984).

Jackson, Messe, and Hunter (1985), in a recent experimental study, examined the effects of allocators' and coworkers' gender and gender role on patterns of reward allocation. Gender role refers "to levels of masculine and feminine desirable social traits . . . that is, traits stereotypically associated with males and females, respectively." The authors employed tests for establishing the masculinity or femininity of male and female subjects who allocated rewards to coworkers whose inputs were less than their own. The findings indicated that feminine workers, regardless of their gender, received more generous allocations than masculine coworkers. Allocations to androgynous workers were intermediate. Males and females did not differ in their allocations, nor had the gender roles of the allocators any influence on the distribution of rewards. The authors suggest that these results indicate that "factors in the situation, (in particular, coworker characteristics) exert a more potent influence on distributive justice behavior than do dispositional characteristics of allocators" (ibid., p. 340). Still, the authors caution that it is not clear yet whether the findings are generalizable to same-sex dyads and to situations in which the coworker's performance is equal or better than the allocator's performance.

OPEN-ENDED FIELD RESEARCH

The wealth of experimental data presented leaves us with a nagging question: How well do these data reflect "real life" situations? Here and there we were able to present some evidence from field studies pertaining to some of the specific aspects investigated by the experimental studies. But this is obviously far from being adequate. We would like to know much more: especially, do employees really tend to lean mostly on the contribution rule when judging the fairness of their pay, as the experimental studies suggest? Are other distributive principles applied under particular circumstances as other experimental studies suggest? Do the underlying principles applied in actual practice vary from culture to culture, and are they affected by any personal predispositions or characteristics?

Unfortunately, the very few pertinent field studies cannot provide an adequate answer to any of these questions. They can, however, illuminate some of them. Two of these field studies were conducted by Rossi and colleagues (Jasso and Rossi, 1977; Alves and Rossi, 1978). These studies aimed at investigating the fairness judgments of earned income. Both studies, carried out in the United States, had an identical design but were based on different samples. Jasso and Rossi's study was based on a cross-sectional city sample while Alves and Rossi's study was based on a nation-wide sample. Participants were required to judge the income fairness of vignettes described in terms of age, sex, family status, number of children, occupation, education, income, and welfare status (do receive/do not receive welfare). The results of both studies were very similar. One major finding was that the income fairness judgments tended to be based on two major distribution principles—merit and need—with the former carrying the greater weight. A second major finding was that much social consensus existed regarding these criteria and their application: The respondent's characteristics explained only a very slight percentage—about 1 percent—of the total variance in the fairness judgments of earned income.

Merit and need also emerged as the two principles guiding the fairness judgment of pay of a sample of 140 blue-collar and white-collar industrial employees in Israel

(Dornstein, 1985). This finding emanates from a content analysis of responses by participants to an open-ended question asking "What is a fair wage/salary?" The results indicated that participants tended to refer in their responses to a variety of work-related contributions as well as to a variety of personal and family needs. But in this study the findings indicated a lesser degree of social consensus than the Rossi and colleagues' studies. Specifically, the analysis of the findings indicated that contributions were relatively more emphasized by white-collar employees and those with relatively higher incomes, and less emphasized by the older employees and by those with larger families. Opposite relationships were obtained in regard to needs: These were relatively more emphasized by older employees and employees with larger families, and less emphasized by white-collar employees and employees with relatively higher incomes. A possible explanation for the lesser degree of social consensus found in the Dornstein study as compared to the Rossi and colleagues studies is that "bystander" judgments like those elicited by the Rossi and colleagues studies are less affected by self-interest factors and factors reflected in the concrete employment situation.

NOTES

1. Goodman and Friedman in their review refer to an earlier (1970) version of this study.

2. Specifically, it is proposed that: (1) Equitable allocations ensure the most efficient allocation of resources since essential resources are allocated proportionally to usefulness. (2) Equitable allocations reward the good performers and punish the poor performers, thus sustaining the high-productive motivation of good performers and spurring the poor performers to improve their performance. (3) By linking rewards and performance, equitable allocations encourage productive behavior.

3. See Major (1987a) for a detailed review.

6 The Standards of Comparison

INTERNAL STANDARDS VS. COMPARISONS WITH OTHERS

Social comparisons are, as indicated, a basic tenet of all justice theories. Some theorists, however, proposed that individuals may also use other referents such as internal standards when evaluating their rewards. Pritchard (1969) even argued that "the 'internal standard' is a very powerful concept" (p. 205) and that it is more likely to be used in the employment situation than social comparisons. This challenge to the social comparison thesis seems a natural starting point for reviewing the empirical evidence on the subject of comparisons in pay-fairness evaluations. The major questions here are: Do individuals indeed tend to refer to "internal standards" when evaluating the fairness of their pay, and if so what exactly is the nature of these standards? How widespread is the use of internal standards, or what is the relative weight of internal standards compared with other comparison standards? Do internal standards serve as substitutes for social comparisons or do they complement them? In the first instance, the focal question is: Under which conditions are internal standards substituted for social comparisons or vice versa? In the second instance the focal question is: What are the specific functions of internal standards as opposed to social comparisons in the process of evaluation?

The few empirical studies on internal standards cannot answer all these questions, but they can shed some light on a few. We shall start the review with the experimental studies and continue with the evidence emanating from pertinent field studies.

Experimental Studies

One of the earliest experimental studies was conducted by Weick and Nesset (1968). Subjects were given a questionnaire describing 20 pairs of hypothetical work situations and were asked to indicate the situation in which they would feel most comfortable. The described situations were constructed to compare preferences between Own-equity (when Person's input/outcome ratio is unity); Comparison-equity (when Person's ratio is equal to Other's ratio); and Own-comparison equity (when Person's own ratio is unity and also equal to Other's ratio). After each pair of items, subjects marked one of ten possible adjustments they would make to the situation they least preferred. These "adjustments" represented different modes of inequity reduction (e.g., persuade coworker to work less energetically; request higher wages, etc.). The coworker was described as similar to Person in such background characteristics as age, education, sex, social background, family responsibilities, and seniority.

The results of this study indicated that, given the choice, subjects preferred Comparison-equity to Own-equity, and Own-comparison equity to Own-equity. They suggest that individuals are more troubled by inequitable comparisons with others than with own inequity. In terms of our basic question—internal standards versus comparisons with others—the results indeed intimate a predominance of the latter but do not negate the possibility of internal standards.

Researchers have pointed out some problems with the methodology used in this study. For example, Pritchard (1969) noted that the findings are weakened by the use of fictitious situations. He also noted that individuals may have responded to the questions according to perceived socially desirable norms rather than according to "genuine" feelings. The latter problem, argues Pritchard, combined with the fact that subjects were usually told that the purpose of the experiment was to study "how much you worry about the other guy" and "how affiliative you are with others," could have created a bias in favor of comparison equity.

Austin and McGinn (1980) noted that Weick and Nesset (1968) only measured preferences for different variations of justice and injustice rather than fairness and satisfactions.

Another study on the question of internal standards versus social comparisons—and one using a different methodology—was conducted by Lane and Messe (1972). The authors manipulated the sum of money given to subjects fulfilling the role of reward allocators: some subjects were given an amount to distribute which, if divided equally, would give each individual the reward that other persons from the same population would perceive as fair (sufficient reward condition): Other subjects were given sums to distribute that were either double or half that amount (over- and insufficient reward condition).[1] The results indicated that, compared with the sufficient reward condition, subjects allocated proportionately more money to themselves in the insufficient reward condition and in the oversufficient reward conditions. These results were largely unaffected by the manipulation of another experimental variable—level of inputs (i.e., high, low, explicit-low input conditions). The authors argued that the results obtained "support the own-equity–other-equity position of Weick which states that persons compare i/o ratios to socially derived internal standards" (Lane and Messe, p. 231).

Austin and Susmilch (1974) noted that some methodological flaws in the Lane and Messe (1972) study render the data ambiguous. For example, they argued that the absence of manipulation checks raises the question of whether the independent variables were successfully operationalized. The authors also argued that the insufficient and oversufficient conditions might have been too discrepant from the sufficient condition. As a result, the researchers may have unwittingly aroused suspicion among their subjects.

Ross and McMillen (1973), in their experimental study, compared the effects on pay satisfaction of an external social comparison and an internal standard. Subjects, assigned the role of workers in a factory game, were rewarded with either a uniformly low, a uniformly high, or a decremental (gradually declining) pattern of payment. In each payment condition, half the subjects were provided with an external comparison level: information about the maximum and minimum payments supposedly received in previous task groups. The findings indicated that when such information was available, the low-payment group produced the most dissatisfaction with rewards whereas the decremental schedule produced intermediate levels of dissatisfaction. In the absence of information on external referents, however, the decremental schedule produced the most dissatisfaction. In this condition, high payments failed to produce greater satisfaction than low payments. The findings of this experiment suggest that other referents, when present, have a stronger impact on pay satisfaction than internal standards based on past outcomes.

In their experimental study, Austin and McGinn (1980) claim to have conducted an "unequivocal test" of the relative impact of social comparisons versus comparisons with one's previous rewards on the fairness judgments of rewards. The study consisted of two experiments. In the first—a role-playing questionnaire study—participants read one of nine versions of a story about a hypothetical person who was rewarded either more, the same as, or less than he had expected, and either more, the same as, or less than another person who had performed similarly in the situation. Subjects were asked to imagine themselves in the role of this person and to judge both the fairness of the reward and how satisfying it would be. Person and other were described as very similar in all respects, including their capability of performing their job. Their inputs too were described as equal. The results of the experiment showed that underrewarded persons that is, persons receiving less than the other person who had performed similarly were, indeed, less satisfied than equally rewarded persons, as equity theory predicts; overrewarded persons, however, were not. In line with Blau's (1964) expectancy theory, persons who got more than they expected were not noticeably more satisfied than those who got exactly what they expected, whereas persons who got less than expected were less satisfied than those who got what they expected. In summarizing the results of this experiment, the authors argued that these results "suggest that individuals want both congruency with others on the basis of investments brought to the situation, and with their internal standards—not necessarily anything more and certainly not anything less on either dimension" (Austin and McGinn, 1980: 434).

To rule out the potential biases stemming from the "relatively uninvolving" role-playing methodology, the researchers conducted a second experiment in which subjects were told they were participating in an experiment on "simulated work settings." In the first phase of the experiment—designed to build an expectancy for a certain reward—subjects performed their tasks alone, in separate rooms, and were rewarded after each task. At the end of this phase, subjects were given short questionnaires asking them how satisfied they were with their reward, and how much they expected to receive for the task to follow. The expected reward for the next task served as manipulation check for the expectancy variable. At the end of the first phase subjects were assembled; the confederate asked the subject how much he had received for the tasks performed and claimed to have received the same amount, thus providing a "fair social context."

In the next phase, subjects worked together and all received the same reward for each task performed; rewards were dispensed openly. The subject's reward relative to "partner" (confederate) was manipulated by varying the amount the confederate appeared to receive. The confederate's job was to ensure equality of performance. After completing the last task, subjects were required to complete a questionnaire rating their rewards on fairness as well as satisfaction. The results were found to be consistent with those of the first experiment. Satisfaction with rewards was found to be significantly affected by both social and expectancy comparison in an additive fashion. Whereas social comparison explained more of the satisfaction ratings than of the fairness ratings, fairness ratings were significantly affected only by social comparisons.

In discussing the theoretical implications of the study, the authors argued that the results are a "reminder of the importance of moral evaluations in social relations, which prove in many situations, to be the most powerful determinant of individuals' emotional reactions to outcome configurations" (Austin and McGinn, 1980: 439). Moreover, while the results suggest that previous rewards are unrelated to moral evaluations when a salient social comparison is available and appear to support Blau's position that simple expectations do not provide a legitimate basis for moral evaluations of desert, the "data should not be interpreted to mean that people will *never* transform their expected rewards into deserved ones" (p. 440). The authors suggest that two sets of circumstances should facilitate the transformation of expectancies into internal standards of deserving: (a) situations where there are no social comparisons available. In such a situation individuals may feel that they deserve what they are accustomed to; (b) situations where information processing is affected by nonrational elements.

Austin and McGinn's (1980) findings indicating that the fairness evaluation of rewards are significantly affected by social comparisons, where such comparisons are available, but unaffected by internal standards, are challenged in a recent study of Messe and Watts (1983). The general design of the study was similar to that of Austin and McGinn (1980; second experiment). A major modification was the addition of a third variable to the experimentally induced expectation variable and the comparison-person variable. This third variable was an established standard of equity "that subjects had incorporated from their past experiences and brought with them to the laboratory." The standard was determined by extensive testing of a large sample of individuals drawn from the same population as the subjects in the experiment. The testing aimed at obtaining an estimation of "fair pay" for the kind of work the subjects had to do. There were also some more minor methodological modifications such as using a more sensitive measure of fairness or examining pay levels that were more sharply differentiated, absolutely and relatively. These changes were intended to prevent the danger of moderating the potential impact of internal standards on fairness judgments assumed to have existed in the Austin and McGinn (1980) study. In the first phase of the study where no social comparisons were available, the findings indicated that "both established and induced internal standards of equity affect fairness judgments." These results contrast with those of Austin and McGinn (1980), where experimentally induced internal standards were not found to be significantly related to fairness judgments. In the second phase of the study, where social comparisons were available, the findings indicated the following: (1) For subjects whose pay matched that of their coworker, pay fairness judgments were affected mainly by internal preestablished standards: the pay level closest to the preestablished fair standard was judged to be closest to (and not significantly different from) fair. By contrast, the other two pay levels in the experiment (one substantially lower than the preestablished fair standard, the other substantially higher) were judged to be significantly different from fair. Social comparisons appeared to have little moderating effect on the impact of internal standards in this case. (2) Social comparisons did, however, affect the subjects' fairness judgments when their pay was significantly lower than preestablished equity. In this case, subjects regarded the low pay as less different from the perceived fair pay when their coworker received the same amount than when he/she received more. On the other hand, social comparisons did not appreciably affect fairness judgments when subjects were paid an amount consistent with the internal standard of own equity, and where the coworker's pay digressed from that standard.

Field Research

Only a few pertinent field studies explicitly include the internal standards frame of reference. One study conducted by Goodman (1974) was to answer the question, "what kinds of referents do people use in evaluating their pay?" (p. 170). The sample consisted of 217 managers from a single firm in the United States. Seven referent categories were derived by coding responses to an open-ended question: "You said you were (satisfied–dissatisfied) with your pay. How did you decide you were (satisfied–dissatisfied) with your pay?" (p. 179). Among the seven referent categories, three concern self-references (pp. 180–81): (1) "Self-pay history," referring to "whether past or future job input/outcome ratios were used in evaluating one's pay"; (2) "Self-internal," referring to the individual's perceived worth to the company; (3) "Self-family," referring to the individual's conception of the pay level "needed to maintain the family's standard of living." The results indicate that all three categories of self-referents were selected equally. In addition, self-referents also appeared in combinations such as "Other-self," "System-self," and "Other-system-self." Indeed, most selections were of the combined type: that is, there was a marked tendency to select multiple referents both within and among the Other, System, and Self categories. A major finding was that Other as a referent category was selected primarily in conjunction with a second referent, and its relative frequency did not seem significantly greater than that of other referent categories such as System or Self.[2]

A second field study directly investigating the nature of pay comparisons and including explicitly internal standards is that of Heneman, Schwab, Standal, and Peterson (1980). The study was conducted in the United States and was based on a sample of 127 fulltime workers employed in professional, technical, or managerial jobs in an insurance company, and a sample of 114 employed MBA students in three universities. Participants were requested to indicate how important each of five comparison dimensions was in influencing their own pay satisfaction. One of these dimensions—termed "history"—referred to what the individual had received in the past and had become accustomed to. Another dimension—"cost of living"—referred to the perceived adequacy of the individual's pay to meet current needs. These dimensions paralleled Goodman's (1974) Self-pay history and Self-family respectively. Generally, the findings suggested, like Goodman's (1974), the existence of multiple referents—among them the above mentioned internal standards referring to Self.

Scholl, Cooper, and McKenna (1987) also included internal standards in their recent field study investigating the referents in pay-equity evaluations. The study was based on a sample of about 160 employees in low- to middle-level managerial positions in a financial institution in the United States. Participants were requested to compare their present salary with that of a specified source of comparison. The second best predictor of pay satisfaction was found to be an item measuring self equity—"internal evaluation of self worth." These results, like those of the previously cited field studies, suggest that internal standards fulfill an important role in the process of pay fairness evaluation.

In their recent research on the referents used in the evaluation of pay conducted on a sample of about 360 managers in a nationwide chain restaurant in the U.S., Summers and DeNisi (1990) found that about a third of the participants tended to choose Self referents (e.g., pay in previous jobs or pay needed to maintain one's standard of living) when required to indicate which of a list of nine referents were most important "when you consider your pay."

Two field studies that did not aim at investigating the standards of comparison used in pay-equity evaluations, but are nevertheless directly relevant to the present question, are those of Rossi and colleagues (Jasso and Rossi, 1977; Alves and Rossi, 1978). The researchers used a vignette method to investigate the fairness evaluation of income. Cross-sectional samples of participants were presented with sets of vignettes described in terms of income, occupation, sex, family status, and other potentially income-relevant characteristics, and were asked to judge, on a nine-point scale, the fairness of the income received by the persons described. The authors' reports suggest that they had no particular difficulties in obtaining the required judgments. We deduct from this that the participants (over 800!) must have utilized some readily available internal norms in evaluating the fairness of the vignettes' income. This may be taken as additional support for the importance of internal standards in pay-fairness evaluations.

Discussion

The evidence presented suggests that individuals do indeed utilize certain internal standards in pay-fairness evaluations. The studies by Rossi and colleagues (Alves and Rossi, 1978; Jasso and Rossi, 1977) and by Messe and Watts (1983) suggest quite strongly that individuals base their evaluations on such standards: In all these studies, large samples of individuals had no difficulty in making the fair pay judgments required of them, though no one supplied them with any standards to assist. Moreover, the authors report a large measure of consensus regarding these judgments, which suggest that they are based on internalized social norms. Goodman (1974), Heneman and colleagues (1980), and Scholl and colleagues (1987) provide support for yet some other sorts of internal standards—perceived self-worth or current financial needs.

Only the study by Austin and McGinn (1980) presents some contradictory evidence. In this experimental study, the authors found that the perceived fairness of present rewards was related to the reward levels of social comparisons present in the situation, but not, as might have been expected, to one's past rewards. A closer look at the study's design suggests that these results may be due to some bias toward social comparisons caused by the experimental conditions where past rewards were experimentally induced standards of short duration. Such standards may be expected to have a relatively weak hold on the individual and to succumb easily to more compelling evidence such as the presence of comparison with others. In contrast, norms and values internalized in real life should be able to withstand such pressures and continue to affect the evaluation process. Indeed, some support for this argument may be found when comparing Austin's study with that of Messe and Watts (1983). In the latter, subjects' internalized norms of fair pay, presumably formed in the past and brought along to the experimental situation, were indeed found to have a substantial impact on their fairness judgments of pay received during the experiment.

Regarding the relative importance of internal standards as compared to social comparisons, the available studies—except the Messe and Watts (1983) study—suggest that internal standards are somewhat less important than comparisons with others.

As to the factors explaining variations in the relative importance of internal standards, the available empirical research tells us very little. Indeed, the only studies that contain some relevant data are those of Ross and McMillen (1973) and Messe and Watts (1973) suggesting that the impact of internal standards is lessened when individuals have the opportunity of comparing themselves with others.

It should be noted that the empirical evidence reviewed above is limited in several respects. First, the number of studies is relatively small. Second, the various studies are difficult to compare because of the different explicit or implicit conceptualizations and definitions of the internal standards variable. Third, some of the studies utilize measures of pay satisfaction rather than measures of perceived pay fairness. Some researchers however distinguish between pay satisfaction and perceived pay fairness and argue that different measures should be applied to each (e.g., Martin, 1981). In practice, perceptions of pay fairness have indeed been found to be strongly affected by perceived current equity (e.g., Berkowitz et al., 1987), but some studies that utilized separate measures for pay satisfaction and pay fairness (e.g., Dittrich and Carrell, 1979) show that they are not perfectly correlated and may, on occasion, relate differently to a number of "independent variables." Fourth, some of the field studies are based on somewhat limited one-organization samples.

SINGLE VS. MULTIPLE COMPARISONS

Some of the studies reviewed above indicate that individuals at times use more than one comparison standard. In this section, we seek to clarify this important issue: Do individuals generally use a single referent or do they use multiple referents in their pay-fairness evaluations? Most studies containing relevant data are field studies.

Among the first is one by Finn and Lee (1972), conducted on a sample of 170 professional employees in one organization in the United States. The study aimed at investigating the determinants and correlates of salary equity. One of the variables investigated was "the reference source for salary perception." This was measured by a number of items, some relating to sources external to the organization, others to internal sources. Participants were instructed to check all items that had an important effect on the perceived fairness of their salaries. The authors do not report detailed data about the frequencies of responses in each category but they report that judgments about salary were "largely a function of mixed consideration." In this research, mixed considerations were defined as "checking an equal number of external and internal items or at least two items in each" (p. 289).

Goodman (1974), in his study investigating the referents used in the evaluation of pay, found that participants tended to use multiple classes of referents. Another important finding was that: "Other as a referent class appeared most frequently in conjunction with the other categories; that is, in evaluating their pay people used Others as referents but also used referents related to System and Self" (p. 182). Goodman also found that the different referent categories were relatively independent, each contributing to the pay satisfaction criterion.

That individuals consider relevant several referents simultaneously was also found, as noted, by Heneman and colleagues (1980). Hills (1980), in his study based on a cross-sectional sample of 275 fulltime workers in the United States, also found that individuals, when evaluating if they are fairly paid, tend to compare themselves simultaneously with others in the employing organization and outside it.

In a study on a large sample of over 2,000 employees in a finance company and over 600 employees in the hotel industry in England, White (1981) found that the impact of both external pay comparisons and internal pay comparisons on pay satisfaction is much stronger than the impact of other factors such as fringe benefits or cost of living increases. The author also notes the relevancy in pay satisfaction of self-referent factors such as reward for work done, responsibility, and overtime pay.

Subbarao and deCarufel (1983), in their study on a sample of 700 faculty members in a medium-sized university in Canada, found that faculty members tended to use multiple comparisons when evaluating the fairness of their pay.

In a study based on a sample of 701 employees, skilled nonsupervisory workers, and managers in an industrial firm in the United States, Ronen (1986) found that for both workers and managers pay satisfaction was best explained by the combined effect of Inside Pay comparisons ("How satisfied are you with your pay compared to other employees in this organization performing a similar job as yourself?") and Outside Pay comparisons ("How satisfied are you with your pay compared to others doing a similar job outside this organization?").

Similarly, Scholl and colleagues (1987) found that pay satisfaction was best predicted by several referent categories combined: "system equity" (comparisons with the amount of pay expected from the system); "occupational equity" (comparisons with others doing substantially the same job in other organizations); and "self-equity" (internal evaluation of self-worth).

Finally, in a recent study conducted with a random sample of 135 blue-collar and white-collar employees in four industrial firms in Israel, Dornstein (1988b) also found clear evidence for the existence of multiple referents among both the blue-collar and the white-collar employees.

Some indirect evidence on the tendency to use multiple comparisons was also obtained by Berkowitz et al. (1987) in a study of the determinants of pay satisfaction. A cross-sectional sample of about 250 male employees in a U.S. county were asked to respond to a series of questions about the frequency of pay comparisons with others of different types. A factor analysis of all 29 items involving pay comparisons and other factors thought to be related to pay satisfaction indicated that all items involving comparisons entered into one factor: "Thus someone who claimed to make comparisons with people in his own organization was also likely to say that he made comparisons with people in other organizations, in the same and different occupations, with those who were paid more and with those paid less, and so on" (p. 547). The authors concluded that "in the light of these data it would be unjustified in future research on the selection of comparison others to assume that different types of comparisons are necessarily mutually exclusive" (p. 547).

Summary

The above review suggests that typically more than one referent is involved in pay comparisons. The relatively large number of studies and the fact that they vary widely in their settings, samples, and methods reinforce this conclusion. Still, there are some limitations that dictate caution: Some studies are based on one-organization samples and others deal with pay satisfaction. As noted, some researchers criticize the use of the latter variable as a substitute for perceived pay equity.

The findings suggesting that individuals typically use multiple referents when evaluating their pay lead to several other important questions, one being the existence of a predominant referent or referent category. For example, do employees compare themselves predominantly with others *inside* or *outside* the employing organization? Do they compare themselves predominantly with *similars* or *dissimilars*? In dissimilar comparisons, what is the predominant pattern— upward or downward? What factors account for digressions from the predominant patterns, if such patterns exist? Alternatively, what factors explain variances in comparison patterns if no typical pattern exists? We shall now examine each of these questions in turn.

EXTRAORGANIZATIONAL VS. INTRAORGANIZATIONAL COMPARISONS

Some theorists proposed that the employing organization is likely to fulfill a most important role in social comparisons (e.g., Homans, 1974). How far is there empirical support for this proposition? A number of field studies provide relevant data. Andrews and Henry (1963), in their study based on a sample of about 230 managers in lower- to middle-management positions in five area firms in the United States found little support for this proposition. These authors concluded that, *"Outside* pay comparisons . . . play an important role in the process of individual pay evaluations" (p. 37; emphasis added). Nevertheless, there were significant variations in the choice of referents between the different management levels. For example, outside references were relatively more frequent among the lower-middle management as compared with the other levels investigated. We shall return to these specific findings later. Similarly, Goodman (1974) reports that the Other-outside referent category made the highest contribution to the explained variance in pay satisfaction.

Hills (1980) factor-analyzed the data obtained in relation to 18 referent dimensions and found that the first factor—market comparisons—explained 44.4 percent of the common variance. On this factor, all the external items had significantly higher loadings than the internal items. Heneman and colleagues (1980) found that external comparisons were on average more important in pay satisfaction than internal comparisons. This applied to all three pay dimensions (level, raise, benefits) investigated.

Shirom (1980), in his investigation of a sample of about 170 foremen in a multiplant industrial enterprise in Israel, found that external comparisons occupied a more central place in the participants' frame of reference and contributed relatively more to their feelings of deprivation regarding pay, than internal groups. The author suggests that this tendency may be due to the fact that the upward mobility of foremen in the organizations studied was blocked, and individuals in these positions had no incentive to compare themselves to those above them, but were eager to assert that they earn "comparable wages" to similar others outside the organization.

Subbarao and deCarufel (1983), in their study on a sample of faculty members in a Canadian university, found that outside comparisons were more frequently chosen than inside comparisons, but that comparisons within the faculty were more powerful in explaining the variance of the overall perceptions of pay fairness.

Ronen (1986) found that both outside and inside comparisons contributed significantly to pay satisfaction, but outside comparison correlated higher with pay satisfaction than inside comparison. Scholl and colleagues (1987) likewise found that pay satisfaction is significantly affected by occupational equity (i.e., comparisons with others doing the same job in other organizations) but is not significantly affected by internal comparison.

Cappelli and Sherer (1988), in their recent study based on a sample of about 580 employees working for a major U.S. airline in a variety of jobs, found that market comparisons, (i.e., comparisons with the market rate for comparable jobs and seniority) and comparisons with similar others in other airlines ("wage contours"), provided the strongest predictors for pay satisfaction. In contrast, no significant relationships were found in regard to internal comparisons.

Dornstein (1988b), in her study among blue-collar and white-collar industrial employees, found that in both groups external references were relatively more important than referents within the employing organization. The most important external referents were the average earnings of all employees and the average earnings of those in the same or similar occupational categories.

In another study on a cross-sectional city sample of 220 employees in Israel, Dornstein (1989) found that the perceived fairness of received pay was significantly related to comparisons with two referents, both external: "the average salary in the economy" and "similars in the same industry." These were the only Other-referent categories that emerged as significant.

The findings of Summers and deNisi (1990) differ somewhat from those emerging from the other studies. Thus, these authors found that about a third of the sample of managers investigated by them tended to refer to Self for equity considerations, whereas more than a third (about 38 percent) relied primarily upon a generalized referent, "a referent not specifically inside or outside the focal organization" (p. 504). A smaller percentage (about 20 percent) reported relying primarily on internal referents, and only a few (about 6 percent) reported relying upon referents outside the organization. The authors suggest that the relatively greater importance of intra- versus extraorganizational comparisons may be due to the fact that their sample was drawn from a nationwide restaurant chain, "and the large number of locations (over 200 nationwide) may make comparisons to others inside the organization much more compelling" (p. 509).

Summary

The studies reviewed suggest quite strongly that contrary to expectations external comparisons tend to be relatively more important in the process of pay-fairness evaluation than internal comparisons. Still, here too some caution is necessary on account of some limiting factors mentioned in the previous section.

INTRA-GROUP VS. EXTRA-GROUP COMPARISONS

Only one study known to us investigated the issue of comparisons within one's work group versus comparisons outside it. The study, conducted by Ambrose and Kulik (1988), was based on a sample of about 150 employees from six work groups in a government organization in the United States. It aimed at investigating the degree to which work-group members shared comparison referents and feelings of pay fairness. Participants were asked to describe four job facets, one of which was compensation. After describing each facet they were asked if they compared that facet to the facet of some referent. Those who did were required to describe that referent. A major, and largely unexpected, finding was that referent choices tended to be external to one's work group rather than internal to it. Obviously, much more research is needed before a conclusion on the role of intra- versus extra-group comparisons, can be reached.

COMPARISONS TO SIMILARS VS. COMPARISONS TO DISSIMILARS

The exchange theories predict, as indicated, that individuals are most likely to compare their pay with that of similar others. What empirical evidence is there to support or refute this thesis? Strange as it seems, the existing relevant empirical evidence that may assist us with this question is quite scarce. It is reviewed below.

Field Research

In his large-scale survey, Runciman (1966) found that generally the comparisons made by individuals were "close to the actual situation of the respondent."

In a study conducted by Martin (reported in Martin, 1981: 90–91) on a sample of blue-collar workers and a heterogeneous sample of individuals from working-class neighborhoods, participants were asked to compare their earnings with those of two other individuals of their own choice. The similarity and direction of comparison (upward/downward) was assessed by the participants themselves. As in her experimental studies (see discussion below), Martin found that the most frequent comparison was with upward similars and the second most frequent was with upward dissimilars. These findings, Martin suggests, confirmed the hypothesis about the importance of dissimilar comparisons.

Gartrell (1983) conducted an exploratory study among 98 blue-collar workers in a municipal public works department, aimed at investigating the visibility of others against whom comparison choices ultimately are made. He found that when asked to compare their pay with others outside the department, 77 percent cited wage rates were *superior* to the respondents'. Still, most occupations cited were skilled operatives, transport workers, or laborers and there were few spontaneous references to professional, managerial, or technical occupations. This suggests that the majority of spontaneous comparisons were of the upward-similar type.

In her study on white-collar and blue-collar industrial employees, Dornstein (1988b) found that the most frequent referent category among the white-collar employees was "the average earnings of all employees"—an essentially dissimilar referent. Among the blue-collar employees, the findings indicated that the most important referents were similars outside the organization and the "average earnings of all employees" in combination. Dornstein also found that among the blue-collar employees, a substantial percentage (about 21%) made important dissimilar comparisons—to "officials in government" and "officials in the organization." Additional data from some open-ended questions about groups that "earn more (less) than they deserve" suggested that these comparisons were of a *negative* type: Officials were frequently mentioned by the blue-collar employees as being among those who "earn more than they deserve." This latter finding suggests the existence of negative references, not just positive references as assumed.

In another recent field study, Dornstein (1989) found additional evidence of the importance of dissimilar comparisons. A major guiding hypothesis in this study was that feelings of pay inequity would be positively related to the perception that one's pay compared unfavorably with the perceived average pay of one's reference groups(s). Among the reference groups investigated were various groups of similars and dissimilars. Unfavorable comparisons with dissimilars were found to explain about 28 percent of the total variance in felt inequity, compared with only 4 percent contribution by other, similar comparisons.

Experimental Studies

The question of similarity/dissimiliarity in social comparisons has also been explored by a few experimental studies. In the 1960s, a series of such studies was carried out but their results were inconclusive. The basic design was a "personality" test measuring subjects' traits valued both positively and negatively. Subjects were given false feedback of their scores, which were placed in the middle of the distribution for their group. After receiving this feedback, subjects were told that they may select one or two scores of their group members. The results of some of these studies supported the similarity thesis: Subjects tended to choose others with similar scores for comparisons (e.g., Darley and Aronson, 1966; Wheeler, 1966). Other studies, however, indicated a tendency among the subjects to select the lowest or highest scorers (e.g., Arrowood and Friend, 1969; Wheeler et al., 1969).

A study with a different experimental design was carried out by Martin and colleagues (reported in Martin, 1981: 84–86). The goal was to investigate the existence, importance, and determinants of dissimilar comparisons. One guiding hypothesis was that when valued outcomes are involved, people prefer upward to downward comparisons. These upward comparisons will be with similars as well as with dissimilars, the latter serving as a basis for feelings of relative deprivation. The basic design was a tape and slide display showing participants, typically employees working for a company, a position similar to their own and a superordinate position in a company said to be similar to their own. After being told to react as if they were the occupants of the subordinate position receiving the average pay for that position in the company portrayed, participants were asked to assess the likelihood that the average paid job incumbent at the portrayed company would make each of five comparison choices: with the highest and lowest pay level for that job, and with the highest, average, and lowest pay level for the superordinate position. The results indicated that the most frequent comparison choice was with upward similar, that is, with the highest-paid similar job incumbent in the portrayed company; upward comparisons with dissimilars (superordinate jobs) were selected as a second preference.

In a recent experimental study, Major and Forcey (1985) examined women's and men's comparison preferences when evaluating the fairness of their pay. Subjects working on one of three jobs and privately receiving identical pay were required to rank order their preferences for ascertaining the average pay of "different groups of people who have worked on the three jobs." The subjects tended to select a same-job comparison first, and this was unaffected by the sex linkage of the assigned job. Furthermore, as their second choice, people were more likely to choose a same-job comparison rather than a same-sex but different-job group comparison. In most cases subjects also preferred same-sex comparisons over cross-sex or combined-sex comparisons. The authors suggest that the above findings are indicative of a similarity bias. They also note that "this suggests that people believe that others in their own job are even more relevant as wage comparisons than are others of their own sex. This seems a reasonable inference, since in this experiment, as well as in the paid work force more generally, pay is explicitly related to job assignment whereas sex is not" (p. 402).

Summary

Both the field studies and the experimental studies produce equivocal results about the relative importance of similar versus dissimilar comparisons. This, as well as the paucity of the studies, preclude any firm conclusions about this issue. But the studies suggest quite strongly that, contrary to the exchange theories, dissimilar comparisons are fairly frequent and fulfill an important role in pay-fairness evaluations.

THE RELATIONSHIP BETWEEN EGOISTIC AND FRATERNAL DEPRIVATION

Given that individuals make comparisons with similars as well as with dissimilars, what is the relationship between egoistic deprivation emanating from comparisons with similars and fraternal deprivation emanating from comparisons between one's membership group and dissimilar groups? Some aspects of this question have been explored by Crosby (1982). Specifically, the question was: Do those perceiving a relative deprivation of their group feel aggrieved with their personal situation as well? Common sense suggests an affirmative answer. But this is not what Crosby found in her Newton study. Whereas employed women were most aware and most aggrieved about sex discrimination in employment, they still felt positively about all aspects of their jobs, including pay. Crosby suggests that three factors may help in explaining this paradox (pp. 76–77). First, people compartmentalize their lives and do not easily connect between one aspect and another: Evaluations about one's group position and one's own position are not necessarily connected. Second, it is easier to make deductions about group deprivation than about individual deprivation: When large groups are compared, it is possible to control for relevant dimensions and arrive at comparable averages. But full comparability is difficult when only a few individuals are involved. Third, argues Crosby, not noticing that one is being mistreated may serve the purpose of self-protection, of not having to hunt for a villain, and of "protecting smooth interaction at work" (p. 77). Crosby reasons that as a result of these difficulties, fraternal deprivation will be more frequent than personal or egoistic deprivation. Also, because of the same difficulties, feelings of personal deprivation are likely to be unstable.

THE COGNITION OF FRATERNAL DEPRIVATION

What cognitive processes are involved in recognizing the existence of fraternal deprivation? Is there empirical support for the proposition of averaging away idiosyncracies? How many cases of obvious discrimination does it take for the recognition of fraternal deprivation? Two experiments conducted by Crosby and colleagues addressed these questions (Crosby, Burris, Censor, and MacKethan, 1986a; Crosby, Clayton, Hemker, and Alksnis, 1986b). In one experiment (Crosby et al., 1986b) undergraduate subjects were asked to assess the likelihood of gender bias in salaries on the basis of information supplied to them about 10 departments in a fictitious company. The information supplied consisted of the salaries of males and females in each department, and the characteristics of each individual in relation to four criteria serving as bases for wage determination. Several cases of discrimination against women were included in the information supplied. All subjects received the same information, but it was presented to them differently: One group of subjects obtained all the information on a single sheet (total picture format); the other group received it on separate sheets for each department (dribble format). The results indicated significant differences in the perception of sex discrimination. As expected, subjects possessing the total picture format perceived significantly more gender bias than subjects under the dribble format.

In a second experiment (Crosby et al., 1986a) undergraduate subjects were supplied with information about eight individuals (two women and six men) who competed for a job/promotion with an individual of opposite sex, and won. Subjects also were supplied with information about the decision of an "outside consultant" supposedly hired to determine the impartiality of the selection process on the relative standing of each contestant in each contest situation relative to four equally weighted hiring/promotion decision criteria. All subjects received identical information indicating that the number of times a male was judged superior by the outside consultant equalled the number of times a female was judged superior. The information was presented to one group of subjects in a way that spread out female superiority instances so that one could not easily identify a clear-cut case where a superior women lost out to a man. In other conditions, one could see one, two, or three cases of discrimination against women. A control group received information in aggregate form. The results indicated that two cases of obvious discrimination were enough to allow the subjects to perceive a degree of discrimination that did not differ significantly from the one perceived by the control group. In both cases the discrimination perceived was significantly higher than in the other groups that received information in a more disjointed form. The overall conclusion from these experiments is that it is easier to perceive discrimination when information is presented in a more aggregate form than when it is presented in an atomized form.

CONCEPTIONS ABOUT INTERGROUP DIFFERENTIALS
AND THEIR EFFECTS

In a recent investigation, Dornstein (1990c) focused specifically on the thesis that fair pay conceptions also include conceptions about fair-pay differentiation among occupations. The study was based on about 5,550 judgments elicited from a cross-sectional city sample of about 220 employees concerning the fair-pay gradings of occupations (50 occupations representing the major occupational categories). A cluster analysis and other analyses of these judgments produced the following findings: (a) individuals discern between *groups* of occupations that are ordered in a hierarchical fashion; (b) the major discernible groups are the professions, the semiprofessions, administrative personnel, skilled and semiskilled manual workers; (c) the perceived just pay differentials are significantly greater between these major groups as compared with the differentials within each group;

(d) individuals in lower socio-economic position perceive the just *overall magnitude* as relatively smaller than individuals in higher socio-economic positions. These latter differences stem mainly from the fact that individuals of lower socio-economic status perceive relatively higher just levels of pay for the lower-level occupations as compared with the latter.

The author concludes that these findings support the basic thesis proposing that employees may be sensitive to the overall configuration of the reward system and the magnitude of differentials within it, and that pay systems aiming at a measure of perceived pay fairness must take into consideration the prevalent conceptions about the contours of just pay differentiation between groups of occupations, about the perceived just pay hierarchy between the groups, and about the overall magnitude (lowest–highest point of the entire scale).

Martin (1981) focused on the thesis that the *magnitude* of differentials vis-à-vis dissimilar groups may affect feelings of equity. To investigate these issues, Martin (1981) conducted a series of experiments exploring the effect of two types of inequality between groups: economic inequality—the magnitude of inequality between occupational groups—and inequality based on a definition of group membership (e.g., sex, race). The magnitude of this second type of inequality was measured in terms of extent of segregation between the groups (e.g., sex segregation between managerial and operative positions).

One study (Martin, 1982) was based on a sample of skilled blue-collar employees (technicians) and had a design similar to the one described earlier (see "Comparisons to Similars versus Comparisons to Dissimilars"). Briefly summarized, the design involved a videotape that realistically portrayed two jobs: a highly skilled blue-collar technician's job; and a low-level management job, that of a supervisor. A specific feature of this experiment was that participants received one of four pay plans in which the average pay level for the focal position (technicians) was identical but which differed in the magnitude of pay inequality (low–high) *between* the two occupational groups (technicians/low-level managers) shown in the videotape, and *within* the blue-collar job category. After being told "to react as if he were a technician receiving the average pay for technicians" in the company portrayed, participants were required to indicate which of the portrayed pay levels the technician depicted was most likely to compare to his own. Participants were also requested to compare the pay of technicians as a group with that of supervisors as a group and to rate the extent to which this pay comparison was dissatisfying, unexpected, and unjust. The findings indicated that the magnitude of in-group or between-group inequalities did not significantly affect the choice of comparison others. The predominant pattern was as expected: first choice—upward similars; second choice—upward dissimilars. However, "when the labor/management pay differential was large rather than small, the blue-collar subjects' comparisons of their pay levels with managerial pay levels caused significantly more dissatisfaction and significantly stronger perceptions of injustice" (Martin, 1982: 118).

The findings of a survey conducted by the author among the blue-collar experimental sample, a middle-management sample, and a heterogeneous sample recruited by newspaper advertisements were congruent with and support the experimental results described above: "Upward dissimilar comparisons were selected almost as frequently as upward similar comparisons" (p. 120).

The effect of group-membership segregation was explored by Martin and colleagues (1981) in a similar experiment involving female secretaries as subjects. In the videotape scene presented to subjects, the magnitude of the occupational sex segregation between the female secretaries and the executives at the company portrayed was manipulated. In the segregated condition all executives were males; in the partially integrated condition a third of the executives were females. The results of this study were similar to those obtained for the blue-collar sample: The female secretarial subjects in the segregated condition found comparisons with executive pay levels significantly more dissatisfying and unjust.

Martin (1981: 93) summarizes her findings by responding to the following questions: "What does it take to get people to question expected economic inequalities, to compare their meagre incomes to those of dissimilar, more prosperous people and to find those comparisons dissatisfying and unjust?" Her answer has three parts:

1. Most people will make comparisons to dissimilar, more prosperous people, provided they are given more than one opportunity to make a comparison.

2. Those upward, dissimilar comparisons will cause dissatisfaction and the perception of injustice if the comparer is exposed to large rather than small amounts of inequality.

3. Those feelings of fraternal deprivation will be pessimistic, by definition, only if the perceived injustice is expected. People with an external locus of control will be more likely to consider an inequality they expected to be unjust.

CHANGES IN REWARDS AND THEIR EFFECTS

How do changes in rewards through time affect the pay-fairness evaluation process? Relative deprivation theorists made some major propositions concerning this issue. Some of these propositions served as bases for recent empirical research. An experimental study by deCarufel and Schopler (1979) examined the effects of improvement in the case of an initially disadvantaged party. It addressed to Gurr's (1970) thesis that feelings of relative deprivation may arise when one's outcomes are increasing, but at a slower rate than one's feelings of entitlement. He called this *progressive deprivation*. The experiment involved subjects working on a clerical task in a simulated industrial setting. A fictitious allocator paid the subjects periodically; the payments always unfair at the beginning. In the subsequent pay periods, subjects were paid either an amount equal to the allocator's, an equal amount plus some compensation for past inequity, or the same amount as originally. In all cases, the total amount the allocator received surpassed what the others received. The results indicated that an improvement in pay was associated with greater satisfaction and perceived fairness when this improvement was arbitrarily granted by the allocator or was forced by a threat from the disadvantaged party. Subjects who received an "equal +" pay rise following appeals to fairness showed no improvement whatsoever in satisfaction. The explanation was that pay raises that followed the appeal to fairness created the feeling among the affected subjects that the right to higher pay was indeed legitimate. This sense of legitimacy, combined with the perception that the pay received still fell short of the perceived fair rate, caused a lack of satisfaction with the improved pay. This lack of satisfaction was not observable among the other subjects, who received pay raises arbitrarily or following threats and hence could not attribute these raises to the fulfillment of a just claim.

The findings of the above study also support Gurr's (1970) thesis of *aspirational deprivation*, defined as a state in which expectations are rising but outcomes are not. Subjects who appealed to fairness but whose pay was not improved showed strong feelings of discontent. Presumably, an appeal to fairness based on a case of obviously unfair pay created the expectation of an improvement; when this did not materialize, resentment grew.

What happens when outcomes fall but expectations do not? Gurr termed such a situation *decremental deprivation*. An experimental study by Ross and McMillen (1973) generally tends to support this thesis. In this study subjects were assigned the position of workers in a factory game and, when rewarded with a decremental pattern of payment, were found to be less satisfied with their rewards than subjects who received either a uniformly high or a uniformly low reward. However, the effect of a decremental pattern of reward was found to be less when an external comparison standard was provided. In groups receiving information about the minimum/maximum payment accorded to similar others in the past, those receiving a uniformly low payment were less satisfied than those working under a decremental schedule. The highest satisfaction in this case was found among those receiving a uniformly high payment.

The so called J-curve hypothesis was also put to an experimental test. According to this hypothesis, individuals experiencing a period of steady rise in outcomes followed by a sudden and sharp drop-off are likely to experience a feeling of relative deprivation caused by a widening gap between expectations that continue to rise and outcomes that have leveled off. In an experiment conducted by Ross, Thibaut and Evenbeck (1971) boy subjects engaged in a rope-pulling contest received ever-increasing rewards from the "manager," actually the experimenter. Then the manager suddenly started giving fewer and fewer rewards. The results indicated that those subjects who had been led to believe that they were "competent" tended relatively more to feel indignant about the allegedly unfair treatment, and were relatively more inclined to retaliate against the manager than their less-competent colleagues.

THE DETERMINANTS OF PAY COMPARISONS

Even if certain modalities in the choice of social comparisons are discernible at times, there are still substantial interindividual variances to be explained. Why do some individuals choose certain referents while others choose different ones? What factors determine the choice of a particular referent? These questions are obviously at the heart of the social comparison issue. An overview of the relevant empirical studies suggests that satisfactory answers to these questions are not yet available. The existing studies are limited in number and scope and address only a small portion of the variables which, according to prevalent theory, may be of relevance. Before reviewing these, it seems important to mention a unique study by Gartrell (1983) investigating the process whereby individuals become *aware* of others from among whom comparison referents are ultimately chosen. The major findings indicated first, that awareness of others outside the employing organization is largely based on one's personal situation: Friends, relatives, and acquaintances are the major sources of knowledge about the wages of outsiders. Moreover, knowledge about others in higher-status occupations is largely dependent on "strong" ties such as relatives or close friends. The mass media is also an important source of information about professional salaries.

Regarding awareness of others inside the employing organization, the findings indicated that participants were "best informed about the wages associated with positions near their own in the wage structure" (Gartrell, 1983: 130). Second, the findings indicated that awareness is affected by social and physical proximity. Third, information was also found to be dependent on the "visibility" of others in the organization. Altogether the findings indicated that awareness is largely a "by-product" of social interaction inside and outside the organization. Differences in status and power act as barriers to such interaction and to the information that may be gained through it. In this respect, Gartrell's findings are in line with those of Runciman (1966) who found that most of the participants in his large-scale study "suggest, or directly state a comparison based on a particular feature of the respondent's personal situation" (p. 229).

Regarding knowledge of the internal wage structure, Gartrell (1983) found widespread ignorance of this issue. The author thought this ignorance quite reasonable: The individuals investigated could gain only very little by knowing the overall wage structure in their organization and hence acted rationally in avoiding the costs involved in gathering this information.

Whether Gartrell's findings are generalizable or not remains open at this stage. As the author himself notes, the limitations of his study are only too obvious: The sample was limited to one organization and to its lower-level employees. Awareness of others may be differently affected in other organizations and among higher organizational echelons. But Gartrell's study is important in focusing attention on a series of factors that may affect the informational inputs about others, including the will to invest effort and incur costs in gathering the relevant information.

We turn now to a review of the specific factors that have been found to influence the actual process of social comparisons rather than the mere awareness of others. The review is arranged according to the major variables investigated, starting with the personal background characteristics.

Personal Background Characteristics

The major variables investigated in this context were education and age.

Education. Several studies have investigated the relationship between level of education and pay comparisons. They suggest that formal education is positively related to outside comparisons. Thus, Andrews and Henry (1963) found that "the greater a man's education, the more likely he was (1) to compare his pay with persons outside the company, and (2) *not* to compare himself with his peers within the company" (p. 31). Similarly, Goodman (1974) found that educational level is related to the selection of Outside-others; persons with lower educational levels selected only half as many outside as inside referents. The tendency among the more highly educated to select outside referents was more pronounced for the professional occupations (e.g., staff, engineering) than for nonprofessional line occupations. Hills (1980) found that those who tend to choose family and friends as referents have relatively lower educational levels than those emphasizing other types of referents. Heneman and colleagues (1980) found that individuals with high school education placed a greater emphasis on current needs than did those with higher levels of education.

Age. Very few studies report findings relating to the relationship between age and referent choices and even these present equivocal evidence. Andrews and Henry (1963) report that age seemed to affect the comparison process little, except for a consistent tendency among the youngest age group, in particular those with college degrees and post graduates, to choose outside reference groups with particular frequency. Hills (1980) reports that individuals who stressed Self in the past as comparisons were relatively younger.

A possible explanation for the above findings is that the young are relatively new in the organization and in the world of work. Newness in the organization might explain the tendency to lean on outside comparisons, while newness in the world of work might explain the tendency to choose oneself in the past as a standard: Here the conception of self-worth perhaps leans on achievements that are at least partly outside the occupational area.

The above explanation and the underlying findings require however some caution in view of the fact that another study (Heneman et al., 1980) found no significant relationship between age and the importance attached to various types of referents.

Position in Organization

Several studies examined the effect on pay comparisons of various aspects of position in the organization such as relative pay level, level in hierarchy, and boundary and nonboundary role.

Relative Pay Level. Patchen (1961), in one of the earliest and best-known studies on pay comparison and their determinants, found that

> men's wage position relative to those like themselves (in age, seniority, education, and family) is an important determinant of the comparison they choose, while their absolute wage position (pay rate) has, in itself, little influence on the choice of comparisons. Men whose earnings are lower than most others like themselves tended to make dissonant comparisons. (p. 104)

Patchen also found that relative wage position interacts with two other factors. One is *felt personal responsibility* for one's fate. Those who were doing relatively poorly on earnings were less inclined to make dissonant comparisons if they accepted personal responsibility for their present position. "But low-earners who blame others (such as their employer) for their present position can use dissonant comparisons as protest and as a claim to higher status" (p. 195). This interpretation is in line with the instrumental thesis stating that social comparisons may be based on instrumental considerations such as ego-protection or self-enhancement (Austin, 1987).

The second factor found to interact with relative pay position is *advancement prospects*. Employees in a relatively low pay position who had good advancement prospects were less inclined to choose upward dissonant comparisons than those with poor advancement prospects. "Only when the combination of low relative earning and the lack of clear opportunity to raise one's position were both present, did a big jump in the choice of dissonant comparisons occur" (Patchen, 1961: 105).

The relative pay level emerged as a significant determinant of social comparisons also in Goodman's (1974) study. Specifically, the findings in this study indicated that individuals on lower salary levels were more likely to select Other-inside referents than those on higher salary levels. According to the author, this finding reflects the fact that, given the pyramidal shape of most organizations, low-paid individuals may have more potential inside referents to select from.

Another finding of the study indicated that salary levels and salary raises were positively related to the selection of self-pay history and family referents. The author asserts that these findings support the thesis that comparisons enhancing self-esteem will be selected and those lowering it will be avoided: low salary individuals and high salary individuals with low raises will avoid choosing self-pay history or family referents since such comparisons are likely to have a negative effect on their felt self-esteem. In contrast, high salary individuals with high raises will be inclined to choose such referents for the opposite reason.

Summers and DeNisi (1990) in a replication of Goodman's study found, contrary to Goodman, that pay level was not significantly related neither to a selection of Other-inside referents nor to a selection of self-pay history or family referents.

Heneman and colleagues (1980) found that the higher the salary level, the greater the importance of external comparisons—for all three pay components investigated (level, raise, benefits). Heneman and colleagues suggest that higher salary individuals have skills more identifiable as "professional" rather than "organizational" and that the labor market would be better defined for such skills which "would seem to permit, and indeed even invite, greater importance being attached to external comparisons" (p. 214).

Dornstein (1988b) found that a relatively low-perceived pay position is associated with a tendency to compare with similars inside the organization. This finding supports the author's hypothesis that instrumental, self-protection tendencies, will have "the effect of narrowing the range of comparison and of bringing them closer to one's own level" (p. 225).

Hierarchical Level. Andrews and Henry (1963) found that lower-middle management was more likely to make external comparisons with others outside the company than were middle and lower management. These authors also found that middle management tended to compare its pay with those on a lower level, while members of lower management were more concerned with keeping up with their peers. The authors cautioned, however, that their findings regarding middle management might be biased since middle management in their study included local management in branch plants. Possibly, they argued, in larger operating units, the emphasis upon lower-level comparisons might not have appeared. Lawler (1965) in his study of about 560 middle- and lower-level managers in government and privately owned organizations found that managers tended to compare their pay with that of their superiors as well as that of their subordinates. Ronen (1986) found "some indication" for his hypothesis that employees in managerial positions, as compared with skilled nonsupervisory workers, tend to consider peers outside the organization as a more relevant reference group, but this trend "is not as clear-cut as expected" (p. 344).

In contrast to the above studies, Oldham and colleagues (1986), in their research on 265 employees in data processing units from 20 departments of a large state government in the United States, found no evidence that job level—an employee's level in the formal hierarchy—has any effect on the choice of social comparisons.

Boundary Position. Goodman (1974) hypothesized that occupancy of a boundary position i.e., a position that involves interaction with individuals in a wide range of organizations, would be positively related to the selection of outside referents. The rationale behind this hypothesis was that boundary-position occupants are relatively more likely than inside-position occupants to have information about outside referents. But the findings did not support this hypothesis, except for staff-position occupants. These were found to select relatively fewer inside referents and relatively fewer System referents, as hypothesized.

Summers and DeNisi (1990), in their replication of the Goodman study found, however, no significant relationship whatsoever between the occupancy of a boundary position and the tendency to compare to outside referents.

Other Work-Related Aspects

Length of Tenure. Several studies explored the relationship between pay comparisons and length of tenure. Goodman (1974) found that, contrary to what might have been expected, tenure does not relate significantly to the selection of Other-inside referents. He suggested that the absence of a significant relationship might be explained by the fact that the tendency of individuals with short length of tenure to select inside referents "as a way to learn about the pay system" is cancelled by the tendency of low-paid oldtimers ("who probably feel inequitably paid") to select "as many inside referents as do people with short length of tenure" (p. 189).

In contrast, Heneman et al. (1980) found that length of tenure is positively related to intraorganizational comparisons in regard to both pay raises and benefits. The authors suggest that "as people become more socialized into, and knowledgeable about, the organization, they turn more toward others within the organization for comparison purposes" (p. 214).

Similarly, Hills (1980) found that length of tenure is negatively related to "market comparisons," that is, external similar/dissimilar comparisons. Hills also found that individuals who stress historical pay, that is, Self in the past, have relatively lower company tenure. This finding coincides with those of Oldham et al. (1986) that employees who used Self-outside referents for pay comparisons had relatively short tenure, whereas those who used Other-inside referents had the longest organizational tenure. These authors suggested that the positive relationship between short tenure and outside comparisons may be explained by the lack of information about inside referents among individuals with short tenure, who thus tend to rely on their own personal experience when evaluating their pay.

Social Influences. The influence of the work group on the choice of comparison others was investigated by Ambrose and Kulik (1988) on a sample of about 150 employees in a government organization. A major hypothesis of this study was that the social environment, in this instance the work group, may affect the comparison process and its outcome in several direct and indirect ways: through overt statements made by group members, through structuring an individual's attention to his environment; through affecting his interpretation of environmental cues; and through influencing the way he interprets his needs. As expected, the findings indicated indeed that work group members tended to agree on referent choices when comparing their compensation.

Pay Secrecy. Lawler (1981) has observed that pay secrecy is widespread in private as well as public organizations. A major advantage of pay secrecy is that it allows management more freedom in the administration of pay and lowers the likelihood of complaints about pay inequity. But how does pay secrecy affect the process of comparison, especially internal comparisons? Does it eliminate such comparisons? What other effects does it have? There are only a few studies that address this question. These focus mainly on the accuracy of perceptions about pay and pay satisfaction under conditions of pay secrecy. Lawler (1972) and

Milkovich and Anderson (1972) found that individuals overestimated the pay of referents at their own and at lower organizational levels, but underestimated the pay levels of referents above them. Mahoney and Weitzel (1978) replicated the former but not the latter results. They also found that these inaccurate estimates are *not* significantly related to pay satisfaction. Subbarao and deCarufel (1983), in their research on faculty members of a Canadian university practicing pay secrecy, found that members used to rely on informal contacts for gathering information on internal pay levels. Altogether these studies indicate that even under conditions of pay secrecy, individuals do not cease to compare themselves with others inside the employing organization, but that such comparisons are often based on inaccurate information. Still, inaccurate information does not seem to lead to dissatisfaction.

Attitudinal Factors

A number of studies investigated the effect on comparisons of certain attitudinal variables such as perceived promotion prospects, perceived locus of control over one's outcomes, and attachment to the organization.

Perceived Advancement and Social Mobility Chances. Patchen (1961) found that perceived advancement chances have different effects on comparisons with others—depending on whether they relate to prospects *within* the organization or outside it. Individuals who had good advancement prospects within the organization tended relatively less to make upward comparisons, and those who made such comparisons tended relatively less to make present dissonant comparisons. By contrast, individuals with the best perceived mobility chances *outside* the organization were more likely than others to make upward dissonant comparisons. Patchen's explanation for these differences was that individuals who believe that they have good chances of promotion within the organization have no incentive to protest their present position: The best way to maximize their chances of promotion is to "stay where they are, work hard and wait." On the other hand, outside advancement chances "can be realized not by staying put and keeping quiet, but by actively fighting for a raise." Those who perceive themselves as having good outside advancement chances would be motivated to protest their present status. Upward dissonant comparisons can serve this purpose, which would explain why those with best perceived outside-advancement chances tended to make such comparisons.

Hills (1980) found that individuals who see few chances for advancement in their organization stress historical self-pay. Hills does not offer an explanation for this finding. Contrary to Hills, Heneman et al. (1980) found a positive relationship between an emphasis on historical self-pay and likelihood of promotion. They also found a positive relationship between likelihood of promotion and an emphasis on personal comparisons; that is, comparisons with friends, relatives, and family members. The explanation for the historical self-pay dimension may be that "high promotables place greater emphasis on their past treatment because they have constantly viewed such treatment as a signal regarding their promotion chances'' (p. 114). As for the personal comparison dimension, ''those who feel more promotable may see personal comparisons as more important because a promotion will serve to enhance their status and pay in relation to friends, relatives and family members'' (pp. 114–15).

Dornstein (1988b) found among white-collar employees a significant positive relationship between perceived good promotion prospects and a tendency to compare with similars inside the organization. No such relationship was found among blue-collar employees. Dornstein also found, among both blue-collar and white-collar employees, a positive relationship between perceived good chances of social mobility and the tendency to compare with similars (inside and outside the organization). Generally, Dornstein's findings are in line with those of Patchen and his interpretation: Individuals with perceived good advancement prospects have little incentive to make dissonant comparisons and to protest their present position, and will thus focus their attention on a narrower range of comparisons than those who wish to protest their present position.

Perceived Locus of Control. As indicated, Patchen (1961) found that individuals feeling responsible for their relatively low pay were less inclined to make dissonant comparisons than those in a similar pay position but not feeling responsible for their fate. The effect of perceived locus of control, that is, perceived responsibility for one's outcomes was also investigated by Martin in an experimental field study (Martin, 1981: 86–88). The experimental design was basically similar to the one described above. (see ''Comparisons to Similars vs. Comparisons to Dissimilars''). The subjects were highly skilled blue-collar employees in a manufacturing organization. Analysis of the comparison choices indicated, as hypothesized, that the expected pattern of comparisons (most frequent first choice—upward similar, most frequent second choice—upward dissimilar) did not hold for one experimental group only: the ''internals''—those feeling responsible for their outcomes. These, in contrast to the other subjects, tended to restrict their first and second choices to similars. This finding strongly supported Patchen's findings: Perceived responsibility for one's outcomes tends to restrict the scope of one's comparisons to similar others.

Organizational Attachment. Dornstein (1988b) investigated the relationship between friendship ties in the organization—one measure of organizational attachment—and patterns of comparison with others. The hypothesized positive relationship between number of friendship ties in the organization and a tendency to compare with others inside the organization was confirmed among the white-collar but not among the blue-collar participants. But satisfaction with various major aspects of the work situation—another index of organizational attachment—was found, as hypothesized, to be positively related to comparisons with similars inside the organization and negatively related to dissimilar comparisons, among both groups of employees.

Knowledge of Reward Range

Several experimental studies investigated the relationship between social comparisons and the availability of information on the existing range of rewards. Wheeler and colleagues (1969) attempted to determine how knowing or not knowing the range (lowest/highest value) of an outcome affects the choice of referents. Subjects were tested for the presence of a positively or negatively valued trait, and were then divided into groups which obtained information about the approximate range of the group's score and groups that did not obtain such information. Subjects were then required to make a first and second choice of the scores in the group they would most like to see. The results indicated that subjects in the positively valued trait condition who did not obtain information on the group's score range tended to choose first the highest group score. Those who obtained information on the score range tended to choose first a similar higher score. The authors concluded that, "when choosing a referent person, an individual's first need is to determine the boundaries of the scale. His second is to determine whether he is more like those better off than himself or more like those worse off, and he is primarily concerned with those better off" (p. 231).

Arrowood and Friend (1969) criticized the conclusions of Wheeler and colleagues, suggesting that a desire for knowing scale boundaries does not accord well with the tendency to require information about the highest score as a first choice. They argued that this finding fits better with a twofold explanation suggested by Thornton and Arrowood (1966): (1) That the information afforded by a positive instance is more useful for self-valuation or more readily interpretable, and (2) a self-enhancement tendency which predicts the choice of a desirable other. Arrowood and Friend also suggested that "choosing the next-best-off other could confirm dissimilarity just as easily as confirming similarity" and is hence no proof for "the dominant motive . . . to determine the degree of similarity with very similar others (Wheeler et al., 1969: 228)" (Arrowood and Friend, 1969: 236–37). Arrowood and Friend (1969) offered the following alternative interpretation. Individuals are interested first in establishing how much of the valued outcome they have, and this can be established by comparison with a positive instance. Second, individuals are interested in knowing how far they are from the "good guys" and this can be found out by comparison with the desirable goal: "People will choose the highest numerical score because of the information afforded by a positive instance. People will compare in the positively valued direction in order to place themselves relative to where they wish to be" (p. 239).

Summary

The findings reviewed suggest that many factors may determine the choice of referents in pay-fairness evaluation. Moreover, many of these factors are related in one way or another to the employment context. However, the overall impression is that no aspect seems to have been investigated thoroughly enough to allow any firm conclusions, and much more research is needed before a solid body of knowledge about the determinants of pay comparisons crystallizes.

NOTES

1. The perceived fair amount was established by previous research.
2. See also our discussion on Goodman's study in the following sections.

7 The Underlying Dimensions of Evaluation

This chapter concerns the empirical evidence relating to the dimensions underlying the process of pay-fairness evaluation. As noted, theorists do not agree on this issue. There is no agreement on whether a single predominant such dimension exists or several, on the nature of these dimensions, whether social consensus on these dimensions should typically be expected, and the factors underlying social consensus or dissensions. Also, if more than one dimension is involved, how are the various dimensions weighted and combined.

Empirical studies that may shed some light on these questions are few. Most of them, with one major exception, are field studies. The exception is studies dealing with the issue of input integration; that is, the way(s) in which the various dimensions are combined and integrated: Most of these studies are of an experimental nature. We turn now to the studies themselves.

THE PERCEIVED RELEVANT DIMENSIONS

As noted, the various theories have different conceptions of the relevant dimensions of evaluation. For example, the exchange theorists believe that these dimensions are the perceived contributions to the exchange. A representative list of what these might be was offered by Adams (1963a):

> On the man's side of the exchange are his education, intelligence, experience, training, skill, seniority, age, sex, ethnic background, social status, and very importantly, the effort he expends on the job. Under special circumstances other attributes will be relevant: personal appearance or attractiveness, health . . . they are what he perceives as his contribution to the exchange. (p. 422)

Status value theory, to take another example, has a different view on the subject: Any characteristic that "involves two or more states that are differentially valued" can potentially serve as a status characteristic and, as such, a basis of reward expectations.

The different conceptions about the potentially relevant dimensions are important since they implicitly or explicitly guide most of the empirical studies pertaining to the subject: Studies influenced by a particular theory tend to focus on the dimensions perceived as relevant by that theory and to ignore other dimensions lying outside its scope. This bias is especially significant in studies employing a design that is based on researcher-determined lists of potentially relevant dimensions. As it happens, these studies constitute the great majority of all the empirical studies on the subject. The fewer studies employing different methods—more open-ended and less liable to biases stemming from researcher orientation—therefore deserve special attention.

Some first notions about the dimensions perceived as relevant by employees evaluating the fairness of their pay come from early studies that inspired the initial theoretical formulations. For example, Homans (1974) reports that in his case study (see Homans, 1953) in the Customer Accounting Division of the Eastern Utilities Company, the most important dimensions used by the ledger clerks, when comparing themselves with the cash posters, were seniority, chance for advancement, variety, responsibility, and autonomy. Jacques (1970), for his part, found that the major dimension underlying evaluations of pay fairness is time span of discretion on the job. These early findings have become the cornerstone of the respective theories they helped to develop.

Later studies, in the 1970s and 1980s, were conducted after the various theories had become established. They went beyond the exploratory phase and rested on the foundations laid by others. Where the theory specified a priori the nature and basic character of the evaluation dimensions, it seemed logical to proceed with investigating lists of evaluation dimensions that derived from the theory instead of utilizing an open-ended approach, which is not as neat and convenient. The investigations aimed at establishing the *perceived relevancy* of the listed dimensions and the *relative importance* attached to each. Most of the studies, as will become evident, were inspired by the exchange theories and in particular by equity theory. But there are also a few studies that have a different orientation. Some of the studies reviewed have even been inspired by external, outside-the-field research contexts: They are presented here since they contain data directly relevant to the issues discussed. The description following is, as usual, in chronological order.

Field Studies

Belcher and Atchinson (1970) investigated the perceived relevant dimensions among four groups of employees (clerical, semiskilled production, technical, engineers) in a large public utility in the United States. Each participant was presented with a list of 18 possible inputs and was required to indicate how much he thought each item was taken into account in the present pay system, how much it should be taken into account, and how important it was to him in determining pay. The findings indicated that quality of work, job knowledge, reliability, and acceptance of responsibility were perceived as the most important inputs.

Marsh and Mannari (1973) carried out a study on a sample of about 1,000 employees in a plant of a large manufacturing organization in Japan. One aim was to investigate what factors *ought*, in the employees' view, to determine their pay. Participants were required to rank in order of importance six factors: education, number of dependents, job and skill classification, ability, seniority, and contribution to company profits. The rank order obtained for all participants (from highest to lowest) was ability, skill, job classification, seniority, contribution to company profits, education, number of dependents. Commenting on the unexpectedly low rank of education (and noting the lack of a correlation between job classification and education) the authors say: "Thus, the respondents appear to be saying: 'Pay should not be based on education as such, but on an individual's skill and the job he holds.' " (p. 29). They also noted that contribution to company profits "could be measuring a number of things: such as company identification; ideological orientation (or job performance) and that its low ranking is hence difficult to interpret. Therefore we cannot be sure what this factor's relatively low rank means" (p. 29).

Rossi and his colleagues (Jasso and Rossi, 1977; Alves and Rossi, 1978) used the vignette technique to determine how individuals in the United States (cross-sectional samples) judge the fairness of earnings. The characteristics describing the vignettes were income, education, occupation, sex, ethnicity, number of children, and being on welfare. The findings indicated that "occupation and education dominate other characteristics . . . in influencing distributive justice judgments" (Alves and Rossi, 1978: 551). From among the remaining characteristics investigated, only number of children and being on welfare were found to be statistically significant. The relationships for ethnicity and sex were in the expected direction, yet were not statistically significant: Other things being equal, females and persons of lower ethnicity tended to be judged as relatively more overpaid than males and persons of "higher" ethnicity.

Oldham and colleagues (1982), in their study on the selection and consequences of job comparisons conducted on a sample of 130 fulltime employees (machine operators, inspectors, laborers, clerks, and supervisors) in a large manufacturing organization in the United States, presented participants with a list of seven possible inputs asking them to indicate in regard to each (a) if it was a job requirement (yes/no) and (b) how necessary it was for doing their job. The list included effort, age, education, skill, gender, company seniority, and job seniority. The authors did not report the frequencies obtained in relation to question (b) above, but they note that "employees also were given the opportunity to report on the questionnaire additional job inputs; however, *very few took advantage of this opportunity*" (p. 93, emphasis added). A possible interpretation of this finding is that for most employees investigated, the seven input attributes adequately represented the perceived relevant inputs. Still, it is not clear which of these were actually considered as relevant in pay-fairness evaluation.

Martin (1981: 63) reported the results of a survey study in which subjects were asked to select comparative referents whose pay they would be likely to compare with their own. They were then asked what dimensions they considered when they assessed the overall level of similarity to the comparative referent. The most frequently selected dimensions were occupation, income, age, education, and— for blue-collar and clerical workers only—seniority and productivity. The findings also indicated that "when making comparisons of income, people use on average five, rather than an infinite number of dimensions."

It should be noted that this research, in contrast to the others cited so far, employs a technique able to reflect more accurately the relevant dimensions: Instead of participants receiving a researcher-determined list of dimensions, they may freely report the dimensions taken into account when assessing the degree of similarity to the comparison referents.

A method possessing the same advantage was used by Dornstein (1985) in her study of blue-collar and white-collar employees, who were asked to reflect their ideas about what was fair pay in an open-ended question. A content analysis revealed that the following dimensions were considered as relevant: education, responsibility and authority, dedication to the job, strenuous work, special skills, indispensability, seniority in job, adverse working conditions, inconvenient working hours, length of service, age, and family needs.

Dornstein conducted two other studies on the perceived relevancy and weight of various evaluation dimensions. One (Dornstein, 1988a) investigated which of a number of potentially relevant dimensions of "occupation" serve as significant bases in the pay-fairness gradings of occupations. The dimensions were complexity of work with people, data and objects, education, vocational training, work conditions, the physical demands of an occupation and occupational prestige. Fifty occupations, presumably well known to the public and representing the major occupational categories, were included in the study. The findings, based on the judgments of a cross-sectional city sample of 220 employees in Israel, indicated that occupational prestige, vocational training, physical demands, complexity of work with people, working conditions, and complexity of work with objects were significantly related to the gradings of occupations according to "pay deserved."

In the other study, Dornstein (1990b) employed a vignette technique to investigate the perceived relevancy and weight in pay-fairness judgments of some personal background and task-related characteristics. Participants, about 250 young male adults, were presented with vignettes described as employees earning a specified income and were required to judge its fairness. Apart from income, the vignette also contained information about the worker's sex, formal education, years of vocational training, length of time in the organization, years in that occupation, number of subordinates, physical working conditions, the importance of the job to the organization and the country, and a description of the worker's job in terms of complexity in dealing with data and people. Fairness of pay was judged (in descending order of importance) relative to years in that occupation, absolute amount of pay, physical conditions of the job, education, number of subordinates, complexity of work with data, amount of vocational training and importance of the job to the organization and the country. Length of time in the organization, sex, and complexity of the task in dealing with people were not found relevant. A most interesting and rather unexpected finding was that some aspects such as working with complex data or fulfilling a task important to the organization seemed to be regarded as benefits or positive outcomes rather than inputs requiring to be rewarded. We shall discuss these findings in more detail in a later section.

In their study on judgments of "appropriate" pay for occupations, Mahoney and Blake (1987) found that judgments were significantly related to three factors subsumed under the headings of training, working conditions, and supervision, as well as an additional factor—femininity/masculinity (percentage of females/ males in an occupation).

Experimental studies

Additional information about the perceived relevant dimensions comes from experimental studies. Most of these have already been reviewed extensively in the previous chapters. The studies manipulating performance suggest very clearly that this dimension is considered relevant in reward distribution. But what evidence emerges from these studies about other dimensions? Experimental studies on these are far fewer than those manipulating performance but they do indicate that when information on more dimensions is available it tends to be taken into account in reward allocation. For example, Leventhal and Michaels (1969) found that subjects who had been informed of both performance and amount of time needed took both items into account in distributing rewards. Similar results were reported by Messe and Lichtman (1972), who included time of work needed as a positive contribution (in contrast to Leventhal and Michaels, where time featured as a negative input). Leventhal, Michaels, and Sanford (1972) supplied their subjects with information about performances and effort that were above/below the average and found that allocators used both these types of information in making their allocations.

Törnblom and Jonsson (1985), in an experiment involving the fairness judgments of reward allocations under four conditions defined by two dichotomic variables— competitive/team relationships and one/several participants—found the following rank ordering of justness of allocation criteria:

productivity > effort > ability

This ordering obtained for all except the team/several participants condition. They concluded that "the general pattern of rank ordering was reasonably consistent with previous findings" (p. 256).

Hierarchical Position as an Evaluation Dimension

A few investigations explore in depth the relationship between position in the organizational hierarchy and level of pay judged appropriate for the various positions.

Kuethe and Levenson (1964) presented some exploratory findings on this question from a study based on a sample of 110 students. Participants were presented with a series of organization charts depicting hierarchical relationships among positions in an organization. The structures were varied to permit analysis of the estimated worth of positions according to *number of supervised* and according to *direct* or *indirect* supervision. The salary of one position directly below the position of the head of organization was indicated on all charts and was identical on all of them. The salary for all other positions was left blank. Participants were required to estimate the salaries of the blank positions and were instructed "to assume that the more responsibility a person has, the higher his salary." The major findings were as follows:

1. Holding the number of subordinates constant, indirect supervision commands a higher salary than direct supervision.

2. Additional direct subordinates increase a position's salary.

3. A middle-level position without subordinates is perceived as qualitatively different from a position with subordinates: Some ascribe more value to it. Generally, these positions evoke the greatest disagreement regarding their worth.

4. The salary of the organization head is positively correlated with both number of levels and number of subordinates; number of levels has a greater impact than number of subordinates.

The above findings presumably reflect how individuals judge responsibility of supervisors and show the importance of the following elements (other things being equal): directness of supervision (negative); number of directly supervised (positive); absence of subordinates for middle-echelon positions (varying); and number of echelons and number of subordinates (both positive) for the top-level position.

Mahoney (1979b) replicated the Kuethe and Levenson (1964) study with two different samples: (1) 98 upper-division students of business administration and (2) 58 compensation administrators. The results of these studies essentially confirm those of Kuethe and Levenson; concerning differentials between reporting levels. The results "imply clear distinctions of worth among the different levels of the hierarchy, distinctions of about 33 percent measured on a continuous scale of monetary compensation" (Mahoney, 1979b: 737). The author is inclined to interpret these findings as being in line with relationships reported from psychophysics research, indicating that the amount of increase in stimulus level is some constant proportion of the previous level of stimulus (Torgerson, 1958). In Mahoney's view,

The scale appropriate for distinguishing among organizational positions on dimensions other than hierarchical level (e.g., subordinates supervised) is different and inadequate to account for the differentials associated with organization level. The organization level of a position, whatever it connotes regarding position content, clearly is a significant influence on the imputed *worth* or *status* of the position in the organization (p. 737; emphasis added).

It is interesting to note that Mahoney's findings are very similar to those obtained by Jacques (1970), who found that the perceived just difference between one's pay level and the adjacent pay levels in the hierarchy is about 33 percent along the whole hierarchy.

The importance of just interlevel pay differentials is also evident in Lawler's (1965) study on managers' perception of their own and their superiors' and subordinates' pay. The findings indicated that managers, unaware of the actual salaries of the adjacent levels, tended to perceive them as too close to their own pay level. This was particularly true in regard to downward differentials. A significant positive correlation was found in both private and public organizations between the perception of a too-small downward pay differential and dissatisfaction with own pay. This latter finding suggests the existence of notions of "proper" pay differentials between levels.

Social Status as an Evaluation Dimension

In his list of potentially relevant inputs, Adams (1963a: 422) explicitly includes social status. But, as observed, status value theorists like Berger, Zelditch, Anderson, and Cohen (1972) criticize exchange theorists for including social status and other status characteristics such as age, sex ethnicity, and so on, in their list of inputs/investments, arguing that the exchange formulations cannot properly account for the significance of these characteristics in reward allocation and reward evaluation since the relationship between them and productive contributions is vague and difficult to prove (p. 126). These authors propose, instead, that status characteristics are directly relevant to the allocation and evaluation of rewards. What empirical evidence is there to support this argument? Very few empirical studies exist to supply some relevant data. Generally, they hold that status does indeed serve as a basis for reward evaluation.

The most direct evidence comes from the studies of Rossi and colleagues (Jasso and Rossi, 1977; Alves and Rossi, 1978) on the fairness judgments of earnings, and from Dornstein's study (1988a) on the pay-equity evaluation of occupations. The Rossi and colleagues studies found that "occupation" operationalized as *occupational prestige* constitutes a major element in the fairness evaluation of earnings.

Dornstein (1988a) investigated which of a number of potentially relevant dimensions of "occupation" serve as significant bases in the pay-fairness gradings of occupations. Occupational prestige was found to be a major determinant, alone accounting for about 79 percent of the variance in the average pay gradings; the other factors representing various contributive elements related to an occupation, such as years of training, complexity of work with data/people/objects typical of an occupation, and so on, when added to the equation raised the figure to about 90 percent. In the latter equation, the combined standardized weight of the contribution elements amounted to 75 percent of that of occupational prestige!

Finally, Mahoney's (1979) conclusion that the consistent and uniform percentage pay differentials considered as fair between levels in the hierarchy are more in line with "a general theory of hierarchical order" than a theory of executive compensation, also tends to support the thesis that status *per se* is a relevant dimension in pay fairness evaluation.

Evidence somewhat contradicting the thesis that status as a symbolic characteristic serves as a basis for pay-fairness evaluations comes from an experimental study by Parcel and Cook (1977). Three variables were experimentally manipulated to test their effect on reward allocation in dyads working jointly on a task. These were social status (operationalized as ability scores), relevance (operationalized as relevance of the ability for performing the collective task) and performance feedback. The findings indicated generally that status differentials in themselves, as well as differences in the relevance of abilities to task performance, did not significantly affect the distribution of rewards, which tended to be equal on average. However, "the addition of performance feedback resulted in an increased adoption of the equity-contribution rules, marked differentiation in reward allocation, and thus clear alignment of the status and reward hierarchies" (Parcell and Cook, 1977: 323). The authors conclude "that congruence of the alignment of status and reward ranks occurs under conditions which are somewhat more limited than the status congruence and equity perspectives have previously indicated. Information concerning respective contribution to the group task is necessary to effect the predicted congruence" (p. 323).

An experimental study that fully exposes the difficulty in reaching some definite conclusions on the issue was conducted by Evan and Simmons (1969). The major hypothesis was that levels of performance would be affected by incongruencies/congruencies among competence, authority levels, and pay. Specifically, underpaid subjects, that is, subjects who received pay that they were led to believe was lower than matched their level of competence/authority, would exhibit a lower performance level compared with individuals equitably paid, that is, led to believe that they were receiving pay that matched their competence/authority. Conversely, it was expected that overpaid subjects would exhibit a higher performance level than individuals equitably paid. The results of the experiment involving the manipulation of competence (operationalized as ability to perform the relevant task) and pay were indeed according to what was expected. But the results of the experiment involving the manipulation of authority (operationalized as bestowal of a supervisory title—"assistant supervisor") and pay were not. Contrary to expectations, the experimentally manipulated incongruencies between pay and authority had no significant effect on the subjects' performance. The authors suggested that the subjects bestowed with the supervisory title may not have felt that they had any actual authority since they were not given an opportunity to actually exercise it. Support for this interpretation comes from data indicating that those bestowed with the title of supervisor "reported that their job titles were not appropriate." Presumably, the feeling that their titles were inappropriate prevented reaction to incongruencies between title and payment. If so, the findings tend to support the argument that *actual contribution* (in this case actual performance of the supervisory task) is a necessary condition for the alignment of status and rewards: Where there was only the title but no actual supervision, subjects apparently did not react with a feeling of underpayment when paid less; that is, when paid the rate due to "ordinary" workers. This conclusion, however, does not emanate from the results involving the manipulation of competence and pay. Here, performance levels varied as predicted in response to incongruencies between pay and ability; actual contribution was immaterial. A possible explanation for the above apparent paradox is that in the first experiment involving competence subjects were led to believe that pay was granted on the basis of competence test results and so reacted to incongruencies between pay and competence. On the other hand, in the experiment involving authority, the subjects given the title "supervisor" were led to believe that their jobs were usually paid more because they differed from their coworkers' jobs, which were described as more routine and to be performed under the assistant supervisor's direction. The task of actual supervision was thus part and parcel of the job definition. When during the experiment only the title was given but no supervisory responsibilities were demanded, subjects probably felt that the contribution matching their title is lacking and so did not react to incongruencies between their title and their pay.

Obviously, more empirical evidence is needed to substantiate the above line of reasoning, and, even more important, to test the conditions under which an alignment of pay and status is an integral part of the expectations for fair pay. Still, even at this stage, when empirical evidence is scant, it seems important to note that some significant difference between the field studies of Rossi and colleagues (Jasso and Rossi, 1977; Alves and Rossi, 1978) and of Dornstein (1988a), and the experimental studies of Parcel and Cook (1977) and of Evan and Simmons (1969), may have affected the results. In the field studies, social status is operationalized as the social prestige of occupations. Occupational prestige, as a wealth of studies shows, is a major dimension of social status in all modern societies and as such is most deeply embedded in the social structure of these societies. On the other hand, in the experimental studies social status is an artificial, experimentally created, construct in a test situation. It seems quite reasonable to think that the effect on pay-fairness judgments of a status element deeply rooted in the social fabric of society will be far greater than that of an artificially created social-status construct of ability differentials.

SOCIAL CONSENSUS ON RELEVANT DIMENSIONS

As indicated, there is much theoretical disagreement on the question of social consensus regarding the dimensions underlying judgments of pay fairness. Empirical research has therefore a crucial role to fulfill in disentangling this issue, but unfortunately the available evidence, as will become shortly evident, is rather fragmented, fraught with contradictions, limited in scope, and does not allow a firm conclusion. We turn now to the studies themselves.

One of the first systematic studies is by Belcher and Atchinson (1970), who found that the four occupational groups investigated differed significantly in their perceptions of which inputs should be included and what weight should be given to each in determining their pay. For example, clerical workers assigned a significantly higher degree of importance to "acceptance of responsibility," "judgment," "oral communication skill," and "quality of work performed" than did production workers.

Van Knippenberg and Van Oers (1984) in a field study among a sample of social psychiatric nurses (SPNs) and baccalaureate nurses (BNs) found significant differences between these groups in the importance attached to various inputs. The BNs, perceived by all as the theoretically more-trained group, were found to value "theoretical insight" more than the SPNs. By contrast, the latter, perceived to be superior on interpersonal relations, were found to attach much higher value to "interpersonal relations" than the former. The authors argue that these findings "corroborate the validity of a notion . . . that group members are inclined to exaggerate and upgrade the things their own group is relatively good at" (pp. 359–60).

Significant differences are also reported by Dornstein (1985) in her study on white-collar and blue-collar employees in four industrial organizations. The findings of this study indicated that the white-collar and the blue-collar employees tended to differ in the emphasis placed on various inputs when discussing the concepts of fair pay. For example, white-collar employees tended to emphasize relatively more "responsibility and authority" and "indispensability to the organization" while blue-collar employees tended to emphasize relatively more "difficult working conditions" and "inconvenient working hours." Dornstein suggested that these findings support her thesis, derived from the instrumentality proposition emphasizing self-enhancement and ego-protection tendencies (e.g., Austin, 1977), that employees will tend to consider as most relevant and most important those dimensions which are central to, and which best characterize, their work. Here are some of her comments:

It is interesting to note that the standards emphasized by each group are not only central features in the jobs performed by it, but also differentiate most sharply between the two groups. Thus, unpleasant physical conditions are thought to be part and parcel of blue-collar industrial jobs while the opposite is true in relation to white-collar jobs. On the other hand, authority and responsibility are almost exclusively vested in white-collar positions while blue-collar jobs involve little authority and demand only very little responsibility. (Dornstein, 1985: 326)

The findings of Belcher and Atchinson (1970) may be interpreted in a similar vein. For example, "responsibility," "judgment," and "oral communication skill" are clearly some of the core inputs required by white-collar employees, but not those of production workers. Also, "quality of work performed" measurements are considerably more often applied to white-collar than to blue-collar jobs.

Some findings, however, contradict at least *prima facie* the findings cited above. For example, Rossi and colleagues (e.g., Jasso and Rossi, 1977; Alves and Rossi, 1978) show that only very little—about 1 percent—of the variance in vignette earnings is explained by respondent characteristics such as sex, race, education, income, and prestige, and by respondent-vignette characteristics interaction.

In her study on the pay equity gradings of occupations, Dornstein (1988a), like Alves and Rossi (1978), found that only a very small proportion—about 2 percent—of the variance in the pay-fairness gradings of various occupations is accounted for by the respondents' personal and work-related characteristics (e.g., sex, socio-economic status, education, age, time on the job, organizational tenure, number of subordinates, and size of the employing organization). Of these, only socio-economic status, education, and number of subordinates were found to be statistically significant. Specifically, the findings indicated that individuals of relatively low education and socio-economic status tend to attach greater importance to vocational training than the other status groups. Similarly, individuals in positions of authority tend to attach relatively more importance to physical demands than those without authority.

In another study, examining the pay-fairness judgments of vignettes described as job occupants with differing job-related personal and work-related characteristics, Dornstein (1990b) found no significant evidence whatsoever for the impact on these judgments of the personal background characteristics of the individuals exercising the judgments.

A possible explanation for the discrepant findings of the above studies regarding social consensus on evaluation dimensions is that some of them focused basically on the actual employment situation in which they were conducted while others focused on "constructed" or hypothetical situations. Thus, social dissensus was found in those studies carried out in concrete employment contexts—Belcher and Atchinson's (1970) with four occupational groups, Van Knippenberg and Van Oers's (1984) with psychiatric and baccalaureate nurses, and Dornstein's (1988b) with blue-collar and white-collar industrial employees. In contrast, social consensus was found in the studies of Rossi and colleagues and in Dornstein's (1990b) study employing both a vignette method, and in Dornstein's (1988a) study on the pay gradings of occupations. Quite possibly, in hypothetical situations and "constructed" situations, individuals' judgments mostly reflect accepted social norms, whereas their judgments in concrete employment contexts also reflect the effect of situational factors such as the nature of their jobs and working conditions and their work-related self-interests.

AMBIGUOUS EVALUATION DIMENSIONS

As indicated, some theorists (e.g., Weick, 1966) argued that some evaluation dimensions may be ambiguous; that is, may be assigned (by different individuals or under different circumstances) to either side of the input/output ratio. If this is true, we may wish to know what causes their assignment to one or the other side of the equation. But first we must obviously enquire if there is any empirical evidence to substantiate the argument of ambiguity. Only a few empirical studies exist that can shed some light on this question. One of them conducted by Tornow (1971), investigated the effect of perceived inputs and outcomes on equity/inequity perceptions. In an attempt to measure a person's differential perception of various potentially ambiguous job characteristics, 340 job elements (generated in a previous stage of the study) were presented to a large sample of college sophomores who were required to classify them into inputs and outcomes. Twenty-four items were identified as ambiguous; that is, tended to be classified variously as inputs or outcomes. Among them were such elements as dedication, reliability, high job involvement, complex work, work challenge, have sole responsibility for the job, making many decisions, keeping abreast of a variety of subjects, cooperating with many people, and so on.

Some additional empirical evidence for the existence of ambiguous dimensions, albeit less direct, comes from Dornstein's (1990b) study investigating the relevancy in pay-fairness judgments of a series of task-related and personal characteristics. Some dimensions investigated, specifically working with complex data and fulfilling a task important to the organization, correlated negatively with the fairness evaluation of pay: The more complex and important the tasks, the lower the amount of pay considered fair. These results suggest that the above dimensions tended to be regarded as benefits or positive outcomes rather than inputs requiring reward. Indeed, regarding complex work, these findings fall in line with Tornow's (1971): Complex work is included in his list of ambiguous inputs.

In Greenberg's (1986a) experimental study on performance evaluations, subjects performed a task that had an ambiguous performance referent, which made it difficult for them to tell how well they were doing until they were told. Subjects were given either very negative or very positive feedbacks about their performances and were either paid or not paid for their work. The focal-dependent variable was a composite satisfaction index. The results indicated that high pay elicited more satisfaction than low pay overall, but this was qualified by performance feedback: Satisfaction with low pay was greater when subjects believed that it resulted from low performance evaluations rather than from high evaluations. In the no-pay condition it was found that satisfaction was closely associated with performance feedback and that levels of satisfaction were as low or as high as they were when pay and performance evaluations were congruent. According to the author, this finding suggests that performance evaluations served as ultimate outcomes: When they were low they seemed to serve as negative outcomes making workers feel dissatisfied and when they were high they served as positive outcomes making workers feel highly satisfied. The overall conclusion is that "evaluations of performance can serve as ultimate outcomes themselves, or as penultimate outcomes (acting as inputs, creating expectations for monetary rewards)" (Greenberg, 1986a: 7).

What explains this ambiguity and what circumstances explain the assignment of the ambiguous elements to one or other side of the equation? So far, empirical research has little to offer in reply. The only relevant data come from Tornow's (1971) study showing that individuals may be grouped into Type-*1* persons and Type-*0* persons, based on their tendency to interpret a majority of ambiguous job elements in terms of inputs or, conversely, in terms of outcomes. This finding suggests that the assignments of ambiguous job elements to one rather than the other side of the equation is due to certain (unidentified) personal characteristics. As Tornow argues in support of his work: "The underlying assumption . . . is that, given an ambiguous stimulus field, the individual will provide a structure that reflects his own personality (cf. Murray, 1938)" (Tornow, 1971: 619).

THE EFFECT OF UNCERTAINTY ABOUT CONTRIBUTIONS

People often have more information about outcomes than about contributions or performances to which outcomes are supposed to be related. How, if at all, does such a situation affect fairness judgments? Bierhoff, Buck, and Klein (1986) argue that in this case people are likely "to use outcome information as the basis for a reversed equity script: those who have more must have performed better" (p. 174). A number of experimental studies tend to support this hypothesis. For example, in an experimental study performed by Lerner (1965), subjects observed two coworkers performing a task. Half of the subjects heard later that Bill would be paid whereas the other half heard that Tom would be paid. When asked afterward to rate the workers' contribution to the task, subjects tended to view the worker who got paid as more productive.

In another experimental study conducted by Cook (1975), subjects performing a task received no feedback about their performances in the first phase of the experiment. In the next phase, however, they were given higher rewards than their partners. An examination of the reward distribution for the first phase indicated that self-allocations were nearly as high as in a "defined equity condition": apparently, as expected, the reward distribution in the later phase served as a cue for performance differentials in the first phase.

In a later experimental study by Bierhoff and Kramp (1982), two independent experiments were performed which had the following basic design. Subjects read an account of the rewards distributed (equal/unequal) and of the prevailing relationships (cooperative/competitive) in a task group. They were then required to estimate the likelihood that each of a number of specified performance configurations would fit the reward distribution described. The results indicated that the unequal-reward distribution tended to invoke the equity rule: Distributions tended to be interpreted as the result of unequal contributions. In contrast, the equal-reward distribution situation tended to be interpreted as the result of equal or moderately unequal contributions. Also, in the team condition there was a marked tendency to attribute a greater likelihood to the less skewed, more equal, performance configurations

THE INTEGRATION OF VARIOUS DIMENSIONS
OF EVALUATION

The empirical evidence suggests that multiple dimensions are involved in pay-fairness evaluations. How are these dimensions integrated to produce an overall equity judgment of justice evaluation? Farkas and Anderson (1979) addressed this question. In their study two possible solutions were evaluated. One solution, the *input integration model* assumes that "all relevant stimulus information about the person would be integrated to obtain a single value of deservingness" (p. 879). Such a solution would obviously be hard to apply to qualitatively distinct dimensions. The second solution, the *equity integration model*, assumes a two-step process: first, a separate outcome estimate is derived for each single input value: Then these estimates are combined (averaged or otherwise) to arrive at a final equity judgment. The latter model, the authors suggest, facilitates the problem of integration "because both steps involve quantities that are naturally comparable. Thus, equity integration is a psychologically attractive way to handle multidimensional input" (p. 713).

Two experiments were devised to investigate the issue. The leading hypothesis was that input integration will prevail when the input dimensions are similar while equity integration will predominate when they are dissimilar. In both experiments, subjects received information on the inputs of persons working together on a common task and were required to divide a fixed reward among them. In one experiment, the information specified effort (how hard each person had tried) and performance (how much each person had accomplished). In the second experiment, two pieces of performance information about each person were supplied, making the input information homogeneous. The authors concluded that the result "agreed very well with the hypothesized rule of equity integration when the input dimensions were dissimilar. When the input dimensions were similar, the results agreed moderately well with the hypothesized rule of input integration, although there were small, worrisome discrepancies" (Farkas and Anderson, 1979: 879).

Support for the equity integration model comes also from two field studies by Rossi and colleagues (Jasso and Rossi, 1977; Alves and Rossi, 1978), in which a number of models were tested to find one that best fitted the data obtained.

The findings indicated that this was a simple *additive model* of fairness that involves several calculative stages in which "the amount of just remuneration to a set of claims are calculated and summed" (Jasso and Rossi, 1977: 647).

Vecchio (1984) hypothesized that a power function model represents more adequately the input/outcome integration process than a simple multiplicative or simple additive function model. The power function model has the feature of increasing the relative weighting of the elements which are most salient for the protagonist.

The equations for the three alternative models are presented below: Model (1) represents the simple multiplicative function; Model (2) represents the power function; and Model (3) represents the simple additive function.

$$(\text{Model 1}) \quad \frac{\Sigma(O.R)_a}{\Sigma(I.R.)_a} = \frac{\Sigma(O.R)_b}{\Sigma(I.R.)_b}$$

$$(\text{Model 2}) \quad \frac{\Sigma O_a^R}{\Sigma I_a^R} = \frac{\Sigma O_a^R}{\Sigma I_b^R}$$

$$(\text{Model 3}) \quad \frac{\Sigma O_a}{\Sigma I_a} = \frac{\Sigma O_b}{\Sigma I_b}$$

where O and I represent outcomes and inputs, and a and b represent the protagonist and the referent other respectively. R denotes the relevance or appropriateness which the protagonist attached to the specific outcomes and incomes. The predictive utility of the three models was tested with survey data obtained from a sample of about 100 employed students. Participants were presented with a list of inputs and outcomes and were asked to rate each input listed according to (1) the extent they perceived themselves as possessing it; and (2) the extent they thought it should serve as a basis for compensation. Similarly, they were required to respond to the same questions in regard to a person whose pay they typically compared theirs with. In regard to the outcomes listed, participants were also asked to state (1) the extent to which they perceived themselves as compensated for each; and (2) the extent they thought it appropriate or relevant to be compensated for each. These questions were repeated in regard to the person whose pay they typically compared with. Several affective measures including perceived pay equity were used to test the predictive utility of the above models. The results indicated that the model represented by the power function was the best predictor. Still, the author cautions that this model

should not be viewed as a simple and straightforward representation of cognitive processes. It must be remembered that any cognitive model attempts a paramorphic representation of an underlying process. Certainly, it is doubtful that an individual would consciously calculate a power function (Vecchio, 1984: 279–80).

Do rewards have any effect on input intergration? Cook and Yamagishi (1983) hypothesized that multiple distribution rules will be used in a situation in which the reward is a fixed sum, exogenously determined. In this case, the authors argued, distribution rules would be selected in order to maximize the amount of reward that the allocator could claim, regardless of the type of input. It was hypothesized that high-input individuals, who could claim more than an equal share of the fixed reward if an equity-contributions rule were used, would select the *equity* rule as the basis for allocation. By contrast, individuals whose input levels were so low that the use of the contribution rule would entitle them to less than an equal share of the available fixed sum, were predicted to select an *equality* rule as the basis for allocation. Multiple rules were not expected to be used in the situation in which the amount of the reward to be allocated was dependent upon the individuals' level of contribution. In this case, it was expected that contribution would have a greater effect on the equity judgment than information on another input—an attribute. However, allocators whose relative level of contribution was low were expected to assign greater weight to the attribute in the allocation decision than allocators with high levels of contribution, if it increased the reward that they could claim.

An experiment conducted by the authors and aiming to test these hypotheses tended, generally, to support them: It indicated that in the fixed-reward condition, level of contribution (operationalized as actual performance) was assigned more weight in the allocation decision than level of attribute (operationalized as ability). In the dependent reward condition, differential weights were assigned to the two inputs, as anticipated: "A slight anomaly" in the data was that the low-ability high-performance subjects allocated slightly more to themselves than did the high-ability high-performance subjects, contrary to prediction. The authors suggest that this finding may indicate that an "effort" credit is granted to individuals with low ability who perform well in spite of their ability. These results

> suggest that the multidimensional input situations are more complex than currently conceived in existing theoretical work on this topic. The main finding that emerges from our investigation is that, under certain conditions (specified here in terms of the type of reward to be allocated), multiple distribution rules come into play in allocation decisions based on multiple inputs. Since much of the research has been conducted in fixed-reward situations, the possible confounding of rule integration with input integration must be examined more closely. Furthermore, the difference between the actual participants' allocation decisions and third-party judgments must be investigated, since the results of our study may not replicate any of the findings derived from research on bystander allocation decisions or equity judgments (Cook and Yamagishi, 1983: 123–24).

Another study was conducted by Kayser and Lamm (1980), who hypothesized that the relevancy of inputs in reward allocations would be determined also by such factors as the degree to which they are perceived as being under the person's volitional control and the type of outcome to be allocated—gains or losses. Specifically, they hypothesized that an input perceived to be under the volitional control of a person will lead to more unequal allocations than an input perceived as not being under his volitional control. A second hypothesis related to the distribution rules applied. It was hypothesized that, under a condition where inputs are perceived as partly equal and partly unequal, there will be a stronger tendency to follow the equality rule than the equity rule: Following the equality rule would be consistent with both the equity principle (taking into account the equal inputs of the parties) as well as the equality principle. By contrast, disregarding the fact that some inputs are equal, and dividing outcomes in accordance with the ratios of the unequal inputs, would create a dissonance which presumably allocators would wish to avoid. A third hypothesis was that there will be a relatively stronger tendency to follow the equality rule when dividing losses than when dividing gains: A loss can be more easily attributed to extraneous factors and hence inputs lose some of their "relevancy" in the allocation decision. These hypotheses were tested in a series of experiments conducted among male and female subjects in Germany. The subjects had to decide how gains/losses should be divided among vignettes described as two partners selling a brochure containing an essay written by both of them. The inputs of the partners that were experimentally manipulated were effort (time spent on the essay) and ability (represented as a score on a task-relevant ability test). The findings tended to support the hypotheses as follows: They indicated that differences in effort were taken more into account than differences in ability. They also indicated that under a condition of effort-differences/ability-equality or ability-differences/effort-equality there was a marked tendency, as expected, to prefer the equality rule over the equity rule. This finding suggests, say the authors, that the allocation decisions do not reflect a step-by-step processing of information: "Assumptions about different weights of different dimensions have only limited use; the weight differences observed in conditions with one-dimensional information supplies are 'overrun' by constellation effects when more complex information is given" (Kayser and Lamm, p. 12).

Thus, the overall constellation of inputs is a dimension which in itself affects the input-relevancy perception. A third finding was that, as expected, under a condition of loss there was a relatively greater tendency to follow the equality rule than under a condition of gain. The authors conclude that the causal importance of a factor is not identical with its being an "effector." Rather, the interaction between the two "varies with the type of input constellation (simple and complex), with the type of input dimensions (effort and ability) in the information supply, as well as with type of performance outcome (gain or loss)" (p. 12).

Does the *multiplicity of dimensions* have any effect on the input integration? Von Grumbkow and Wilke (1978) conducted an interesting experiment that sheds some light on this question. They hypothesized that in a complex multiple-dimension situation, individuals have more opportunity to escape from a presented dimension. It was further hypothesized that individuals will be more inclined to escape a given dimension if the results of utilizing it are unpleasant. Specifically, it was hypothesized that feelings of underpayment (presumed unpleasant) will be of lesser magnitude in a complex situation as compared with a simple situation. The results indicated, as expected, that in a complex/underpaid situation subjects perceived relatively less inequity and tended relatively less to respond with lowered productivity as compared with their partners in the simpler/underpaid situation.

THE SUBSTITUTABILITY OF PAY WITH OTHER POSITIVE OUTCOMES

While all exchange formulations emphasize the need to investigate empirically the perceived relevant outcomes, most of the information on this topic, with a few exceptions (e.g., Belcher and Atchinson, 1970), comes from outside the field; from studies of job attitudes and job satisfaction. Because job satisfactions has been extensively studied (e.g. Locke, 1976) long lists of factors which may be regarded as rewarding outcomes from the job are available. But for researchers interested in the perceived equitability of the employment exchange such lists are only the beginning of a series of most important questions. One question of particular importance to the present issue—the fairness judgments of pay—is: Are outcomes substitutable with one another and, if yes, to what extent? Obviously, where pay is perceived as substitutable with other positive outcomes, this may greatly affect pay-fairness judgments. For example, two individuals with identical pay, identical preferences, and identical perceptions about the form and components of the equity formula may judge the fairness of their pay differently, depending on the presence or absence of other positive outcomes at work.

Because so little research attention has been paid by researchers in this field to the issue of outcomes, little is known about these and other important questions relating to outcome. The only exception is some empirical evidence on job status and status symbols at work and its relationship with pay. Job status and work-related status symbols are included in the list of potentially relevant outcomes presented by Adams (1963: 423). Other exchange formulations (e.g., Blau, 1964; Homans, 1974) also regard job status as potential outcome. Empirical research tends to support this position. Belcher and Atchinson (1970) investigated the perceived relevant positive outcomes and found status to be a significant outcome in a list spanning 19 such outcomes. Empirical research also indicates that job status and work-related status symbols are perceived as substitutes of pay. For example, in a study conducted by Greenberg and Ornstein (1983) subjects working on a task were given extra job responsibilities with no additional payment for them, but were bestowed with a high job title that was either earned on the basis of their superior performance or unearned—bestowed for no apparent reason. Subsequent production and attitude measurements indicated that the subjects who received the earned title maintained their pretitle level of performance and felt equitably paid despite their increased responsibilities and lack of additional compensating payment. The bestowal of an unearned title, however, at first was associated with an improvement of performance and feelings of overpayment but subsequently led to a sharp drop in performance and feelings of underpayment. The authors suggest that the earned title was perceived as "adequate compensation for the additional inputs to keep workers feeling equitably paid" (Greenberg and Ornstein, 1983: 285). The unearned titles were, however, not recognized as desired outcomes as a consequence of which the additional responsibilities were perceived as inputs not compensated for. A major resulting implication is that attribution plays an important role in the perception of inputs and outcomes and that the administration of these factors may be an important determinant of how they are perceived; that is, as inputs or conversely as outcomes. Another important implication is that a worker's title

> may operate as a status symbol (Dandridge et al., 1980). We see from both studies that for a status symbol to be perceived as rewarding by the recipient, the basis for its bestowal must be recognized as legitimate. Indeed, we found that only titles believed to be earned on the basis of one's performance helped define the status value of the symbol. Thus, whether or not a job title will be recognized by its holder as a symbol of his or her status appears to depend on the holder's belief about the basis of the title's bestowal. (Greenberg and Ornstein, 1983: 296)

Support for the above thesis comes also from Evan and Simmon's (1969) study described earlier.

According to the above findings, the reply to the question posed—Is job status perceived as a substitute for pay—seems to be yes, *provided* that the status is perceived as bestowed legitimately.

Nor should Greenberg and Ornstein's (1983) warning about the nature of their study be overlooked: These are short term laboratory studies "that leave unanswered important questions. . . . For example, the question of how long an unearned title can compensate for added responsibilities." (p. 296).

Another study that supplies some more indirect evidence on the relationship between status symbols and feelings of equity is Greenberg's (1988) field research investigating the relationship between a status symbol—office space—and productivity. Employees who during a refurbishing of offices were temporarily reassigned to higher-status offices were found to increase their performance levels relative to employees reassigned to equal-status offices, whereas those reassigned to lower-status offices decreased their performance levels.

Part IV Conclusions and Implications

8 Summary and Conclusions

This chapter focuses on the conclusions that may be drawn from the empirical research presented so far and relates them to the questions raised in Chapter 4. This task requires an evaluation of the studies presented. From among the many possible criteria of evaluation, those that seemed most important were chosen as follows. It is proposed that, other things being equal, the conclusions derived from a set of pertinent studies should be regarded with more caution as the number of studies is fewer; their equivocality, is greater; the field studies are fewer and the bias in favor of experimental studies is greater; the variety in methodologies employed is less and the doubt about their soundness or suitability is greater; the variety in research settings is less, and the bias in favor of small and selective samples of participants is greater. With these criteria in mind, we turn to a brief review of the main findings and the conclusions emanating from them.

THE UNDERLYING DISTRIBUTION PRINCIPLES

A primary question relates to the norms of distribution or distributive rules underlying the fairness evaluation of pay. Here, a major distinction was made between monistic theories, which propose a single distributive principle, and theories proposing a variety of such principles. The latter suggest that the principle applied in a particular situation will depend on a number of contextual and personal characteristics, a view that essentially transforms the nature of the question asked: The point at issue now is which factors are responsible for which distribution rule, rather than which distribution rule predominates. An extension of this position suggests that evaluations may be guided by several distributive principles in combination.

The bulk of the studies that can shed some light on this controversy are experimental and may be roughly divided into those influenced by equity theory and those influenced by the thesis that the rules applied will be affected by, and may vary according to, a variety of contingent factors.

Studies Focusing on the Contribution Principle

The experimental studies testing some major propositions of equity theory tend largely to affirm these propositions. A relatively large number of studies basically support the proposition that individuals believing that they are inequitably rewarded will attempt to adjust their inputs to the rewards offered: Inputs will be raised in response to induced overpayment and will be lowered in response to induced underpayment. A smaller number of experimental studies tend to support the proposition that perceived inequity will be associated with a tendency to withdraw or leave the field.

The abundance of experimental studies inspired by equity theory contrasts sharply with the scarcity of field studies on the theory. Of the two field studies reviewed that focused on the effect of inequity on performance, only one yielded results in line with the basic thesis. The other suggested that future expectations for improvement mitigated the reactions of the underrewarded participants. This post-hoc interpretation more than reversing the impression left by the slight support of the field studies turns attention to the importance of studying the time dimension in pay-equity conceptions—a factor which, as noted, was largely ignored by equity theory.

There is a greater number (five) of field studies focusing on withdrawal as affected by perceived inequity and these tend largely to support the basic thesis. Specifically, they indicate that individuals perceiving themselves as underrewarded are more likely to want to quit or to actually quit, if given the choice, than their partners.

How should the above result be interpreted? Should they be taken as proof for the validity of equity theory arguing that the sole guiding principle underlying pay-fairness evaluations is the contribution principle and disproof of the competing theories? A major limitation of these studies—their being mostly experimental—suggests a negative answer to this question. By their very nature, experimental studies can be useful for testing certain propositions derived from a theory but cannot serve as sufficient proof for the validity of the theory, and cannot effectively invalidate other competing theories. The more limited conclusion emanating from these studies is that the contribution principle does indeed affect the fairness evaluation of pay.

A similar conclusion also emerges from a different experimental research strategy, one that focuses on the individuals' preferred mode(s) of reward allocation rather than on their reactions to a given reward distribution. In these studies, data are collected on the fairness judgments of a given reward distribution, or on the actual or preferred mode(s) of reward allocation in task groups, by individuals given to manipulated information on the performance/contributions of reward recipients. Seven such experimental studies were reviewed. Generally, they indicate a preference for a mode of reward distribution that accords relatively higher rewards to higher performers/contributors than to lower performers/contributors.

Studies Focusing on the Effect of Contextual Variables

The opponents of equity theory attempted to produce empirical support for their view that a variety of factors may influence the rules applied in a particular situation. This line of mostly experimental research utilizes generally the reward allocation paradigm in its various forms for studying, with the aid of experimental manipulations, the conditions under which the contribution rule applies or conversely other rules take over. These studies indicate that a number of factors tend indeed to affect, as suggested, the type of distribution rules used in the allocation of rewards in task groups. Here is a summary of the main findings relating to the various factors.

The Social Relationships among Group Members. The major postulate guiding these studies is that reward allocation patterns will depend among others on the nature of social relationships prevailing in the task group such as the patterns of interaction, the nature of interpersonal attitudes, and the anticipated longevity of relationships. These studies, summarized in Table 8.1 tend generally to confirm the underlying hypotheses.

The studies indicate that the contribution principle tends to be preferred where individual work or interindividual competition are emphasized; whereas in task groups that are defined as teams, or where interdependencies among members are emphasized, or where members feel drawn together by a "common fate," the preferred principle is equality.

Similarly, the studies indicate that reward allocations tend to follow the equality rule in contexts where friendly relationships prevail, or where harmony is emphasized, or where individuals perceive similarities between themselves and others in the group; whereas the equity rule tends to be followed where individuals perceive themselves as strangers, or as dissimilar, or where performance rather than harmony are emphasized.

Actual or anticipated long-term relationships were found to be associated with a tendency to prefer equality, especially among high-level performers. In contrast, interactions of short duration were found to be associated with a tendency to follow the equity rule.

The Group Goals. A number of experimental studies, summarized in Table 8.2, investigated the impact of group goals on the preferred mode of reward allocation.

Generally, these studies suggest that where maximizing production is a major goal, reward distribution tends to follow the equity rule. But, when conflict avoidance is a major goal, reward distribution tends to follow the equality rule rather than the equity rule. Where motivating performance is an important goal, reward distribution tends to favor the weaker performers, whereas when efficient

Table 8.1
The Effect of Social Relationships on Preferred Distribution Rule(s)

Independent Variables	Preferred Distribution Rule(s)	Number of Studies
Individual work Interindividual competition	Contribution	
versus		5
Teamwork Member interdependency Felt "common fate"	Equality	
Friendly relationships Group harmony Perceived similarity with others	Equality	
versus		10+
Conflictual relationships or estrangement Perceived dissimilarity	Contribution	
Long-term relationships	Equality	
versus		3
Short-term relationships	Contribution	

Table 8.2
The Effect of Group Goals on Preferred Distribution Rule(s)

Independent Variables	Prefered Distribution Rule(s)	Number of Studies
Maximizing production	Contribution	4
Conflict avoidance	Equality	1
Motivating performance	Favors weaker performer	1
Efficient resource allocation	Favors most efficient allocators	2
Membership control	Favors those whom group wishes to retain or to encourage to join it	4

resource allocation is a major goal, resource allocation tends to favor those members perceived as contributing most to this goal. Finally, when membership control is a major goal, reward distribution tends to be in favor of those whom the group wishes to retain or to encourage to join it.

It should be noted that in the typical research design of these studies, the subjects acting as resource allocators are explicitly briefed about the major group goals. It would be quite reasonable to assume that such a design raises the subjects' awareness of the instrumental value of resource allocation and enhances their motive to follow instrumental rather than justice considerations when allocating rewards. Hence, great caution is needed when interpreting the results of these studies, especially when explicit measures of the perceived fairness of allocations are lacking, because these results may in fact not reflect justice considerations but rather purely instrumental considerations.

Resource Scarcity or Abundance. Six experimental studies were reviewed that investigated the effect of resource scarcity or resource abundance on preferences for a given distribution rule. These studies suggest that the equity rule tends to be followed in reward allocation only when resources are sufficient but not when they are scarce or abundant. The evidence about the effect of the latter conditions is equivocal. Earlier studies suggest that under such conditions there is a tendency to prefer one's self- interests. A recent study, however, suggests that these findings may not apply in nondyadic situations and that in larger groups there will be a tendency to prefer the equality rule. In addition there is some evidence suggesting that resource scarcity interacts with other contextual variables such as membership control goals: under relative resource scarcity the tendency to discriminate in favor of the more productive and mobile members is greater than under relative resource abundance.

Perceptions about Contributions. Seven experimental studies investigating if and how perceived contributions influence attitudes toward distribution principles suggest that such perceptions may indeed have an important impact. Some results (one study) suggest that the existence of a *performance maxima* may be associated under certain circumstances with a higher emphasis on the contribution principle. Other results (six studies) suggest that the equity principle is preferred when individuals perceive themselves as responsible for the results produced, whereas the equality principle is preferred (especially by high performers) when causality is determined externally. There are also some indications (one study) that the effect of the "locus of control" variable is mitigated by stringent environmental pressures, such as high pressure for performance. Under such conditions, the contribution principle tends to predominate, regardless of locus of control considerations.

Some of these studies also suggested that contributions perceived as highly performance-related tend to elicit reward allocations that are based on the equity principle whereas contributions that are perceived as less relevant lead to the use of the equality principle.

Other Situational Variables. Only two field studies present some evidence about the effect of a most important variable—*tradition*. They suggest that individuals tend to prefer reward distribution patterns to which they are accustomed.

A single study investigating the effect of *hierarchical position* on the preferred rules suggests that these preferences may vary with one's position in the organization's hierarchy. While managers generally preferred the contribution rule, they differed in their preferences as to the specific applications of this rule. Individuals in subordinate positions seemed, however, to be highly influenced by social-relationship considerations and did not discriminate between equity and equality.

Studies Focusing on the Effects of the Sociocultural Context

Are the distribution rules underlying pay-fairness evaluations influenced in any way by the surrounding sociocultural context? The pertinent studies are relatively few, mostly experimental, and vary greatly in the variables investigated and the cultures compared—a combination of traits that obviously does not facilitate their evaluation. The overall, and highly tentative, conclusion emanating from these studies is that the underlying justice norms may indeed be influenced by sociocultural factors. For example, studies investigating the reaction of individuals to various modes of inequity (three studies) suggest that these reactions may vary because input/outcome relationships are interpreted differently in different cultures. It is suggested that the reasons for these different interpretations may be that individuals from different cultures vary in their tendency to associate higher rewards with higher required inputs, in their sensitivity toward the input/outcome linkage, or, thirdly, in the value they place on high-input as opposed to high-outcome situations.

Studies utilizing the reward allocation paradigm reveal that in task situations there is generally a tendency, across cultures, to prefer the contribution rule over the equality or need rule but that intercultural differences may affect the degree to which there is a tendency to differentiate, in a given situation, between the rules. For example, studies indicate that individuals in cultures with an emphasized collectivist orientation are more willing to give consideration to need or to favor in-group equality than individuals in individualistic-oriented cultures. Studies also indicate that conceptions of need may vary from one culture to another.

Some interesting findings emanate from cross-cultural studies investigating the effect of certain interactional variables (e.g., direct vs. mediated exchange; competition vs. cooperation; reactions toward in-group vs. out-group members) on reward allocations. These findings indicate that individuals from other cultures, when compared with American individuals, react as expected, and similarly to the American individuals. An additional and perhaps somewhat surprising finding emanating from these studies is that subjects from other cultures tend to differentiate more between the varying situations as compared with the American subjects. The above findings are important in a twofold sense: First, they provide cross-cultural support for some theses that have been tested mainly among

U.S. subjects; second, they suggest that the socio-cultural context may affect the intensity of reaction to a given situational variable rather than its direction.

Generally, the review of existing cross-cultural studies, perhaps even more than the review of studies in other areas, leaves a strong "taste for more": the review shows very clearly the existence of a vast area which is virtually unexplored and which, if investigated more intensively, can greatly improve our understanding of the subject.

Studies Focusing on the Effect of Personal Characteristics

Most studies in this area employ the reward allocation paradigm and concentrate mainly on differences between the sexes, and to a lesser extent on the effects of a Protestant Ethic orientation. Other personal characteristics are largely uninvestigated.

Sex Differences. A major finding of these studies is that women, especially when their inputs are greater than their partner's, tend generally to allocate less rewards to themselves.

Recent research effort has been spent mainly on investigating the reasons for this behavior. The theory that the reason lies mainly in certain value orientations in which women differ from men found little support in the pertinent studies. In contrast, a series of other studies support an alternative thesis suggesting first that women's sense of personal entitlement with respect to pay is lower than men's, and second that the reason for this lies in the standards of pay comparisons utilized by women. The first element is supported by a number of experimental field studies showing that, other things being equal, women have lower pay expectations than men. The second part of the thesis is supported by two complementary lines of investigation. One focuses on the prevalent pay norms for men and women. The pertinent experimental and field studies (six) indicate that, other things being equal, the pay norms for women are lower than those for men, which suggests that women are likely to have lower *internal* pay standards for themselves. The other line of investigation focuses on the social comparison standards utilized by the sexes. The pertinent studies indicate a tendency among individuals of both sexes to compare with similars, including similars in sex. These findings suggest that women will have lower *social* comparison standards than men since their referents— other women—earn on average less than comparable men.

There are also some indications (two experimental studies) that women tend to differentiate relatively less than men between the contribution and equality norms and may consequently be less sensitive to contribution differentials. This may also explain to some extent the tendency among women to allocate themselves less when their contributions surpass their partner's.

The Effects of a Protestant Ethic Orientation. All the (six) pertinent studies reviewed tend to support the thesis that a Protestant Ethic (PE) orientation will be associated with a strong preference for the equity principle. Specifically, the studies indicate that individuals scoring high on the PE scale tend relatively more than the low PE scorers to prefer the equity principle when performance is perceived as attributable to internal factors, that is, factors controlled by the performing individuals.

Summary and Discussion

The above summarizing review of empirical research suggests that the contribution principle does indeed occupy a most important place in the process of pay fairness evaluation, but that other distribution principles may apply too. Which rule(s) is(are) actually applied would depend on the nature of the situation, the personal characteristics of the participants, and perhaps also on the specific sociocultural context. A number of major weaknesses in the research reviewed suggest that these conclusions should be regarded with caution. One such major weakness is that inferences about the guiding principles are mostly based on indirect rather than direct evidence (e.g., investigating performances under varying conditions of pay equity or investigating reward allocations under varying input and contextual conditions). A second major weakness is that most pertinent studies are experimental, and most propositions investigated in them still must pass the test of field research and "real-life" situations. A major deficiency in this context is that experimental studies do no reflect the potential impact of numerous contextual variables that operate in real-life employment settings. A third major weakness is that certain major lines of investigation are not well explored even in the experimental sense. This applies to all areas where the number of studies is altogether very small. This attenuates even further the conclusions that arise from the pertinent studies. A fourth weakness, especially of the experimental studies, is that most of them ignore the time dimension; according to a number of theorists this is a severe drawback since pay-fairness perceptions may be affected by past as well as future elements. Fifth, the experimental studies, especially those using the reward allocation paradigm, have been found deficient also for disregarding the possibility that studying only one factor at a time may be misleading since factors may interact and produce thereby different results from those emerging in single-factor studies. For example, reward-allocation studies have been criticized for assuming isomorphism between individual and group goals and for operationalizing only one goal at a time (e.g., Cook and Hegdvedt, 1983: 226–27.)[1] In the area of the cross-cultural comparisons there are additional weaknesses. The overall impression is that these are dominated by an ad-hoc approach and suffer direly from a lack of theoretical guidance. They rarely utilize a theoretical definition of the main independent variable—culture— and do not always provide a sound theoretical foundation for the variables investigated.

Some important questions are largely unexplored. The studies reviewed focused mostly on theses involving the contribution and equality principles. As a result, the question asked if other distribution principles are or are not relevant remains largely unanswered. For example, all the monistic theories exclude the need principle, but is this principle really irrelevant? The few experimental studies, mostly focusing on cross-cultural differences, suggest that considerations of need may not be totally irrelevant in pay-fairness evaluations, but these studies are insufficient for a well-founded answer on this question.

Another question left open is: Do individuals, when faced with a complex situation with conflicting demands, compromise in some way by applying more than one principle simultaneously, or do they perhaps choose a single principle? In the latter case what factors determine which principle is chosen? The answers to these questions are obviously of utmost importance given the fact that real-life situations lack the simplicity of experimental designs and are usually rather complex.

Indeed, the dearth of field studies that can shed some light on the above questions is sorely felt. The very few available studies open new vistas. They suggest first that individuals do indeed apply more than one principle in pay-fairness evaluations and that, though the equity or contribution principle occupies a predominant position, other principles are involved as well. As such, these studies, like those investigating the effect of contextual factors, tend to undermine the position of all the monistic theories proposing the relevance of only a single distributive principle. Second, the studies suggest that pay-fairness evaluations may be also guided by need as well as social-ranking considerations. As such, they complement the findings emanating from the experimental studies that display the relevance in particular contexts of the equality principle. Moreover, they suggest that the need and social-ranking principles are applied in a more universal form, regardless of particular contextual factors, and thus support the arguments of relative deprivation theorists that pay-fairness evaluations may be affected by considerations relating to the consummatory value of pay as well as the argument of status value theorists arguing for the relevance of social-ranking considerations.

The above studies, few as they are, and the findings emanating from them, deserve special attention not only because they are field studies and can be assumed to reflect real-life situations much better than the experimental studies, but also because from them we learn directly about the pay-fairness judgments of individuals and the factors underlying these judgments rather than having to make deductions from studies reporting reactions to inequity or preferences in reward allocations.

Apart from their relevance to the issue of the distribution principles underlying pay fairness evaluations, the above studies are also most important in regard to another major issue—that of social consensus on the distribution rules applied in the process of pay-fairness evaluation. Their importance lies in the fact that the experimental studies lack some essential features for dealing with this question. For example, a major limitation of experimental studies is that they use relatively small numbers of participants and lean heavily on one segment of the population—students—whereas investigating the consensus question would require relatively large, cross-sectional samples, like those employed by the above field studies, which could well reflect the population and its various segments.

The problem is, however, that the findings of the above field studies relating to this latter question are somewhat equivocal: Whereas some studies suggest a good deal of consensus, others show some distance between groups of employees. It was argued that this equivocality may be due to the differences in research methods and research settings. Specifically it was suggested that the consensus emanating from studies involving "bystander" judgments may reflect agreed social norms, whereas the dissensus emanating from studies carried out in actual work-settings may reflect the effect of some elements related to one's work situation and one's self-interest. If this is indeed so, do the findings imply the existence of a broad consensual normative framework within which actual views are coloured by certain situational and personal self-interest elements?

THE STANDARDS OF COMPARISON

It was indicated that while all the principal theories regard social comparison as a primary basis for pay-fairness evaluations there is no agreement on the exact nature of these comparisons, nor on the possibility that other standards of comparison may be applied as well. The review of the pertinent empirical evidence centered on a number of major questions arising in relation to these issues.

Internal Standards vs. Social Comparisons

One such question relates to the proposition that individuals may use an internal standard in evaluating their rewards. Altogether, eleven pertinent studies—five experimental and six field—were reviewed. These are not completely equivocal, and some have methodological problems as well. The general impression emanating from them, however, is one of support for the above proposition. Specifically, they suggest that individuals' pay-fairness evaluations may be guided by certain internalized social norms, by comparisons with self in the past, by conceptions of self-worth, or by conceptions of the adequacy of pay for fulfilling one's perceived financial needs.

The questions that follow are: What is the importance of internal standards relative to social comparisons? Is there any support for Pritchard's (1969) argument that in the employment situation internal standards are more likely to be used than social comparisons? Or conversely, do the findings support the theories arguing that social comparisons are at the center of the pay-fairness evaluation process? The pertinent evidence suggests that social comparisons fulfill a relatively more important role than internal standards but, given the nature of the evidence, this conclusion must be regarded as highly tentative.

Other important questions i.e., whether social comparisons and internal standards are complementary or substitutes for each other, and related questions, are not directly addressed by any of the pertinent studies. They will have to be one of the targets of future research.

Single vs. Multiple Standards

Do individuals tend to use one or several comparison standards? Eight relevant studies, all field studies, were reviewed. These suggest that frequently more than one referent is used. For example, social comparisons are frequently coupled with various internal standards or system comparisons. Moreover, social comparisons of one type are often coupled with social comparisons of another type; comparisons with similar others are coupled with dissimilar social comparisons, and comparisons with others in the organization are coupled with comparisons with others outside it. These findings are most important and require explanation. Why is there a tendency to use multiple referents? Do these findings suggest that a single referent does not suffice for a full evaluation? Do they suggest that different standards or referents fulfil different functions for the individual using them? These questions have not received much attention in the pertinent theoretical literature. The empirical findings showing the frequency of multiple comparisons, however, attest to the importance of these matters, theoretically as well as empirically.

Inside-Outside Comparisons and Similar-Dissimilar Comparisons

If more than one social referent is involved in pay-fairness evaluations, is there a predominant pattern? Are similar comparisons more frequent than dissimilar comparisons as the exchange theories suggest? Are inside comparisons more frequent than outside comparisons as several theorists propose?

A number of studies were reviewed that relate to the issue of similar versus dissimilar comparisons. These studies (five field and six experimental) suggest that comparisons with dissimilars, including the average earnings in the economy, occupy a most important place in the evaluation process. These findings refute the proposition of exchange theories stating that similar comparisons are at the heart of the reward-evaluation process, and support relative deprivation theory arguing that dissimilar comparisons and comparisons with the average reward level may be of no lesser importance. Still, the equivocality of evidence regarding the relative importance of similar versus dissimilar comparisons precludes any conclusions, even tentative, about this particular issue. Perhaps, as some theorists propose, similar and dissimilar comparisons fulfill a different function and are hence likely to be used simultaneously. Indeed, the high frequency of multiple social comparisons suggests that this is indeed a possibility, but further research effort is necessary to validate this proposition.

Eleven field studies were reviewed that relate to the issue of intra-versus extra-organizational comparisons. These studies generally suggest that comparisons outside the employing organization are more frequent and important then comparisons inside it. This finding is rather surprising and is contrary to what might have been expected from prevalent propositions such as the social proximity thesis, or the thesis proposing that individuals sharing an employing authority will tend to compare with each other. But the fact that it derives mainly from field studies that employed different methodologies, were based on samples of participants of a varied nature, and were conducted in a variety of settings (some even outside the United States—a somewhat atypical feature) strengthens our faith in its validity.

Even more intriguing and contrary to expectations are the findings of a field study indicating that individuals tend to compare with others outside the work group rather than inside it. But here judgment must be withheld until more evidence is available.

Fraternal Deprivation: Its Cognition and Its Relationship with Egoistic Deprivation

The findings indicating that individuals compare themselves with dissimilars and are hence exposed to fraternal deprivation raise two major questions: What cognitive processes are involved in recognizing the existence of fraternal deprivation? What is the relationship between fraternal deprivation and egoistic deprivation: Are individuals experiencing fraternal deprivation also likely to feel personally deprived? Only two studies address these questions. One experimental study suggests that atomized information impedes the recognition of fraternal deprivation whereas concentrated information facilitates it.

Another (field) study suggests that fraternal deprivation is unrelated to egoistic deprivation: Individuals may feel that the group to which they belong is deprived without feeling that they personally are discriminated against. It has been suggested that several factors may obstruct the recognition of egoistic deprivation: the difficulty of making deductions about such deprivation; a tendency to self-protection and a preference for smooth interaction; and the compartmentalization of the various life aspects. These propositions bring us back to the question of the relative frequency of similar versus dissimilar comparisons and the need to investigate it in more depth in extensive field studies.

Conceptions about Intergroup Differentials and their Effects

One field study found support for the thesis that employees have conceptions about the nature of fair-pay differentiation between occupations and groups of occupations and about the overall magnitude of pay differentiation.

The findings of two experimental field studies suggest that the magnitude of intergroup differentials does indeed play an important role in felt inequity, which tends to be greater the larger the magnitude of intergroup differentials and intergroup discrimination.

Changes in Rewards and their Effects

What is the effect of changes in received rewards on perceived pay fairness? The pertinent studies are very few and all are directed to testing certain hypotheses advanced by relative deprivation theory (e.g., Gurr, 1970). Thus, support for the progressive deprivation hypothesis was found in one experimental study indicating that feelings of deprivation, of being unfairly treated, may not be alleviated by increasing rewards if this increase is at a slower rate than feelings of entitlement. The same study also indicated that individuals whose expectations for the alleviation of an existing deprivation were raised but were not fulfilled are likely to feel deprived, and tends thus to support the aspirational deprivation hypothesis. An additional experimental study indicating that a decremental pattern of payment is associated with pay dissatisfaction lends support to the decremental deprivation hypothesis. Finally, one experimental study found support for the *J*-curve hypothesis stating that individuals experiencing a steady rise in outcomes followed by a sudden and sharp drop-off are likely to experience a feeling of relative deprivation.

The Determinants of Comparisons

Ascertaining and describing the existing patterns of comparison is obviously important but not enough. There is the question of understanding the underlying processes. What explains the tendencies of individuals to choose (a) particular referent(s)? The review of pertinent studies suggests that at present we can offer only some tentative, rudimentary answers to these questions. The evidence stems mostly from field studies, but there are also some illuminating experiments.

Personal Background Characteristics. Only two such characteristics have received some attention in the pertinent empirical research. One is *level of education*. According to the three field studies reviewed, level of education seems to be positively related to comparisons with others outside the organization. One field study suggests that level of education is negatively related to comparisons with others belonging to one's close social circles such as friends and family.

Of the three field studies investigating the impact of *age*, only two found some significant relationships. One of them found that individuals who tend to make comparisons with self in the past are relatively younger than their colleagues. The other found that there is a relatively greater tendency among the younger, especially more educated, employees to make outside comparisons. It was suggested that these findings reflect the fact that young employees, with little knowledge about others in the organization and in the world of work, are less likely to compare themselves with others in the organization and more likely to rely on self-comparisons.

Organizational Position. Four field studies were reviewed that investigated the relationship between *relative pay position* and social comparisons. Two of them suggest that pay level is positively related to a tendency to compare with others outside the organization. Several explanations are offered for this finding. One is that higher-salary individuals have fewer comparison opportunities in the organization because of its pyramidal shape. Another is that higher-salary individuals have skills more identifiable as "professional" than "organizational"; for such skills, it is argued, the external labor market is more relevant. A third explanation is that high-salary individuals as compared with low-salary individuals are less prone to a narrowing of comparison horizon following ego-protection needs.

One field study also found an interaction between low pay and two other variables. The findings suggest that lower-paid individuals who have little advancement chances and/or feel no personal responsibility for their low-pay position are relatively more inclined than their colleagues to make "dissonant" comparisons, that is, comparisons to similar others earning more than themselves. These findings fall in line with the instrumental thesis according to which comparisons serve a variety of purposes; for example, to bolster protest against the present situation. Another finding in line with the instrumental thesis is that high salary and high-salary raise individuals tend to refer relatively more to their own past pay and to their standard of living—comparisons that are likely to enhance and bolster their felt self-esteem.

The findings of the four field studies dealing with the relationship between social comparisons and *organizational level* are generally inconclusive and do not allow any conclusions on this subject, except perhaps that individuals in managerial positions tend to make upward as well as downward comparisons.

Two field studies investigating the hypothesis that *boundary position*, that is, a position that involves interaction with individuals in a wide range of organizations will be positively related to outside comparisons found no support for it.

Other Work-Related Aspects. From among the three field studies investigating *tenure*, two found a significant positive relationship between length of tenure and the tendency to make comparisons with others inside the employing organization. It was suggested that these findings reflect an increasing socialization into, and an increasing knowledge of, the employing organization among higher-tenure individuals.

One field study investigating the *influence of the work group* on social comparisons found that work-group members tended to agree on referent choices. Several group-dynamic factors were suggested as an explanation for this finding.

Four field studies investigating the effect of *pay secrecy* found that it does not impede individuals from making internal comparisons, but that such comparisons are often based on inaccurate information. Inaccurate information was, however, not found to lead to pay dissatisfaction.

Attitudinal Factors. Prominent among the studies investigating the relationship between attitudinal factors and social comparisons are the studies dealing with *perceived advancement* and *social mobility* prospects. Altogether, five such field studies were reviewed. All of them found certain significant relationships but these were not always consistent. Two studies suggest that individuals with scant internal-promotion prospects tend relatively more than their partners to make upward and dissonant comparisons. It was suggested that nonpromotables may be motivated to make such comparisons as a means of protesting their present position.

The findings of one study indicating a positive relationship between perceived good social mobility chances and a tendency to compare with similars may be interpreted in a similar vein.

The studies investigating the relationship between perceived promotion chances and inside versus outside comparisons are equivocal: One study found a positive relationship with internal comparisons whereas another study produced mixed results.

Outright contradictory results emanate from the two studies examining the relationship between perceived promotion prospects and a tendency to relate to past self-pay: While one study suggests a positive relationship, the other suggests a negative relationship.

Altogether, the prevalent studies on the effect of perceived promotion and social-mobility chances suggest that this is a promising research avenue, but that much more research effort must be invested before any firm conclusions can be drawn.

Two field studies investigating the relationship between comparisons and *perceived locus of control* suggest, as may be expected, that individuals feeling responsible for their outcomes tend significantly more than their partners to compare with similars.

One field study examining the relationship between *satisfaction* with various aspects of the work situation and social comparisons found, as expected, that individuals satisfied with the organization tend relatively less to make dissimilar outside comparisons and are relatively more inclined to make similar inside comparisons.

One experimental study examining the effect of knowing/not knowing the *range of outcomes* on comparison choices indicates that individuals who lacked information of the reward range tend to be interested above all in the highest reward level, whereas those who possessed such information were mostly interested in a similar higher score. There are disagreements among researchers as to the interpretation of these results.

Summary and Discussion

The studies investigating the comparison standards utilized in pay-fairness evaluations reveal a more variegated and complex picture than most theories would suggest. They show that individuals may use a variety of comparison standards such as system, various internal standards, and various social referents. Moreover, they indicate that there is a marked tendency to use multiple referents—a phenomenon that still awaits investigation in more depth. Generally, the studies tend to refute the argument proposing that comparison tendencies are idiosyncratic: The studies investigating the determinants of comparisons, even if few and insufficient, suggest quite clearly that specific contextual factors influence this process and give it direction.

The studies investigating the comparison trends suggest tentatively that social comparisons are more prominent than other types of comparisons. They tend to negate the exclusivity of similar social comparisons and point very clearly to the importance of dissimilar comparisons in the process. Moreover, individual's conceptions of pay fairness seem to be affected also by the magnitude of intergroup differentials and by changes through time in reward level.

Nevertheless, the overall impression is that available research has only skimmed the surface of the comparison issue and that much more effort needs to be invested. While the majority of studies in this area are field studies, which may be considered an advantage, the number of studies is altogether too small to generate full confidence in their results. Also, some lines of investigation such as those dealing with the use of internal standards, the cognitive processes underlying comparisons, or the effect of changes in rewards are tipped toward the experimental and still await supporting evidence from field studies.

Regarding the determinants of comparisons, empirical research is far behind theory and there is great potential for expansion. Moreover, what is presently available is not always firmly founded and requires more supporting evidence. In addition, the multiplicity of determinants suggests that research models different from those employed in the past must be used. Thus, studies must control for the effects of factors external to those investigated and must employ multivariate models that allow an investigation of the interactive effects between the variables investigated.

THE DIMENSIONS OF PAY-FAIRNESS EVALUATION

It was indicated that, while most theories propose that the fairness judgment of rewards is based on the evaluation of "deservingness" relative to a number of perceived relevant dimensions, it falls to empirical research to determine what these dimensions are in actual practice, how they are weighted and combined, how well they are universally agreed, and if they are not, what explains the disagreements. An overview of the relevant empirical data indicates that satisfactory answers are not yet available. Still, there are some promising beginnings that deserve attention.

The Perceived Relevant Dimensions

The empirical evidence in this area has the advantage of deriving mostly from field studies. A major limitation, however, is that most of these studies have used researcher-determined lists of dimensions. Another major limitation is that these lists have been compiled selectively, each being based on a particular theoretical orientation specifying what the relevant dimensions might be and excluding dimensions that do not fall within this range. The few studies that have avoided this bias deserve hence special attention.

The list of relevant dimensions emerging from the pertinent studies is not short: One study even came up with a list of close to 20. But for the above limitations, a comparison across studies could be very useful for gaining an idea about the relative importance of the dimensions involved. But as matters stand, such a comparison seems rather futile. At this point, a better strategy seems to be to regard the various studies as complementary and thus gain an overall impression about the dimensions that are generally considered relevant.

This latter strategy leads inexorably to the conclusion that the dimensions considered as relevant extend over all three major bases of evaluation suggested by Berger and colleagues (1983) rather than just one basis. They include *diffuse characteristics* such as age, sex, and marital status; *ability characteristics* such as occupation, education, skills and training, and tenure; and *performance-related contributions* such as effort and productivity. But, beyond this general picture, what other information about the underlying evaluation dimensions does the available empirical research offer?

Social Status as an Evaluation Dimension

The place of social status in pay-fairness evaluation is most intriguing. The close relationship between social prestige and income is well-known and has been documented by numerous studies. But what place does social status occupy in the process of pay-fairness evaluation? Is it a relevant dimension, and if so, is it merely one of many others, as equity theory argues, or is it the most important and perhaps sole dimension, as status value theory argues? Four pertinent field studies suggest that social status is one of a number of evaluation dimensions but a most important one. Two experimental studies, however, indicate that higher status should be perceived as associated with superior contributions to group goals in order to earn a higher reward value. On the other hand, the findings emerging from other experimental studies suggest that there is a tendency to attribute higher contributions to individuals receiving higher rewards in the absence of exact information on contributions to group performance. How may all these results be interpreted and reconciled? We suggest that they do not necessarily contradict each other, but seem to illuminate some of the underlying dynamics, through time, of the relationship between status and reward evaluations. As status value theory suggests (Berger et al., 1983) higher status seems legitimized by higher contributions; higher contributions legitimize higher rewards; higher rewards become associated with higher contributions and higher status. At any given point in time individuals tend to react according to these mental associations induced during the process of socialization: They evaluate the fairness of rewards according to perceived social status and they associate higher status as well as higher rewards with higher contributions. However, these reactions may change if and when individuals acquire information contradicting the customary underlying assumptions about contribution-status-reward linkages. Indeed, in one study cited (Evans and Simmons, 1969), individuals invested with high authority ($=$ high status) made above-average contributions, but when they realized that this authority was "hollow" that is, could not actually be exercised their contributions dropped to the level of others of lower status!

Social Consensus on Evaluation Dimensions

A question of major importance is whether social consensus on the perceived relevant dimensions is to be expected or not. As noted, theorists disagree on this, and these disagreements await resolution by empirical research. Existing research, however, has produced equivocal result: Some studies indicate a high degree of social consensus while others indicate a substantial measure of dissensus. It was suggested that perhaps these inconsistencies are only apparent and that, in fact, owing to different methodologies, studies indicating consensus were not measuring the same thing as those indicating dissensus. Specifically, it was argued that a picture of social consensus emerges from hypothetical-situation studies where participants probably tended to base their judgments on accepted social norms. By contrast, a picture of dissensus emerges from concrete-situation studies where, in all probability, participants' views also reflected the effect of situational factors and their self-interests. This argument, logical as it may be, still does not permit any firm conclusions about this important, but somewhat neglected, subject. These will have to wait for the results of future research.

Ambiguous Evaluation Dimensions

Another important question relates to the proposition of theorists that some dimensions of evaluation may be ambiguous; that is, may be viewed as outcomes or as inputs. Ambiguous dimensions are obviously a potential source of uncertainty in the evaluation process, and one would like to know as much as possible on this topic. Unfortunately, what is available here is also somewhat disappointing. Only one field study addresses this question directly, and it tends to support the basic proposition. It indicates that such elements as dedication, reliability, high job involvement, complex work, challenge, responsibility, making many decisions, keeping updated on a variety of subjects, and cooperating with many people may indeed be perceived as inputs *or* outcomes. It also indicates individuals may be predisposed or inclined to interpret elements as inputs or outcomes. Some limited additional support for the thesis emerges from another field study where complex work and fulfilling a task important to the organization unexpectedly emerged as negatively correlated with level of pay. Obviously, much more effort needs to be invested in investigating the very existence of ambiguity and the factors underlying it.

Criteria for Evaluating Interlevel and Intergroup Differentials

Hierarchy is a major feature of employing organizations. What are the criteria applied when evaluating interlevel pay differentials? Three experimental field studies focusing on responsibility as an aspect of hierarchy have consistently found that, other things being equal, perceived fair-pay level is positively related to indirect supervision and number of subordinate levels and negatively related to direct supervision. For top-level positions, the perceived fair-pay level was positively related to number of subordinate levels and to total number of subordinates. Substantial inconsistencies revealed themselves in regard to middle-level positions without subordinates.

In addition, the above studies suggest that certain fixed-percentage differentials are considered as just when judging the fairness of interlevel pay differentials. This implies that hierarchical levels are regarded not only as differential "bundles of responsibility" but also as differential statuses that need to be adequately distinguished from each other.

Organizational tasks are differentiated also in the functional sense and the question of pay differentials arises also in regard to this aspect. What criteria are applied when the fairness of pay differentials between jobs and occupational groups in the organization is evaluated? Again, empirical evidence is insufficient. One field study suggests that in the overall configuration there are some contours *between* which larger differentials are accepted and *within* which only relatively small differentials are tolerated. These findings are most intriguing but must be pursued further. In particular, it is important to establish what determines the notions of closeness or remoteness between tasks and occupational specialties.

The Effect of Uncertainty about Contributions

When information about rewards is available but there is uncertainty about contributions or performances, how does this affect the fairness evaluation of rewards? Three experiments were reviewed suggesting that in such a situation there is a tendency to attribute higher performances or higher inputs to recipients of higher rewards.

The Integration of the Various Dimensions

Given that pay-fairness evaluations involve multiple dimensions, how are these integrated to produce an overall estimate of deservingness? An experimental study and a large-scale field study provide some evidence regarding the integration of similar and dissimilar dimensions. Essentially, they support the hypothesis that when dimensions are similar an input integration model pertains; that is, a model in which inputs are summed to obtain a single value of deservingness. However, when dimensions are dissimilar an equity integration model pertains; that is, a model in which separate reward estimates for each dimension are derived first, and are then combined to produce a final evaluation of deservingness.

A series of experimental studies focused on other aspects of the question. One study focusing on the integration formula applied suggests that a power function model represents more adequately the integration process than a simple additive or multiplicative model. Another suggests that the weighting of dimensions and the distribution rules followed may vary according to whether rewards are fixed or depend on the participants' contributions. In fixed-reward conditions individuals low on certain potentially relevant dimensions tend to prefer the equality rule, whereas individuals high on such dimensions prefer the equity rule. In dependent-reward conditions the tendency is generally the equity rule. In this case, contributions to performance usually tend to be assigned higher weights than attributes such as ability. However, individuals with relatively low contributions tend to assign to an attribute higher weights than individuals with relatively high contributions—if this increases their rewards.

Other experiments indicate the effect of other factors. One experiment suggests that dimensions that are perceived to be under volitional control (e.g., effort) are assigned higher weight than dimensions not perceived to be under such control (e.g., ability). Also, there is a tendency to follow the equality rule when individuals are equal on some dimensions but not on others. These findings suggest that the overall constellation of inputs, not merely the nature of individual inputs, affect the input-relevancy perception as well as the distribution rule preferred.

Another experiment on the complexity of evaluation dimensions supports the hypothesis that in a complex situation it is easier to escape from a presented dimension. In accordance with this hypothesis the results indicate that there is less felt inequity in a complex situation than in a simple situation.

All these findings are intriguing but obviously need the support of additional studies, especially field studies, before firm conclusions can be drawn.

The Substitutability of Pay with Other Rewards

Is pay substituable with other rewards? Which other rewards? Under which conditions? Empirical studies on this are extremely rare. The two pertinent experimental studies reviewed suggest that status and status symbols perceived as legitimate may serve as a substitute for pay. This is a promising beginning that still awaits further development in the future. At the moment, any conclusions seem premature.

Summary and Discussion

The studies concerning the perceived relevant evaluation-dimensions suggest they may be of a varied nature including diffuse social characteristics, ability characteristics, as well as contributive factors. Still, because of the methodological biases of most past studies, firm conclusions about the specific dimensions involved and especially their relative weights seem premature. This latter issue then, awaits more thorough clarification in future research, as do other focal issues. For example, more effort has to be invested in the question of social consensus about evaluation dimensions. The data now available suggest that while there may be broad consensus on the relevancy of certain dimensions, the respective weights attached to some of them may vary profoundly. Moreover, virtually very little is yet known about inter-cultural variation in the perceived relevant dimensions and their weights.

The thesis that certain dimensions are ambiguous finds some support, but it falls to future research to pinpoint the factors that generate ambiguity and those factors that determine each such dimension as an input or as an outcome.

Intergroup differentials and interlevel differentials seem extremely important in the overall process of evaluation but more knowledge must be accumulated concerning the criteria applied in making judgments about just differentials, especially intergroup differentials.

Similarly, research concerning the importance of social and organizational status in the process of pay-fairness evaluation suggests that these dimensions are indeed important but much more needs to be known about their weights in the overall process and possibly, according to recent research, also about the contextual factors that may influence their relevance.

Finally, most studies on the integration of various dimensions are experimental and this area direly needs the support of suitable field studies.

GENERAL CONCLUSIONS

It is obvious by now that our subject is far more complex than the initial formulations imply. The data presented, for all their deficiencies, suggest that these formulations and their ramifications could be regarded as complementing each other in many respects rather than as competing with each other. This conclusion applies to all three major aspects considered: Thus, the data for the underlying distribution rules suggest that pay-fairness evaluations include considerations about the contributive value of rewards as the exchange theories suggest, as well as their status and consummatory value, as the status value and relative deprivation theories suggest. They also indicate that the rules applied are contingent on certain contextual and personal characteristics. The data for standards of comparison suggest that individuals tend to make comparisons with similars, as the exchange theories argue, as well as with dissimilars, as relative deprivation theory argues. Moreover, in the general process of comparison certain elements ignored by the exchange formulations but emphasized by relative deprivation theory, such as the overall reward configuration and certain elements within it (e.g., intergroup differentials, average reward levels and scale extremities), as well as changes through time in rewards appear most important. Finally, the data for evaluation dimensions suggest that these may vary and may include those emphasized by the exchange formulations, but also other dimensions such as diffuse social characteristics and other social-status elements.

But above all, the data confirm that the underlying model of determinants is much more complex than envisaged by the initial formulations combined, and that elements from more recent theoretical work done under the aegis of the various theoretical streams may be of great relevance in understanding the subject.

Apart from the drawbacks already noted in the more detailed expositions presented in the foregoing, it is important to note that most of the studies were conducted in Western countries, particularly the United States. The question thus arises of how far findings that seem quite well founded in respect of the various evaluative components are generalizable across cultures? Indeed this cross-cultural perspective should be another important area of future research.

NOTE

1. See also the methodological comments in Goodman and Friedman (1971). Carrell and Ditrich (1978), and Cohen (1978).

9 Implications and Applications

In this chapter we discuss some tentative implications and potential applications of the materials presented so far for pay policy and pay administration. This may not be easy: The available data cover some ground but leave large areas completely unexplored. In areas where investigation has begun there are some promising developments but also many open questions. Where tentative answers to some questions can already be discerned there is still the need for more verification and more groundwork. The area as a whole suggests some provisional contours but much is still obscure. The dangers of a journey through such territory are obvious and some may even call it premature. Others will perhaps be willing to see the heuristic value and advantages of such an endeavor: to inspire and perhaps redirect some prevailing thoughts on the subject, and above all to reveal some of the potential inherent in a better understanding and improved knowledge of it.

We have argued that the review of both theory and empirical research suggest that it may be more fruitful to regard much of the work done in the wake of different paradigms as complementary rather than competitive. Here we wish to gather the fruits of this approach: to examine the implications of the empirical findings as if they flow from a unified body of research rather than from separate lines of thinking. The discussion will highlight those aspects where, following available empirical evidence, a reorientation in actual practices aiming at a measure of perceived pay fairness is called for.

THE UNDERLYING DISTRIBUTION NORMS

It was suggested that employers and compensation specialists when dealing with questions of pay fairness are guided by the idea that the employment situation is an exchange and that a measure of pay fairness can be achieved by equating or coming close to equating the values of contributions made and rewards offered (e.g., Belcher and Atchinson, 1975). This idea is well matched by the various exchange formulations of justice. No wonder that equity theory—the most developed among the exchange theories—has become an integral part of compensation theory. Indeed, there are few recent textbooks in this field that fail to relate to it extensively.

It was further suggested that the exchange perspective has led practitioners to view some issues and practices in pay policy as relevant to the question of pay fairness and others as irrelevant. Thus, issues that do not touch upon contribution-reward linkages but relate to other issues such as the buying power of pay or the organization's ability to pay are considered to be outside the scope of the pay-fairness issue. However, available empirical evidence suggests that the prevalent conceptions of what does and what does not belong to the issue of pay equity and pay fairness may be misplaced, mainly because the contribution principle is but one of the principles guiding pay-fairness notions.

A Variety of Underlying Distribution Norms

Thus, evidence that, in evaluating the justness of their pay, employees also relate to its consummatory value rather than merely its exchange value implies that issues related to this value, such as COLA allowance, minimum wage, personal budget and standard of living, are directly relevant to, and cannot be separated from, the issue of pay fairness. Specifically, wages that fall below an acceptable minimum standard of living, wages with buying power eroded by inflation and not adjusted to their previous real level, and wages that do not match the standard of living and personal budget expectations of employees may become sources of felt deprivation among them. The implication is that organizations striving for a measure of perceived pay fairness among their employees must consider these factors and shape their pay policies accordingly. It seems important to note here that the oft-heard argument in this context that standard of living conceptions are entirely subjective (e.g., Patten, 1977) and cannot therefore serve as bases for pay policy formation, seems rather ill-founded and is refuted by pertinent sociological studies. These show that conceptions about what constitutes a minimum or an adequate standard of living are far from idiosyncratic and reflect rather commonly held social beliefs shared by relatively large numbers of individuals belonging to a given social stratum (e.g., Esterlin, 1973; Rainwater, 1974).

The Impact of Contextual Factors

Empirical evidence from research on the effect of contextual factors suggests that, beyond considerations relating to the consummatory value of pay, pay-fairness evaluations may also be affected by a variety of contextual factors. Under certain circumstances individuals may prefer an equal distribution of rewards and a compression of wage differentials rather than a distribution that follows the equity rule. This implies that pay policies aiming at a measure of perceived pay fairness may have to take into account these contextual factors.

Task Interdependency and Cooperation. According to available evidence, a major factor of this sort is the social relationships prevailing in, and perhaps also between, task groups. Specifically, where task interdependency is high, where results are dependent on team effort, and where cooperation and harmony are highly valued, there are signs of a tendency to prefer an equal reward distribution. The implication is that under such conditions, pay policies based on individual contributions and leading to relatively large wage differentials may be misplaced.

Indeed, in the area of incentive pay plans, it has long been recognized that an efficient and viable plan must take into consideration such variables as task interdependencies and teamwork (e.g., Patten, 1977: 416–18; Lupton and Bowey, 1983: 65–67). This recognition has come about gradually as the result of trial and error following the failure to achieve consistent success with individual incentive plans. Quite often, such plans emerged as sources of conflict and demoralization caused by earning differentials within the group in which the plan was applied, and between it and adjacent nonincentive groups. Quite often, the results were output restriction and "large and growing incentive yields accompanied by low and declining effort levels; and high proportions of payments of average earnings and other guarantees for non-incentive employees" (Patten, 1977: 396). That learning process resulted in some important recommendations; for example, to institute group incentive plans rather than individual incentives where jobs within the work group are highly interdependent and where results depend on the effort of the entire group (e.g., Lawler, 1971). As to conflicts arising among work groups that are interdependent, the solutions are less clear mainly because such more-general solutions require some understanding of the underlying processes and are difficult to reach through a process of trial and error.

The findings about preferred distribution principles illuminate somewhat the underlying processes and offer an explanation for the problems encountered in incentive plans: They suggest that these may be related to the perceived fairness of a distribution rule in a particular situation. Moreover, and their major contribution lies here, they also suggest that factors such as the degree of interdependency within and among work groups, the degree of member and group cooperation, and the degree of intermember and intergroup harmony should be considered not just in pay incentive plans but also more generally, in decisions about pay differentiation within and among work groups.

Most interesting in this context are the findings of a recent field study by Pfeffer and Langton (1988) indicating that actual pay patterns are indeed affected, in the way predicted, by task interdependency, teamwork, and member cooperation. Specifically, the study investigated a number of contextual variables that might affect salary inequality within academic departments and was based on a sample of about 1,800 such departments in 303 colleges and universities in the United

States. One of its major findings was, as predicted, that salary inequality was positively related to a tendency of faculty members to work individually and negatively related to a tendency to cooperate with each other. It would of course be most interesting to know whether these patterns reflect any purposeful and cognitive action of the pay-policy makers in the organizations investigated or if they reflect an inherent process, but the study does not report any data on this issue.

Compressing wage differentials obviously presents a dilemma vis-à-vis the need to give recognition to high performers. Leventhal and colleagues (1976b) suggest that the solution may lie not in total equality, but in a pattern of not too large differentials that would "equalize the psychic gratifications of members rather than their actual incomes." This suggestion still has to be put to empirical test and its parameters to be specified more accurately.

Friendship Relationships. The empirical evidence suggests that the equality principle is preferred over the contribution principle in contexts where friendly relationships prevail or are emphasized or where members perceive similarities between themselves and others. These findings and their implications should be looked at from the perspective of the impressive array of organizational behavior studies, starting from the renowned Hawthorne studies (Roetlisberger and Dickson, 1939), and showing the great importance of work-related friendship relationships to employees and the profound impact these relationships have in turn on organizational members' attitudes and behaviors, and through them on the functioning of the organization and it units (e.g., Trist and Bamforth, 1951; Gross, 1953). The major lesson of these studies is that organizations must pay close attention to these effects and take them into account in shaping their organizational policies, since ignoring them can be rather costly to the organization. The particular implication of the findings reviewed in the present work is that where friendship relationships prevail, pay policies should be wary of creating substantial pay differentials since such differentials may run counter to the fairness perceptions of members and lead to a variety of costly reactions.[1] That organizations tend, indeed knowingly or unknowingly, to follow this principle in actual practice emerges again from the findings of the Pfeffer and Langton (1988) study on pay differentiation in academic departments. Specifically, the findings indicate that the greater the social contact among department members the lower the degree of wage inequality in the department.

The Goals Pursued. The evidence emanating from resource allocation studies indicates that preferences regarding distribution rules are significantly affected by the group goals toward which allocators orient themselves, such as maximizing production, avoiding or reducing internal conflicts, efficient resource allocation, or membership control. A major implication of these findings is that organizations aware of the instrumental value of certain patterns of reward allocation and wishing to utilize them for the pursuit of certain organizational and/or subunit goals, might be more successful in this endeavor if they persuade their members of the importance of these goals and achieve a measure of membership identification with them. Under these conditions, members might be more willing to accept and perhaps even see as justified reward allocation rules that otherwise may be perceived as unjust and unfair.

Resource Abundance or Resource Scarcity. According to the available evidence, perceptions about the fairness of a given distribution rule may also be affected by resource scarcity or resource abundance. Specifically, in conditions of sufficiency the contribution rule seems to be preferred but in conditions of scarcity or abundance the equality principle takes precedence. The implication is that under extreme conditions, of resource scarcity or resource abundance, employees might expect the employing organization to forego the contribution principle in favor of more equality and smaller pay differentials. For example, when scarce resources dictate a reduction in pay, larger cuts in the pay of the better paid employees are likely to be perceived as fairer and are less likely to arouse feelings of relative deprivation generally than an even, all-around pay cut. Conversely, when resources are abundant, the lower-paid employees may expect an improvement in their pay regardless of contribution. Moreover, the studies suggest that organizations operating one-time profit sharing schemes, that is, sharing with their employees "abundant" resources, may be expected to follow the equality principle rather than a differential allocation.

The Nature of Contributions. The evidence suggests that the perceived fairness of a distribution rule is also affected by the nature of contributions. Specifically, when contributions are perceived as relatively less relevant to performance there is a greater tendency to favor the equality principle. One implication is that when performance cannot be related easily to contributions, equal pay or small pay differentials will be perceived as fairer than relatively large pay differentials. This implication is directly relevant to the difficulty of many employing organizations of gauging employee contributions. It is typical of professionally staffed service organizations such as hospitals, schools, welfare agencies, and the like, but it is also common in manufacturing organizations: "The difficulty of gauging employee contributions, particularly in manufacturing firms, where it has become increasingly hard to identify at what precise point in production there is an employee action that interferes with or improves quantity or quality." (Patten, 1977: 360). The available evidence suggests that, under such conditions, a pay system based on large pay differentials between individuals performing the same or similar jobs may be difficult to defend and may arouse strong feelings of inequity and should hence be avoided.

Organizational Position. The empirical evidence suggests that the preferred distribution principle for system-wide incentives as well as the choice of specific criteria for applying the principle may vary among echelons in the organization. This implies that organizations should be alert to such preferences in their decisions on incentive plans of this sort and, in any event, should beware of applying one or other principle in blanket fashion.

The Sociocultural Context

Studies on cross-national comparisons, few and inconclusive as they are, still create the impression that individuals from different sociocultural backgrounds may in some cases diverge in their views about what constitutes just distribution principles. This implies that organizations with employees of various sociocultural backgrounds, for example, multinational corporations or organizations drawing their workforce from culturally nonhomogeneous settings, should in their pay policies recognize that a policy that has proven itself in one country and in regard to employees of a particular sociocultural background may not be as successful, in terms of perceived fairness, in another country or with employees from a different sociocultural background.

Personal Characteristics

Indications that personal characteristics such as sex or a Protestant Ethic orientation may affect preferences about distributive justice principles suggest that these characteristics may be important in devising a pay policy aiming at perceived fairness. Huseman and colleagues (1987) proposed an analytical construct—the equity sensitivity construct—to reflect the equity sensitivity of individuals as it is affected by a variety of relevant *individual* characteristics. The view of these authors is that equity sensitivity is a *trait* rather than a state, implying that preferences emanating from equity sensitivity might be expected to be relatively stable and change only "rarely and only as the consequences of grossly significant changes in the situation" (p. 232). Investigating individuals' equity orientations and using the results for devising a suitable pay policy may thus be useful for a pay policy aiming at perceived pay fairness. Nor should such a practice be too difficult to implement since selective recruitment and promotion policies make it unlikely that personal characteristics will be dispersed at random in the employing organization.

THE STANDARDS OF COMPARISON

The prevalent conception of employing organizations about pay comparisons is that a single type of referent—individuals performing a similar job—is involved in the process. Guided by this idea, organizations conduct external surveys to gather information intended to assist them in determining "comparable wages" for their workforce, and try internally to align the pay of similar jobs. Available evidence implies that these strategies and the basic underlying concept do not conform closely with reality. Thus, there are strong indications that individuals may also compare with dissimilars and may also use other standards such as Self or System in evaluating the fairness of their pay. The evidence also suggests that individuals tend quite often to make multiple rather than single comparisons, and that reference patterns are not uniform but differ from one situation to another. In general, the implication is that employing organizations, instead of acting according to stereotype notions about who the relevant referents are, should be prepared to monitor the relevant information in regard to their own workforce. The following discussion focuses on some of the more specific evidence that may assist in giving this effort direction and making it more efficient and selective.

Similar vs. Dissimilar and External vs. Internal Comparisons

The evidence suggests that external comparisons are of central importance in the overall process of pay comparisons. One implication is that attempts of employers to establish bargaining norms that focus attention on circumstances at the employing organization (e.g. Freedman, 1985) may not be successful (e.g. Cappelli and Sherer (1988: 689). The evidence also suggests that, besides making comparisons with similars outside the organization, employees also tend to make comparisons with the perceived average earnings of all employees. Presumably, the perceived average earnings serve as a yardstick to assess one's relative position vis-à-vis others "in general" and to obtain a sense of one's general well-being, of how well or how badly one is faring compared with the "average person." Employing organizations aiming at a measure of perceived pay fairness should note this tendency and take it into account in their pay policies. At the very least, they cannot persist in assuming that average-wage trends are irrelevant to the process.

As to the prevailing notion that external wage comparability is essential in achieving a measure of pay fairness, the evidence suggests that since employees may differ significantly in their tendency to make external comparisons this idea may not apply equally to all. According to this evidence, the tendency to chose outside comparisons may be affected by a number of factors such as level of education, pay level, length of tenure, organizational position (e.g., staff boundary position), and satisfaction with the organization. This suggests that there is need for a more selective approach in applying the idea of external-wage comparability and, moreover, that in certain cases more attention should be given to internal comparability instead.

An additional factor is the effect of perceived promotion prospects on pay-comparison tendencies. For example, the evidence indicates that perceived good promotion prospects mitigate the tendency to make upward and dissonant comparisons, while the opposite is true in regard to individuals estimating their promotion prospects as poor. This evidence should alert pay-policy makers to some potential loci of felt relative deprivation in the organization, and perhaps also to the costs (in terms of felt deprivation) of blocked internal promotion.

The Effect of Perceived Intergroup Pay Differentials

The available evidence suggests that policies aiming at a measure of perceived pay fairness should take into account the magnitude of intergroup differentials since these are an important determinant of felt relative deprivation. For example, pay-policy makers should realize that increasing intergroup differentials, even between dissimilar groups, may arouse feelings of relative deprivation among those affected. Here an aspect that is often misconceived by pay-policy makers should be noted. This is the frequent demands from affected groups of employees to preserve traditional differentials relative to other groups of employees whose pay has been raised. These demands are frequently viewed as actions driven by sheer greed and opportunism. The evidence, however, casts them in a different light. It suggests that, whereas traditional differentials may have come to be perceived as just and fair, their enlargement as a result of pay raises to other groups is likely to be perceived as unjust and may lead to the formation of a felt deprivation.

Evidence relating to the cognitive processes involved in the formation of relative deprivation feelings vis-à-vis dissimilars has also an interesting, albeit indirect, implication for pay policies aiming at a measure of pay fairness. It is indicated that aggregated- and concentrated-information facilitates the formation of relative deprivation feelings while atomized information impedes it. One implication is that standardization, namely, the transition from individually based to standardized pay schedules for job occupants, which is an important aim of pay policies and which also necessarily involves a high concentration of information may also unintentionally increase the chances of felt relative deprivation.

Another implication of the findings is that the design of wage/salary systems in an organization should follow the perceived just configuration of pay differentiation between groups of occupations/jobs and the perceived just hierarchy between them: An attempt to differentiate between those perceived as belonging together or to break the perceived just hierarchy may arouse feelings of deprivation among those adversely affected by these policies.

According to the findings, organizations aiming at perceived pay fairness may also have to strike a "delicate balance" between the conception of the lower and higher echelons regarding the just overall magnitude of pay differentiation.

The Effect of Changes in Reward Levels

Some evidence from relative deprivation research and relating to the dynamic aspects of felt relative deprivation draw attention to certain difficulties that pay policies aiming at pay fairness may encounter as a result of these dynamics. For example, a pay raise intended to alleviate a felt deprivation may not achieve this result and may even aggravate this feeling if it only partly meets the expectations for perceived fairness. The reason, according to the evidence, is that an attempt to redress a felt injustice is likely to strengthen the perception that the felt deprivation was justified; this is the case of progressive deprivation. Similarly, actions that raise expectations for the alleviation of an existing felt deprivation (e.g., job evaluation or reevaluation), but do not fulfill these expectations, may worsen the feeling of deprivation; this is the case of aspirational deprivation. Another case is decremental deprivation. For example, organizations attempting to lower, absolutely or relatively, some employees' pay following a lowering of job requirements (e.g., lower skill or responsibility requirements) may stimulate feelings of relative deprivation in the employees affected if pay expectations do not change concomitantly. But a concomitant change in pay expectations may be difficult to achieve because the reward-contribution link is often not well defined.

For example, job evaluation, which is supposed to effectuate such a link, is not a scientific method (e.g., Patten, 1977: 197, 249–50; Lupton and Bowey, 1983: 12) and is often based on "soft" criteria (e.g., Patten, 1977: 294). Also, employing organizations quite often fail to adequately define the desired contributions (Belcher, 1974: 216–217; Belcher and Atchinson, 1975). As a result of these and similar deficiencies in linking contributions and rewards, changes in job requirements may not be perceived as justifying an adjustment in pay; in other words, pay expectations may not change as a consequence of changed job requirements.

THE UNDERLYING DIMENSIONS OF EVALUATION

The Perceived Relevant Dimensions

One problem facing pay-policy makers aiming at a measure of perceived pay fairness is to detect what dimensions are perceived by employees as relevant in pay-fairness evaluation and what their relative weights are. The empirical evidence suggests that, generally, many of the dimensions perceived as relevant by employees are also practically used by employing organizations to build various pay schemes based on contribution-reward linkages. In this general respect, then, it may be said that actual practice does not diverge fundamentally from employees' conceptions. But beyond this generalization, empirical research focuses attention on some specific aspects whereas reorientation may be needed.

For example, the prevalent belief in employing organizations is that pay is to be based primarily on levels of difficulty and importance of jobs (i.e., job evaluation) and on performance on the job (i.e., output and performance measures). In cases where these criteria are difficult to apply or do not seem valid enough (e.g., professional and managerial jobs) ability and personal characteristics are used as approximate substitutes. Available empirical evidence suggests, however, that this approach may lead to substantial discrepancies between the actual bases of pay and those perceived as relevant by the employees. The main reason is that, while employees do indeed regard job difficulty and job importance as well as various performance dimensions as relevant dimensions in pay-fairness evaluations, they do not always seem to agree that these dimensions are the only relevant dimensions or that they should take priority over others such as ability (e.g., education, training, job seniority), occupational status, or a variety of personal characteristics (e.g., sex or age). The resulting discrepancies between employees' conceptions and actual practice may create among employees a feeling of deprivation—of not being adequately rewarded according to the perceived relevant criteria—with all the ramifications of this. The implication is that employing organizations wishing to avoid this must find ways of more carefully aligning the actual pay bases with those perceived as relevant by their workforce.

The empirical evidence reviewed has other important implications. For example, the evidence indicating that usually several evaluation dimensions, not just one, are perceived as relevant, implies that pay schemes geared to one particular dimension, such as certain job evaluation schemes (e.g., Lupton and Bowey, 1983: 20–31), may not adequately fulfill the function of achieving perceived pay fairness since they may miss some of the dimensions considered by employees as relevant and important.

On the other hand, evidence indicating that the number of dimensions perceived as relevant and important is usually not great, suggests that schemes employing a relatively large number of dimensions (and not a few schemes are indeed like this) may also not be conducive to perceived pay fairness and may be even dysfunctional. The reason is that such schemes are likely to include dimensions perceived as irrelevant or only marginally relevant, and are hence likely to cause serious discrepancies between the weight attached by the organization to the various dimensions and those attached by the individuals for whom the schemes are intended.

Furthermore, the available evidence suggests that different groups of employees may have different conceptions of the relevancy and weight of different dimensions. One implication is that pay plans using only one dimension-weight scheme for all jobs in the organization may be inadequate for achieving a measure of perceived pay fairness. Another is that employing organizations cannot rely on preconceived or management-based ideas about the relevant dimensions and their weight but must gather such information from their employees. This activity should also supply the organization with information about employees' perceptions of wage clusters and wage contours, that is, perceptions about jobs that are perceived as alike, belonging to the same or close clusters in respect of pay, and jobs that are perceived as different, belonging to different and remote clusters. These conceptions are important because they contain information about continuities and discontinuities: They indicate the contours within which *same* or similar dimension-weight schemes can and should be applied and outside which *different* dimension-weight schemes should be applied. They also reveal where only relatively small wage differentials will be tolerated (among jobs forming a cluster and among groups of close clusters) and where relatively larger wage differentials might be acceptable (between groups of remote clusters). Indeed, certain job-evaluation schemes actually used by organizations tend to differentiate between types of jobs such as manual versus clericals or professional, managerial and administrative versus lower-level clerical and manual. In another variant, schemes are based on clustering jobs round certain key jobs. The problem is that these schemes generally use internal committees for the range of judgmental tasks involved in applying the scheme. This may result in schemes that do not reflect well the employees' conceptions of job clusters. This danger of arbitrariness is perhaps mitigated, even if not avoided completely, when employees' representatives are consulted or take part in the committees, but is quite serious in the absence of employee representation. In this case, the committee may produce a scheme that falls indeed in line with management's conceptions but counters the employees' fairness conceptions.

Social Status as a Dimension of Evaluation

The available empirical evidence suggests that the practice of basing pay schemes solely on the internal criteria such as job evaluation may miss the aim of a measure of perceived pay fairness because of, among other things, disregarding the fact that social status as reflected, for example, in occupational prestige, is an important dimension of pay-fairness evaluation. For example, such schemes may create situations where some of the workforce may find itself lower down the pay scale than the level dicated by their place in the occupational-prestige scale. Feelings of relative deprivation, of not being properly rewarded, are likely to ensue among those so affected: They may feel that a major criterion of perceived "deservingness" has been ignored and even violated. A paper by Zelditch and colleagues (1966) extending the status value theory to organizations is relevant in this context. Its central concept is the *balanced status structure*. In the authors' view only balanced status structures are viable. A balanced status structure is one in which "each status element is balanced with every other relevant status element" (p. 272). The relevant elements may be external or internal status characteristics and goal objects such as money, office space, or other status symbols. Organizations may achieve a balanced status system by employing selective recruitment and advancement policies that assign individuals with external status characteristics (Ei) to higher ranked jobs in the organization (Ji) and assign higher pay levels (Pi) to higher ranked jobs. Thus, the relative values of E, J, and P are aligned and a balanced status system is achieved. According to the authors, the major mechanism for achieving a match between required contributions and rewards is the internal-status structure. Since this, unlike the external-prestige structure, is under the organization's control, it can be manipulated in a way that will create a fit between required contributive inputs and pay: Jobs that are important to the organization, that entail special and relatively rare qualifications or characteristics or abilities, will receive higher rank and hence higher payment. The need for rewarding differential performances will find its solution in a bonus system: "Organizations may have a system of bonuses that is not associated with status classes" (Zelditch et al., 1966: 282).

Directly supporting the status balance theory is the finding that, in order to earn higher reward value, status must also be perceived as associated with higher contributions. This finding also implies that the practice of "cooling off" individuals at some stage of their careers by awarding them with higher titles and higher salaries but withdrawing from them important responsibilities, or promoting individuals on the pay scale without matching this with increased job requirements, may create feelings of relative deprivation among individuals in adjacent positions.

The available empirical evidence also suggests that the pay of *hierarchical positions* is evaluated from a functional, that is, contributive perspective as well as a status-ranking perspective. The contributive perspective includes, for example, evaluations of various aspects of responsibility, while the status-ranking perspective includes expectations about pay differentials between hierarchical levels that relate mainly to the need to distinguish "properly" and "justly" between different status levels through fixed percentage (roughly 30 percent) differentials. Organizations aiming at a measure of pay fairness should be alert to these distinct perspectives of evaluation and their implications. They must recognize, for example, that position incumbents in the hierarchy seek a just return for their contributions as well as a "proper distance" in pay vis-à-vis their subordinates and may feel relatively deprived if any of these conditions are not met.

Ambivalent Evaluation Dimensions

The findings suggest that a substantial number of evaluation dimensions are ambivalent—that is, may be regarded as input or conversely as outcomes. One major implication is that to prevent feelings of deprivation organizations should be alert to the way these dimensions are perceived by their own workforce. Another major implication is that to prevent inconsistencies organizations must pay great attention to the way they present these dimensions to their employees and to avoid ambivalent messages; for example, presenting greater responsibility as a reward for dedicated work while at the same time emphasizing the greater burden associated with it. These opposing cues may create confusion over standards of fairness in pay followed by the system and may lead ultimately to feelings of relative deprivation among employees, on account of the sense that expectations vis-à-vis the system are not adequately met. The best policy regarding the ambivalent dimensions seems to be one that consistently emphasizes the one aspect that best fits the conceptions of the employees themselves—either input *or* outcome—and that thereby helps prevent ambivalent perception of these dimensions.

The Integration of the Various Dimensions

The findings indicate that a number of factors determine the modes of input integration and the perceived just input/output links. These factors include the degree of input similarity, the degree of perceived volitional control over them, the degree to which they are perceived as contributing directly to performance, and the degree to which reward resources are perceived as linked to contributions. Thus, there is a tendency to prefer the contribution rule when inputs are perceived as being under one's volitional control and as contributing directly to performance, and when resources are perceived as being dependent on participants' contributions. By contrast, there is a tendency to prefer the equality rule when opposite conditions prevail. These findings suggest that, in devising pay and incentive systems, organizations must recognize not only *what* inputs are perceived as relevant, but also the *way relevant inputs are perceived* and the perceived *resource-contribution* links.

Moreover, the evidence suggests that employees may not always agree among themselves on what just input/outcome links are and on what allocation principles should be applied in a particular situation. When rewards depend upon contributions, individuals with low contributions tend to assign lower weight to inputs contributing directly to performance than do with individuals with high contributions. When resources are fixed, individuals low on contributive inputs prefer the equality rule, whereas individuals high on such inputs prefer the equity rule. Organizations should be alert to, and be prepared to deal with, these divergent views and the conflicts they may generate among employees when devising pay schemes linking rewards to contributions or pay schemes based on fixed-sum allocations such as certain bonus schemes.

GENERAL CONCLUSIONS

The above discussion has focused on the implications of the empirical evidence presented and the conclusions arising from it for a pay policy aiming at a measure of perceived pay fairness. Not all may perhaps agree with the proposals advanced and questions may arise over whether the empirical evidence presented is ripe enough for practical applications and over the conclusions themselves. But there can be little doubt about the usefulness of such an exercise in demonstrating that there are no simplistic solutions to the problem of perceived pay fairness and in highlighting the many factors that may require consideration when such a solution is attempted. Moreover, the discussion also suggests that simplistic solutions based on stereotype notions about the factors affecting perceived pay fairness may even be counterproductive.

Beyond, the exercise also suggests that part of the factual knowledge needed for such a solution cannot come from outside but must be gathered by the employing organization itself. The message is that if organizations indeed wish to further the goal of perceived pay fairness they cannot avoid investing some effort in studying the subject among their own workforce.

NOTE

1. Moreover, some research findings indicate that the application of the contribution rule among members of work groups leads to competitive feelings among group members and threatens their friendly relationships (e.g., Deutsch, 1986: Ch. 10).

References

Adams, J. S. (1963a). Toward an understanding of inequity. *Journal of Abnormal Social Psychology*, 67: 422-36.

Adams, J. E. (1963b) Wage inequities, productivity and work quality. *Industrial Relations*, 3: 9-16.

Adams, J. S. (1965). Inequity in social exchange. In L. Berkowitz (Ed.), *Advances in Experimental Social Psychology*, 2: 267-99. New York: Academic Press.

Adams, J. S. and Freedman, S. (1976). Equity theory revisited: Comments and annotated bibliography. In L. Berkowitz and E. Walster (Eds.), *Advances in Experimental Social Psychology*, 9: 267-299. New York: Academic Press.

Adams, J. S. and Jacobsen, P. (1964). Effects of wage inequities on work quality. *Journal of Abnormal and Social Psychology*, 69(1): 19-25.

Adams, J. S. and Rosenbaum, W. E. (1962). The relationship of worker productivity to cognitive dissonance about wage inequity. *Journal of Applied Psychology*, 46: 161-64.

Alves, W. H. and Rossi, P. H. (1978). Who should get what? Fairness of judgments of the distribution of earnings. *American Journal of Sociology*, 8: 541-63.

Ambrose, M. L. and Kukik, C. T. (1988). Referent sharing: Convergence within workgroups of perceptions of equity and referent choice. *Human Relations*, 41: 697-707.

Anderson, B., Berger, J., Zelditch, M., Jr., and Cohen, B. P. (1969). Reactions to inequity (I). *Acta Sociologica*, 12: 1-12.

Anderson, B., and Shelly, R. K. (1970). Reactions to inequity (II): A replication of the Adams experiment and a theoretical reformulation. *Acta Sociologica*, 13: 1-10.

Andrews, I. R. (1967). Wage inequity and performance: An experimental study. *Journal of Applied Psychology*, 51(1): 39-45.

Andrews, I. R. and Henry, M. M. (1963). Management attitudes toward pay. *Industrial Relations*, 3: 29-39.

Andrews, I. R. and Valenzi, E. R. (1970). Overpay inequity of self-image as worker: A critical examination of an experimental induction procedure. *Journal of Organizational Behavior and Human Performance*, 5: 266-75.

Aral, S. O. and Sunar, D. G. (1977). Interaction and justice norms: Cross-national comparisons. *Journal of Social Psychology*, 101: 175–86.

Arrowood, A. J. and Friend, R. (1969). Other factors determining the choice of a comparison other. *Journal of Experimental Social Psychology*, 5: 233–39.

Atchinson, T. J. and Belcher, D. W. (1971). Equity rewards and compensation administration. *Personnel Administration*, 34: 32–46.

Austin, W. (1977). Equity theory and social comparison processes. In J. Suls and L. Miller (Eds.), *Social Comparison Processes*, pp. 279–305. New York: John Wiley.

Austin, W. (1979). Justice, freedom and self-interest in intergroup conflict. In W. G. Austin and S. Worchel (Eds.), *The Social Psychology of Intergroup Relations*, pp. 121–43. Monterey, CA: Brooks-Cole.

Austin, W. (1980). Friendship and fairness: Effects of type of relationship and task performance on choice of distribution rules. *Personality and Social Psychology Bulletin*, 6: 402–08.

Austin, W. and Hatfield, E. (1980). Equity theory, power and social justice. In G. Mikula (Ed.), *Justice in Social Interaction*, pp. 25–62. New York: Springer-Verlag.

Austin, W. and McGinn, N. C. (1977). Sex differences in choice of distribution rules. *Journal of Personality*, 45: 379–94.

Austin, W. and McGinn, N. C. (1980). Internal standards revisited: Effects of social comparisons and expectancies on judgments of fairness and satisfaction. *Journal of Experimental Social Psychology*, 16: 426–41.

Austin, W. and Susmilch, C. (1974). Comments on Lane and Messe's confusing clarification of equity theory. *Journal of Personality and Social Psychology*, 32: 400–04.

Banks, W. C. (1952). The effects of perceived similarity upon the use of reward and punishment. *Journal of Experimental Social Psychology*, 12: 131–38.

Barnard, Ch. (1952). Functions and pathology of status systems in formal organizations. In Ch. I. Barnard (Ed.), *Organization and Management*, pp. 207–44. Harvard University Press.

Baskett, G. D. (1973). Interview decisions as determined by competency and attitude similarity. *Journal of Applied Psychology*, 57: 343–45.

Bass, B. M. (1968). Ability, values and concepts of equitable salary increases in exercise compensation. *Journal of Applied Psychology*, 52: 299–303.

Beal, E. F. (1963). In praise of job evaluation. *California Management Review*, 5: 9–16.

Belcher, D. W. (1974). *Compensation Administration*. Englewood Cliffs, NJ: Prentice-Hall.

Belcher, D. W. and Atchinson, T. J. (1970). Equity theory and compensation policy. *Personnel Administration*, (July–August): 22–33.

Belcher, D. W. and Atchinson, T. J. (1975). Compensation for work. In R. Dubin (Ed.), *Handbook of Work, Organization and Society*, pp. 567–611. New York: Rand McNally.

Berger, J., Fisek, M. H., Norman, R. Z. and Wagner, D. G. (1983). The formation of reward expectations in status situations. In D. M. Messick and K. S. Cook (Eds.), *Equity Theory: Psychological and Sociological Perspectives*, pp. 127–68. New York: Praeger.

Berger, J., Zelditch, M., Jr, Anderson, B. and Cohen, B. P. (1972). Structural aspects of distributive justice: A status value formulation. In J. Berger, M. Zelditch Jr. and B. Anderson (Eds.), *Sociological Theories in Progress*, 2: 119–46. Boston: Houghton-Mifflin.

Berkowitz, L., Fraser, C., Treasure, E. P. and Cochran, S. (1987). Pay equity, job gratification and comparisons in pay satisfaction. *Journal of Applied Psychology.* 72: 544–51.

Bernstein, M. and Crosby, F. (1978). *Relative deprivation: Testing the models.* Paper presented at the American Psychological Association annual meeting, Toronto.

Bernstein, M. and Crosby, F. (1980). An empirical examination of relative deprivation theory. *Journal of Experimental Social Psychology*, 16: 442–56.

Bierhoff, H. W., Buck, E. and Klein, R. (1986). Social context and perceived justice. In H. W. Bierhoff, R. L. Cohen and J. Greenberg (Eds.), *Justice in Social Relations*, pp. 165–86. New York: Plenum.

Bierhoff, H. W., Cohen, R. L. and Greenberg, J. (Eds.). (1986). *Justice in Social Relations*, New York: Plenum.

Bierhoff, H. W. and Kramp, P. (1982). Backward inferences to contributions on the basis of reward allocations. *Proceedings of the 24th Meeting of Experimental Psychologists, 247.* Trier: University of Trier.

Bies, R. J. (1987). The predicament of injustice: The management of outrage. In L. Cummings and B. M. Staw (Eds.), *Research in Organizational Behavior*, vol. 9, pp. 289–319, Greenwich, CT: JAI Press.

Bies, R. J. and Shapiro, D. L. (1987). Interactional fairness judgments: The influence of causal accounts. *Social Justice Research*, 1: 160–69.

Blau, P. (1964). *Exchange and Power in Social Life*. New York: Wiley.

Bond, M., Leung, K. and Wan, K. C. (1982). How does cultural collectivism operate? The impact of task and maintenance contributions on reward distribution. *Journal of Cross-Cultural Psychology*, 13: 186–200.

Bossong, B. (1983). Verteilungspräferenzen, Art der sozialen Beziehung und Bedürftigkeit (Allocation preferences, the type of social relationship and needs). *Zeitschrift für Experimentelle und Angewandte-Psychologie*, 30: 566–72.

Brandt, R. B. (1962). *Social Justice*. New Jersey: Prentice Hall.

Brickman, P. and Campbell, D. T. (1971). Hedonic relativism and planning the good society. In M. H. Appley (Ed.), *Adaptation-level Theory*, pp. 287–302. New York: Academic Press.

Brickman, P., Folger, R., Goode, E. and Shul, Y. (1981). Microjustice and macrojustice. In M. Lerner and S. C. Lerner (Eds.), *The Justice Motive in Social Behavior*, pp. 173–204. New York: Plenum.

Callahan-Levy, C. M. and Messe, L. A. (1979). Sex differences in the allocation of pay. *Journal of Personality and Social Psychology*, 37: 433–46.

Cappelli, P. and Sherer, P. D. (1988). Satisfaction, market wages, and labor relations: An airline study. *Industrial Relations*, 27: 56–73.

Carles, E. M. and Carver, C. S. (1979). Effects of person salience versus role salience on reward allocation in the dyad. *Journal of Personality and Social Psychology*, 37: 2071–80.

Carrell, M. R. and Dittrich, J. E. (1976). Employee perceptions of fair treatment. *Personnel Journal*, 55: 523–24.

Carrell, M. R. and Dittrich, J. E. (1978). Equity theory: The recent literature, methodological considerations and new directions. *Academy of Management Review*, 3: 202–10.

Carter, C. (1986). Layoffs, equity theory and work performance: Further evidence of the impact of survivor guilt. *Academy of Management Journal*, 39: 222–24.

deCarufel, A. (1986). Pay secrecy, social comparison and relative deprivation in organizations. In J. M. Olson, C. P. Herman, and M. P. Zanna (Eds.), *Relative Deprivation and Social Comparison: The Ontario Symposium*, 4: 181–99, Hillsdale, NJ: Lawrence Erlbaum.

deCarufel, A. and Schopler, J. (1979). Evaluation of outcome improvement resulting from threats and appeals. *Journal of Personality and Social Psychology*, 37: 662–73.

Chesler, P. and Goodman, E. J. (1976). Women, Money and Power. New York: Morrow.

Cohen, R. L. (1974). Mastery and justice in laboratory dyads: A revision and extension of equity theory. *Journal of Personality and Social Psychology*, 29: 464–74.

Cohen, R. L. (1978). *A critique of reward allocation research on distributive justice*. Unpublished manuscript, Bennington College.

Cook, K. S. (1975). Expectations, evaluations and equity. *American Sociological Review*, 40: 372–88.

Cook, K. S. and Hegdvedt, K. A. (1983). Distributive justice, equity and equality. *Annual Review of Sociology*, 9: 217–41.

Cook, K. S. and Parcell, T. L. (1977). Equity theory: Directions for future research. *Sociological Inquiry*, 47: 75–88.

Cook, K. S. and Yamagishi, T. (1983). Social determinants of equity judgments: The problem of multidimensional input. In D. M. Messick and K. S. Cook (Eds.), *Equity Theory: Psychological and Sociological Perspectives*, pp. 95–126. New York: Praeger.

Cook, T. D., Crosby, F. and Hennigan, K. M. (1977). The construct validity of relative deprivation. In J. Suls and R. Miller (Eds.), *Social Comparison Processes*. New York: Wiley.

Coon, R. C., Lane, I. M. and Lichtman, R. J. (1974). Sufficiency of reward and allocation behavior. Human Development, 17: 301–13.

Cosier, R. A. and Dalton, D. R. (1983). Equity theory and time: A reformulation. *Academy of Management Review*, 8: 311–19.

Crosby, F. (1976). A model of egoistical relative deprivation. *Psychological Review*, 83: 85–113.

Crosby, F. (1982). *Relative Deprivation and Working Women*. New York: Oxford University Press.

Crosby, F. (1984). Relative deprivation in organizational settings. In L. L. Cummings and B. M. Staw (Eds.), *Research in Organizational Behavior*, 6: 51–93. Greenwich, CT: JAI Press.

Crosby, F., Burris, L., Censor, K. and MacKethan, E. R. (1986a). Two rotten apples spoil the justice barrel. In H. W. Bierhoff, R. L. Cohen, and J. Greenberg (Eds.), (1986). *Justice in Social Relations*, pp. 267–81. New York: Plenum.

Crosby, F., Clayton, S. D., Hemker, K. and Alksnis, O. (1986b). Cognitive biases in the perception of discrimination: The importance of format. *Sex Roles*, 14: 637–46.

Crosby, F. and Gonzalez-Intal, M. (1984). Relative deprivation and equity theories: Felt injustice and the undeserved benefits of others. In R. Folger (Ed.), *The Sense of Injustice: Social Psychological Perspectives*, pp. 141–66. New York: Plenum.

Crozier, M. (1965). *The Bureaucratic Phenomenon*. London: Tavistock Publications.

Curtis, R. C. (1979). Effects of knowledge of self interest and social relationship upon the use of equity, utilitarian and Rawlsian principles of allocation. *European Journal of Social Psychology*, 9: 165–75.

Dandridge, T. C., Mitroff, I. and Joyce, W. (1980). Organizational symbolism: A topic to expand organizational analysis. *Academy of Management Review*, 5: 77–82.

Darley, J. M. and Aronson, E. (1966). Self-evaluation vs. direct anxiety reduction as determinant of the fear-affiliation relationship. *Journal of Experimental Social Psychology*. Suppl. 1: 66–79.

Davies, J. C. (1962). Toward a theory of revolution. *American Sociological Review*, 27: 5–18.

Davis, J. A. (1959). A formal theory of relative deprivation. *Sociometry*, 22: 280–96.

Debusschere, M. and Van Avermaet, E. (1984). Compromising between equity and equality: The effects of situational ambiguity and computational complexity. *European Journal of Social Psychology*, 14(3): 323–33.

Deutsch, M. (1975). Equity, equality, and need: What determines which values will be used as the basis of distributive justice? *Journal of Social Issues*, 31(3): 137–49.

Deutsch, M. (1985). *Distributive Justice*. New Haven, CT: Yale University Press.

Dittrich, J. E. and Carrell, M. R. (1979). Organizational equity perceptions, employee job satisfaction and departmental absence and turnover rates. *Organizational Behavior and Human Performance*, 24: 29–40.

Doeringer, P. B. and Piore, M. J. (1985). *Internal Labor Markets and Manpower Analysis*, Lexington, MA: Heath.

Dornstein, M. (1985). Perceptions regarding standards for evaluating pay equity and their determinants. *Journal of Occupational Psychology*, 58: 321–30.

Dornstein, M. (1988a). Pay equity evaluations of occupations and their bases. *Journal of Applied Social Psychology*, 18: 905–24.

Dornstein, M. (1988b). Wage reference groups and their determinants: A study of blue-collar and white-collar employees in Israel. *Journal of Occupational Psychology*, 61: 221–33.

Dornstein, M. (1989). The fairness judgements of received pay and their determinants. *Journal of Occupational Psychology*, 62: 287–99.

Dornstein, M. (1990a). Perceived fairness of pay incentives and their social bases: A case study among industrial employees in Israel. *Personnel Review*, 19: 27–33.

Dornstein, M. (1990b). The pay equity evaluations of task and task incumbents' characteristics. In E. S. Lea, P. Webley and B. M. Young (Eds.), *Applied Economic Psychology in the 1990's*, pp. 904–30. Exeter, England: Washington Singer Press.

Dornstein, M. (1990c). Perceptions of just pay differentiation among occupations, and their social bases. (Unpublished paper.)

Duchon, D., and Jago, A. G. (1981). Equity and the performance of major league baseball players. *Journal of Applied Psychology*, 66: 728–32.

Dunlop, J. T. (1957). The task of contemporary wage theory. In G. W. Taylor and F. C. Pierson (Eds.), *New Concepts in Wage Determination*. pp. 117–39. New York: McGraw Hill.

Ekeh, P. (1974). *Social Exchange Theory*, Cambridge, MA: Harvard University Press.

Esterlin, R. (1973). Does money buy happiness? *The Public Interest*, 30: 3–10.

Evan, W. M. and Simmons, R. G. (1969). Organizational effects of inequitable rewards: Two experiments in status inconsistency. *Administrative Science Quarterly*, 14: 224–37.

Evans, M. G. and Molinari, L. (1970). Equity, piece-rate overpayment and job security: Some effects on performance. *Journal of Applied Psychology*, 54: 105–14.

Farkas, A. J. and Anderson, N. H. (1979). *Journal of Personality and Social Psychology*, 37: 879–96.

Farrell, D. and Rusbult, C. E. (1981). Exchange variables as predictors of job satisfaction, job commitment and turnover: The Impact of rewards, costs, alternatives and investments. *Organizational Behavior and Human Performance*, 28: 78–95.

Feather, N. T. (1983). Observers' reactions to allocations in relation to input of allocator, type of distribution, and Protestant Ethic values. *Australian Journal of Psychology*, 35: 61–70.

Feather, N. T. and O'Driscoll, M. P. (1980). Observers' reactions to an equal or equitable allocator in relation to allocator input, causal attributions, and value importance. *European Journal of Social Psychology*, 10: 107–29.

Festinger, L. A. (1954). A theory of social comparison processes. *Human Relations* 7: 114–40.

Finn, R. H. and Lee, S. M. (1972). Salary equity: Its determination, analysis and correlates. *Journal of Applied Psychology*, 56: 283–92.

Foa, U. G. and Stein, G. (1980). Rules of distributive justice: Institution and resource influences. *Academic Psychology Bulletin*, 2: 89–94.

Folger, R. (Ed.) (1984a). *The Sense of Injustice: Social Psychological Perspectives*. New York and London: Plenum.

Folger, R. (1984b). Emerging issues in the social psychology of justice. In R. Folger (Ed.), *The Sense of Injustice: Social Psychological Perspectives*, pp. 3–24. New York and London: Plenum.

Folger, R. and Konovsky, M. H. (1989). Effects of procedural and distributive justice on reactions to pay raise decisions. *Academy of Management Journal*, 22: 115–30.

Freedman, A. (1985). *The New Look in Wage Policy and Employee Relations*. New York: Conference Board.

Freedman, S. M. and Montanari, J. R. (1980). An integrative model of managerial reward allocation. *Academy of Management Review*, 5: 381–90.

Friedman, A. and Goodman, P. S. (1967). Wage inequity, self-qualification and productivity. *Organizational Behavior and Human Performance*, 2: 406–17.

Garland, H. (1973). The effects of piece-rate underpayment and overpayment on job performance: A test of equity theory with a new induction procedure. *Journal of Applied Social Psychology*, 3: 325–34.

Garrett, J. B. (1973, August). *Effects of Protestant ethic endorsement upon equity behavior*. Paper presented at the meeting of the American Psychological Association, Montreal.

Garret, J. B. and Bloom, E. J. (1975, August). *Interactive effects of Protestant ethic and task input on reward allocations*. Paper presented at the meeting of the Midwestern Psychological Association, Montreal.

Gartrell, D. C. (1983). On the visibility of wage referents. *Canadian Journal of Sociology*, 7: 117–43.

Gartrell, D. C. (1985). Relational and distributional models of collective justice sentiments. *Social Forces*, 64: 64–83.

Gergen, K. J., Morse, S. J. and Bode, K. (1971). *Overpaid or overworked? Cognitive and behavioral reactions to inequitable payment*. Unpublished manuscript, Swathmore College.

Gergen, K. J., Morse, S. J. and Gergen, M. M. (1980). Behavior exchange in cross-cultural perspective. In H. C. Triandis and R. W. Breslin (Eds.), *Handbook of Cross-cultural Psychology*, 5: 121–54. Boston: Allyn & Bacon.

Goodman, P. S. (1974). An examination of referents used in the evaluation of pay. *Organizational Behavior and Human Performance*, 12: 170–95.

Goodman, P. S. (1975). Effect of perceived inequity on salary allocation decisions. *Journal of Applied Psychology*, 60: 372–75.

Goodman, P. S. (1976). Social comparison processes in organizations. In B. M. Staw and G. R. Salanick (Eds.), *New Directions in Organizational Behavior*, pp. 97–132. Chicago: St. Clair Press.

Goodman, P. and Friedman, A. (1969). An examination of quantity and quality of performance under conditions of overpayment in piece-rate. *Organizational Behavior and Human Performance*, 4: 365–74.

Goodman, P. and Friedman, A. (1971). An examination of Adams's theory of inequity. *Administrative Science Quarterly*, 16: 271–88.

Gordon, M. E. (1969). An evaluation of Jacques' studies of pay in the light of current compensation research. *Personnel Psychology*, 22: 369–89.

Greenberg, J. (1978a). Allocator-recipient similarity and the equitable division of rewards. *Social Psychology*, 41: 331–41.

Greenberg, J. (1978b). Equity, equality and the Protestant Ethic: Allocating rewards following fair and unfair competition. *Journal of Experimental Social Psychology*, 14: 217–26.

Greenberg, J. (1979a). *Scarcity and the distributive fairness of natural resource allocations*. Paper presented at the meeting of the Southwestern Psychological Association, New Orleans.

Greenberg, J. (1979b). Protestant ethic endorsement and the fairness of equity inputs. *Journal of Research in Personality*, 13: 81–90.

Greenberg, J. (1980a). Cognitive reevaluation of outcomes in response to underpayment inequity. *Academy of Management Journal*, 32: 174–84.

Greenberg, J. (1980b). Attentional focus and locus of performance causality as determinants of equity behavior. *Journal of Personality and Social Psychology*, 38: 579–85.

Greenberg, J. (1981). The justice of distributing scarce and abundant resources. In M. J. Lerner and S. C. Lerner (Eds.), *The Justice Motive in Social Behavior*, pp. 289–312. New York: Plenum.

Greenberg, J. (1982). Approaching equity and avoiding inequity in groups and organizations. In J. Greenberg and R. Cohen (Eds.), *Equity and Justice in Social Behavior*, pp. 389–436, New York: Academic Press.

Greenberg, J. (1986a). Determinants of perceived fairness of performance evaluation. *Journal of Applied Psychology*, 71: 340–42.

Greenberg, J. (1986b). Organizational performance appraisal procedures: What makes them fair? In R. J. Lewicki, B. H. Sheppard, and M. Bazerman (Eds.), *Research on Negotiation in Organizations*, vol. 1, pp. 25–41. Greenwich, CT: JAI Press.

Greenberg, J. (1987). A taxonomy of organizational justice theories. *Academy of Management Review*, 12: 9–22.

Greenberg, J. (1988). Equity and workplace status: A field experiment. *Journal of Applied Psychology*, 73(4): 606–13.

Greenberg, J. (1989). Cognitive reevaluation of outcomes in response to underpayment inequity. *Academy of Management Journal*, 32: 174–84.

Greenberg, J. and Cohen, R. (Eds.), (1982a). *Equity and Justice in Social Behavior*. New York: Academic Press.

Greenberg, J. and Cohen, R. (1982b). Why justice? Normative and instrumental interpretations. In J. Greenberg and R. Cohen (Eds.) *Equity and Justice in Social
Behavior*, pp. 437–39. New York: Academic Press.

Greenberg, J. and Leventhal, G. S. (1976). Equity and the use of overreward to motivate
performance. *Journal of Personality and Social Psychology*, 34: 179–90.

Greenberg, J. and Ornstein, S. (1983). High status job title as compensation for underpayment: A test of equity theory. *Journal of Applied Psychology*, 68: 285–97.

Gross, E. (1953). Some functional consequences of primary controls in formal work
organizations. *American Sociological Review*, 18: 368–73.

Gruder, L. L. (1971). Determinants of social comparison choices. *Journal of Experimental Social Psychology*, 7: 473–89.

Gurr, T. R. (1970). *Why Men Rebel*. Princeton, NJ: Princeton University Press.

Hamilton, M. (1966). *A study of management attitudes toward pay*. Unpublished master's
thesis, San Diego State University.

Hegtvedt, K. A. (1987). When rewards are scarce: Equal or equitable distributions? *Social
Forces*, 66: 183–207.

Heider, F. (1958). *The Psychology of Interpersonal Relations*. New York: John Wiley
and Sons.

Heneman, H. G., Schwab, D. P., Standal, J. T. and Peterson, R. B. (1980). Pay comparisons: Dimensionality and predictability. *Academy of Management Proceedings*, 38:
211–15.

Hills, F. S. (1980). The relevant other in pay comparisons. *Industrial Relations*. 19: 345–50.

Homans, G. C. (1953). Status among clerical workers. *Human Organization*, 12: 5–10.

Homans, G. C. (1961). *Social Behavior: Its Elementary Forms*, New York: Harcourt,
Brace Jovanovich.

Homans, G. C. (1974). *Social Behavior: Its Elementary Forms*. (revised ed.). New York:
Harcourt, Brace Jovanovich.

Huseman, R. C. and Hatfield, J. D. and Miles, W. T. (1987). A new perspective on equity
theory. *Academy of Management Review*, 12: 222–34.

Jackson, L. A., Messe, L. A. and Hunter, J. E. (1985). Gender role and distributive justice
behavior. *Basic and Applied Social Psychology*, 6: 329–43.

Jaques, E. (1970). *Equitable Payment*. (2nd ed.). London: Heinemann Educational Books.

Jasso, G. (1978). On the justice of earnings: A new specification of justice evaluation
function. *American Journal of Sociology*, 83: 1398–419.

Jasso, G. (1980). A new theory of distributive justice. *American Sociological Review*,
45: 3–32.

Jasso, G. (1983). Fairness of individual rewards and fairness of the reward distribution:
Specifying the conflict between the micro and macro principles of justice. *Social
Psychology Quarterly*, 46: 185–99.

Jasso, G. and Rossi, P. H. (1977). Distributive justice and earned income. *American
Sociological Review*, 42: 639–51.

Kahn, A. (1972). Reactions to generosity or stinginess from an intelligent or stupid work
partner: A test of equity theory in a direct exchange relationship. *Journal of Personality and Social Psychology*, 21: 116–23.

Kahn, A., Lamm, H. and Nelson, R. F. (1977). Preferences for an equal or equitable
allocator. *Journal of Personality and Social Psychology*, 35: 837–44.

Kahn, A., Nelson, R. E. and Gaeddert, W. P. (1980). Sex of subject and sex composition of the group as determinants of reward allocations. *Journal of Personality and Social Psychology*, 38: 737–50.

Kahn, A., O'Leary, V. E., Krulewitz, J. E. and Lamm, H. (1980). Equity and equality: Male and female means to a just end. *Basic and Applied Social Psychology*, 1: 173–97.

Kashima, Y., Siegal, M., Tanaka, K. and Isaka, H. (1988). Universalism in lay conceptions of distributive justice: A cross cultural examination. *International Journal of Psychology*, 23: 51–64.

Katz, M. G. and Messe, L. A. (1973, May). *A sex difference in the distribution of rewards.* Paper presented at the meeting of the Midwestern Psychological Association. Chicago.

Kayser, E., Feeley, W. M. and Lamm, H. (1982). *Layperson's social psychology of social relationships*. Universität Mannheim: Berichtausdem SFB 24.

Kayser, E. and Lamm, H. (1980). Input integration and input weighting in decisions on gains and losses. *European Journal of Social Psychology*, 10: 1–15.

Kerr, C. (1954). The balkinization of labor markets. In E. W. Bakke et al. (Eds.), *Labor Mobility and Economic Opportunity*, Cambridge: Technology Press of M.I.T.

Kerr, C. (1986). Models of the market. In C. Kerr and P. D. Staudohar (Eds.), *Economics of Labor in Industrial Society*, pp. 197–204. San Francisco: Jossey-Bass.

Kidder, L. H., Belletterie, G. and Cohn, E. S. (1977). Secret ambitions and public performances. *Journal of Experimental Social Psychology*, 13: 70–80.

Kourilsky, M., and Kehret-Ward, T. (1984). Kindergarteners' attitudes toward distributive justice: Experimental mediators. *Merill-Palmer Quarterly* 30: 49–64.

Krupp, S. (1961). *Patterns of Organization Analysis*, New York: Holt, Rinehart and Winston.

Kuethe, J. L. and Levenson, B. L. (1964). Concepts of organizational worth. *American Journal of Sociology*, 70: 342–48.

Lamm, H. and Schwinger, T. (1980). Norms concerning distributive justice: Are needs taken into consideration in allocation decisions? *Social Psychology Quarterly*. 43: (4) 425–29.

Landau, S. B. and Leventhal, G. S. (1976). A simulation study of administrator's behavior toward employees who receive job offers. *Journal of Applied Social Psychology*, 6: 291–306.

Lane, I. M. and Coon, R. C. (1972). Reward allocation in preschool children. *Child Development*, 43: 1382–89.

Lane, I. M. and Messe, L. A. (1971). Equity and distribution of rewards. *Journal of Personality and Social Psychology*, 20: 1–17.

Lane, I. M. and Messe, L. A. (1972). Distribution of insufficient, sufficient and oversufficient rewards: A clarification of equity theory. *Journal of Personality and Social Psychology*, 21: 228–33.

Lane, I. M., Messe, L. A., and Phillips, J. L. (1971). Differential inputs as a determinant in the selection of a distributor of rewards. *Psychonomic Science*, 22: 228–229.

Lansberg, J. (1984). Hierarchy as a mediator of fairness: A contingency approach to distributive justice in organizations. *Journal of Applied Social Psychology*. 14: 124–35.

Larwood, L. and Blackmore, J. (1977). Fair pay: Field investigations of the fair economic exchange. *Academy of Management Proceedings*, 81–85.

Larwood, L., Kavanagh, M. and Levine, R. (1978). Perceptions of fairness with three alternative economic exchanges. *Academy of Management Journal*, 21: 69–83.

Larwood, L., Levine, R., Shaw, R. and Hurwitz, S. (1979). Relation of objective and subjective inputs to exchange preference for equity or equality reward allocation. *Organizational Behavior and Human Performance*, 23: 60–72.

Lawler, E. E. III (1965). Managers' perceptions of their subordinates' pay and their superiors' pay. *Personnel Psychology*, 18: 413–22.

Lawler, E. E. III (1966). Managers' attitudes toward how their pay is and should be determined. *Journal of Applied Psychology*, 50: 270–79.

Lawler, E. E. III (1968a). Equity theory as a predictor of productivity and work quality. *Psychological Bulletin*, 70: 596–610.

Lawler, E. E. III (1968b). Effects of hourly overpayment on productivity and work quality. *Journal of Personality and Social Psychology*, 10: 306–13.

Lawler, E. E. III (1971). *Pay and Organizational Effectiveness*. New York: McGraw-Hill.

Lawler, E. E. III (1972). Secrecy and the need to know. In M. Dunette, R. House and H. Tossi (Eds.), *Readings in Managerial Motivation and Compensation* (pp. 362–71). East Lansing: Michigan State University Press.

Lawler, E. E. III (1981). *Pay and Organization Development*. Reading, MA: Addison-Wesley.

Lawler, E. E. III, Koplin, C. A., Young, T. F. and Fadem, J. A. (1968). Inequity reduction over time in an induced overpayment situation. *Organizational Behavior and Human Performance*, 3: 253–68.

Lawler, E. E. III and O'Gara, P. W. (1967). Effects of inequity produced by underpayment on work output, work quality and attitudes toward the work. *Journal of Applied Psychology*, 51: 403–10.

Lawrence, P. R. and Lorsch, J. W. (1967). Differentiation and integration in complex organizations. *Administrative Science Quarterly*, 12: 1–47.

Lerner, M. J. (1974). The justice motive: 'Equity' and 'parity' among children. *Journal of Personality and Social Psychology*, 29: 539–50.

Lerner, M. J. (1975). The justice motive: Some hypotheses as to its origins and forms. *Journal of Personality*, 45: 1–52.

Lerner, M. J. and Lerner, S. C. (Eds). (1987). *The Justice Motive in Social Behavior: Adapting to Times of Scarcity and Change*. New York: Plenum Press.

Lerner, M. J. and Miller, D. T. (1978). Just world research and attribution process: Looking back and ahead. *Psychological Bulletin*, 85: 1031–51.

Lerner, M. J., Miller, D. T. and Holmes, G. J. (1976). Deserving and the emergence of forms of justice. In L. Berkowitz and E. Walster (Eds.), *Advances in Experimental Social Psychology*, vol. 9: 133–62. New York: Academic Press.

Leung, K. and Bond, M. (1982). How Chinese and Americans reward task related contributions: A preliminary study. *Psychologia*, 25: 32–39.

Leung, K. and Bond, M. (1984). The impact of cultural collectivism on reward allocation. *Journal of Personality and Social Psychology*, 47: 793–804.

Leung, K. and Park, H. J. (1986). Effects of interactional goal on choice allocation rule: A cross-national study. *Organizational Behavior and Human Decision Processes*, 37: 111–20.

Leventhal, G. S. (1976a). The distribution of rewards and resources in groups and organizations. In L. Berkowitz and E. Walster (Eds.), *Advances in Experimental Social Psychology*, vol 9: 92–133. New York: Academic Press.

Leventhal, G. S. (1976b). Fairness in social relationships. In J. W. Thibaut, J. T. Spence and R. C. Carson (Eds.), *Contemporary Topics in Social Psychology*, pp. 211–39. Morristown, NJ: General Learning Press.

Leventhal, G. S. (1980). What should be done with equity theory? In K. J. Gergen, M. S. Greenberg and R. H. Willis (Eds.), *Social Exchange: Advances in Theory and Research*, pp. 27–55. New York: Plenum.

Leventhal, G. S., Allen J. and Kemelgor, B. (1969a). Reducing inequity by reallocating rewards. *Psychonomic Science*, 14: 295–96.

Leventhal, G. S. and Anderson, D. (1970). Self-interest and the maintenance of equity. *Journal of Personality and Social Psychology*, 15: 57–62.

Leventhal, G. S., Karuza, J. and Fry, W. R. (1980). Beyond fairness: A theory of allocation preferences. In G. Mikula (Ed.), *Justice in Social Interaction*, pp. 166–218. New York: Springer-Verlag.

Leventhal, G. S. and Lane, D. W. (1970). Sex, age and equity behavior. *Journal of Personality and Social Psychology*, 15: 312–16.

Leventhal, G. S. and Michaels, J. W. (1969). Extending the equity model: Perceptions of inputs and allocation of rewards as a function of duration and quantity of performance. *Journal of Personality and Social Psychology*, 12: 303–09.

Leventhal, G. S. and Michaels, J. W. (1971). Locus of cause and equity motivation as determinants of reward allocation. *Journal of Personality and Social Psychology*, 17: 229–35.

Leventhal, G. S., Michaels, J. W., and Sanford, C. (1972). Inequity and interpersonal conflict: Reward allocation and secrecy about rewards as methods of preventing conflict. *Journal of Personality and Social Psychology*, 23: 88–102.

Leventhal, G. S., Weiss, T. and Butrick, R. (1973). Attribution of value, equity and the prevention of waste in reward allocation. *Journal of Personality and Social Psychology*, 27: 276–86.

Leventhal, G. S., Weiss T. and Long, G. (1969b). Equity, reciprocity, and reallocating rewards in the dyad. *Journal of Personality and Social Psychology*, 13: 300–05.

Leventhal, G. S. and Whiteside, H. D. (1973). Equity and the use of reward to elicit high performance. *Journal of Personality and Social Psychology*, 25: 75–83.

Levine, J. M. and Moreland, R. L. (1987). Social comparison and outcome evaluation in group contexts. In J. C. Masters and W. P. Smith (Eds.), *Social Comparison, Social Justice, and Relative Deprivation: Theoretical, Empirical and Policy Perspective*, pp. 105–130. Hillsdale, NJ: Lawrence Erlbaum Assoc.

Lipset, S. M. and Trow, M. (1957). Reference group theory and trade union wage policy. In M. Komarovsky (Ed.), *Common Frontiers of the Social Sciences*. Glencoe, IL: The Free Press.

Livernash, E. R. (1957). The Internal Wage Structure. In G. W. Taylor and F. C. Pierson (Eds.), *New Concepts in Wage Determination*. New York: McGraw Hill.

Locke, E. A. (1976). The nature and causes of job satisfaction. In M. Dunnette (Ed.), *Handbook of Industrial and Organizational Psychology*. pp. 1297–1349. Chicago, IL: Rand McNally.

Lord, R. G. and Hohenfeld, R. J. (1979). A longitudinal field assessment of equity effects on the performance of major league baseball players. *Journal of Applied Psychology*, 64: 19–26.

Lupton, T. and Bowey, A. (1983). *Wages and Salaries*. (2nd ed.) Aldershot, Hants: Gower.

Mahoney, T. A. (1979a). Justice and Equity in Compensation. In T. A. Mahoney (Ed.), *Compensation and Reward Perspectives*. pp. 190–93. Homewood, Ill.: R. D. Irwin.

Mahoney, T. A. (1979b). Organizational hierarchy and position worth. *Academy of Management Journal*, 22: 726–37.

Mahoney, T. A. and Blake, R. H. (1987). Judgment of appropriate occupational pay as influenced by occupational characteristics and sex characteristics. *Applied Psychology: An International Review*, 36(1): 25–38.

Mahoney, T. A. and Weitzel, W. (1978). Secrecy and managerial compensation. *Industrial Relations*, 17: 245–51.

Major, B. (1987a). Women and entitlement. *Women and Therapy*, 6(3): 3–19.

Major, B. (1987b). Gender, justice and the psychology of entitlement. *Review of Personality and Social Psychology*, 7: 124–48.

Major, B. and Adams, J. B. (1983). Role of gender, interpersonal orientation, and self presentation in distributive-justice behavior. *Journal of Personality and Social Psychology*, 45: 598–608.

Major, B. and Adams, J. B. (1984). Situational moderators of gender differences in reward allocations. *Sex Roles*, 11: 869–80.

Major, B. and Deaux, K. (1982). Individual differences in justice behavior. In J. Greenberg and R. Cohen (Eds.), *Equity and Justice in Social Behavior*, pp. 43–76. New York: Academic.

Major, B. and Forcey, B. (1985). Social comparisons and pay evaluation: Preferences for same-sex and same-job wage comparisons. *Journal of Experimental Social Psychology*, 21: 393–405.

Major, B. and Konar, E. (1984). An investigation of sex differences in pay expectations and their possible causes. *Academy of Management Journal*, 27: 777–92.

Major, B., McFarlin, D. B. and Gagnon, D. (1984). Overworked and underpaid: On the nature of gender differences in personal entitlement. *Journal of Personality and Social Psychology*, II, 47: 1399–412.

Major, B. and Testa, M. (1989). Social comparison processes and judgments of entitlement and satisfaction. *Journal of Experimental Social Psychology*, 25: 101–20.

Mann, L., Radford, M. and Kanagawa, C. (1985). Cross-cultural differences in children's use of decision rules: A comparison between Japan and Australia. *Journal of Personality and Social Psychology*, 49: 1557–564.

March, G. C. and Simon, H. (1958). *Organizations*. New York: Wiley.

Marin, G. (1981). Perceived justice across cultures: Equity vs. equality in Colombia and the United States. *International Journal of Psychology*, 16: 153–59.

Marin, G. (1985). The preference for equity when judging the attractiveness and fairness of an allocator: The role of familiarity and culture. *Journal of Social Psychology*, 125: 543–49.

Mark, M. M. (1980). *Justice in the aggregate: The perceived fairness of the distribution of income*. Unpublished doctoral dissertation, Northwestern University.

Mark, M. M. and Folger, R. (1984). Responses to relative deprivation: A conceptual framework. *Review of Personality and Social Psychology*, 5: 192–218.

Markovsky, B. (1985a). Evaluating theories of justice and equity. In E. J. Lawler (Ed.), *Advances in Group Processes: Theory and Research*, pp. 197–226. Greenwich, CT: JAI Press.

Markovsky, B. (1985b). Toward a multilevel distributive justice theory. *American Sociological Review*, 50: 822–39.

Markovsky, B. (1988). Anchoring justice. *Social Psychology Quarterly*, 51: 213–24.

Marsh, R. M. and Mannari, H. (1973). Pay and Social Structure in a Japanese Firm. *Industrial Relations*, 12: 16–32.

Martin, J. (1981). A theory of distributive justice in an era of shrinking resources. In L. L. Cummings and B. M. Staw (Eds.), *Research in Organizational Behavior* (vol. 3). Greenwich, CT: JAI Press.

Martin, J. (1982). The fairness of earning differentials: An experimental study of the perceptions of blue-collar workers. *Journal of Human Resources*, 17: 110–22.

Martin, J. and Murray, A. (1983). Distributive injustice and unfair exchange. In D. M. Messick and K. S. Cook (Eds.), *Equity Theory: Psychological and Sociological Perspectives*, pp. 169–205. New York: Praeger.

Martin, J. and Murray, A. (1984). Catalysts for collective violence: The importance of a psychological approach. In R. Folger (Ed.), *The Sense of Injustice: Social Psychological Perspectives*, pp. 95–139. New York: Plenum.

Martin, J. E. and Peterson, M. M. (1987). Two-tier wage structures: Implications for equity theory. *Academic Management Journal*, 30: 297–315.

Masters, J. C. and Keil, L. (1987). Generic comparison processes in human judgment and behavior. In J. C. Masters and W. P. Smith (Eds.), *Social Comparison, Social Justice, and Relative Deprivation: Theoretical, Empirical and Policy Perspectives*. Hillsdale, NJ: Lawrence Erlbaum Assoc.

Masters, J. C. and Smith, W. P. (Eds.), (1987). *Social Comparison, Social Justice, and Relative Deprivation: Theoretical, Empirical and Policy Perspectives*. Hillsdale, NJ: Lawrence Erlbaum Assoc.

Meeker, B. F. (1971). Decisions and exchange. *American Sociological Review*, 36: 485–95.

Merton, R. K. (1957). *Social Theory and Social Structure*. Glencoe, IL: Free Press.

Merton, R. K. and Kitt, A. S. (1950). Contributions to the theory of reference group behavior. In R. K. Merton and P. F. Lazarsfeld (Eds.), *Continuities in Social Research: Studies in the scope and method of the "American Soldier."* Glencoe, IL: Free Press.

Merton, R. K. and Rossi, A. (1968). Contributions to the theory of reference group behavior. In R. K. Merton (Ed.), *Social Theory and Social Structure* (enlarged ed.). pp. 279–334. New York: Free Press.

Messe, L. A. Hymes, R. W. and MacCoun, R. J. (1986). Group categorization and distributive justice decisions. In H. W. Bierhoff, R. L. Cohen and J. Greenberg (Eds.), *Justice in Social Relations*, pp. 227–48. New York: Plenum.

Messe, L. A. and Lane, I. M. (1974). Rediscovering the need for multiple operations: A reply to Austin and Susmilch. *Journal of Personality and Social Psychology*, 30: 405–08.

Messe, L. A. and Lichtman, R. J. (1972). *Motivation for money as a mediator of the extent to which quality and duration of work are inputs relevant to the distribution rewards*. Paper presented at the meeting of Southeastern Psychological Association, Atlanta.

Messe, L. A. and Watts, B. (1983). The complex nature of the sense of fairness: Internal standards and social comparisons as bases for reward evaluation. *Journal of Personality and Social Psychology*, 45: 84–93.

Messick, D. M. and Cook, K. S. (Eds.). (1983). *Equity Theory: Psychological and Sociological Perspectives*. New York: Praeger.

Mikula, G. (1974). Nationality, performance and sex as determinants of reward allocation. *Journal of Personality and Social Psychology*, 29: 435–40.

Mikula, G. (Ed.) (1980). *Justice in Social Interaction*. New York: Springer.

Mikula, G. and Schwinger, Th. (1973). Sympathie zum Partner und Bedürfnis nach sozialer Anerkennung als Determinanten der Aufteilung gemeinsam erzielter Gewinne (Sympathy and the need for social approval as determinants for the allocation of common rewards). *Psychologische Beiträge*, 15: 396–407.

Mikula, G. and Schwinger, Th. (1978). Intermember relations and reward allocation. In H. Brandstatter, J. H. Davis and H. Schuler (Eds.), Dynamics of Group Decision, pp. 229–50. Beverly Hills: Sage.

Mikula, G. and Uray, H. (1973). Die Vernachlässigung der individuellen Leistungen bei der Lohnaufteilung in Sozialsituationen (Neglecting individual performances in the allocation of reward in social work settings). *Zeitschrift fur Sozialpsychologie*, 4: 136–44.

Milkovich, G. T. and Anderson, P. H. (1972). Management compensation and secrecy policies. *Personnel Psychology*, 25: 293–302.

Milkovich, G. T. and Newman, J. M. (1984). *Compensation*. Plano, TX: Business Publications, Inc.

Milkovich, G. T. and Newman, J. M. (1987). *Compensation*. (2nd ed.) Plano, TX: Business Publications, Inc.

Miller, A. H., Bolce, L. H. and Halligan M. (1977). The J-Curve theory and the black urban riots. *American Political Science Review*, 71: 964–82.

Miner, J. B. (1984). The unpaved road over the mountains: From theory to applications. *The Industrial-Organizational Psychologist*, 21: 9–20.

Mirels, H. L. and Garrett, J. B. (1971). The Protestant ethic as a personality variable. *Journal of Consulting and Clinical Psychology*, 46: 40–44.

Montada, L. (1980). Developmental changes in concepts of justice. In G. Mikula (Ed.), *Justice in Social Interaction*, pp. 257–84. New York: Springer-Verlag.

Mowday, R. T. (1987). Equity theory predictions of behavior in organizations. In R. M. Steers and L. W. Porter (Eds.), *Motivation and Work Behavior* (3rd ed.), pp. 91–113. New York: McGraw-Hill.

Murphy-Berman, V., Berman, J. J., Singh, P., Pachauri, A. and Kumar, P. (1984). Factors affecting allocation to needy and meritorious recipients. A cross-cultural comparison. *Journal of Personality and Social Psychology*, 46: 1267–72.

Murray, H. A. (1938). *Explorations in personality*. New York: Oxford University Press.

Oldham, G. R., Kulik, C. T., Stepina, L. P. and Ambrose, M. L. (1986). Relations between situational factors and the comparative referents used by employees. *Academy of Management Journal*, 29: 599–608.

Oldham, G. R. and Miller, H. E. (1979). The effects of significant others' job complexity on employee readiness to work. *Human Relations*, 32: 247–60.

Oldham, G. R., Nottenburg, G., Kassner, M. W., Ferris, G., Fedor, D. and Masters, M. (1982). The selection and consequences of job comparisons. *Organizational Behavior and Human Performance*, 29: 84–111.

Opsahl, R. L. and Dunnette, M. D. (1966). The role of financial compensation in industrial motivation. *Psychological Bulletin*, LXVI: 357–61.

Parcel, T. L. and Cook, K. S. (1977). Status characteristics, reward allocation and equity. *Sociometry*, 40: 311–24.

Patchen, M. (1961). *The Choice of Wage Comparisons*. Englewood Cliffs, NJ: Prentice-Hall.

Patten, T. H. (1977). *Pay: Employee Compensation and Incentive Plans*. New York: Free Press.

Pen, J. (1971). *Income Distribution*. London: Allen Lane.

Pepitone, A. et al. (1967). The role of self esteem in competitive choice behavior. *International Journal of Psychology*, 2: 147–59.

Pepitone, A. et al. (1970). Justice in choice behavior: A cross-cultural analysis. *International Journal of Psychology*, 5: 1–10.

Pettigrew, T. (1967). Social evaluation theory. In D. Levine (Ed.), *Nebraska Symposium on Motivation*, 15: 241–318. Lincoln: University of Nebraska Press.

Pfeffer, J. and Langton, N. (1988). Wage inequality and the organization of work: The case of academic departments. *Administrative Science Quarterly*, 33: 588–606.

Pondy, L. R. and Birnberg, J. G. (1969). An experimental study of the allocation of financial resources within small hierarchical task groups. *Administrative Science Quarterly*, 14: 176–211.

Pritchard, R. (1969). Equity theory: A review and critique. *Organizational Behavior and Human Performance*, 4: 176–211.

Pritchard, R. D., Dunnette, M. D. and Sorensen, D. P. (1972). Effects of perceptions of equity and inequity on worker performance and satisfaction. *Journal of Applied Psychology*, 56(1): 75–94.

Rainwater, L. (1974). *What Money Buys: Inequality and the Social Meaning of Income*. New York: Basic Books.

Reis, H. T. (1984). The multidimensionality of justice. In R. Folger (Ed.), *The Sense of Injustice: Social Psychological Perspectives*, pp. 25–62. New York: Plenum.

Reis, H. T. and Gruzen, J. (1976). On mediating equity, equality and self-interest: The role of self-preservation in social exchange. *Journal of Experimental Social Psychology*, 12: 487–503.

Reis, H. T. and Jackson, L. A. (1981). Sex differences in reward allocation. Subjects, partners and tasks. *Journal of Personality and Psychology*, 40: 465–78.

Reynolds, L. G. (1986). Labor mobility. In C. Kerr and P. D. Staudohar (Eds.), *Economics of Labor in Industrial Society*, pp. 204–06. San Francisco: Jossey-Bass.

Reynolds, L. G., Masters, S. H. and Moser, C. H. (1987). *Labor Economics and Labor Relations*. (9th ed.). Englewood Cliffs, NJ: Prentice-Hall.

Roetlisberger, F. J. and Dickson, W. J. (1939). *Management and the Worker*. Cambridge, MA: Harvard University Press.

Ronen, S. (1986). Equity perceptions in multiple comparisons: A field study. *Human Relations*, 39: 333–46.

Ross, M. and McMillen, M. J. (1973). External referents and past outcomes as determinants of social discontent. *Journal of Experimental Social Psychology*, 9: 437–49.

Ross, M., Thibaut, J. and Evenbeck, S. (1971). Some determinants of the intensity of social protest. *Journal of Experimental Social Psychology*, 7: 401–18.

Rotter, N. G. (1987). Perceived commitment, salary recommendation and employee sex. *Perceptual and Motor Skills*, 64: 651–58.

Roy, D. (1952). Quota restriction and goldbricking in a machine shop. *American Journal of Sociology*, 57: 430–37.

Roy, D. (1954). Efficiency and "the fix": Informal intergroup relations in a piecework machine shop. *American Journal of Sociology*, 60: 255–66.

Runciman, W. (1966). *Relative Deprivation and Social Justice*. London: Routledge and Kegan Paul.

Rusbult, C. E., Insko, Ch. E., Lyn, Y.H.W. and Smith, W. J. (1990). Social motives underlying selective exploitation: the impact of instrumental versus social-emotional allocator orientation on the distribution of rewards in groups. *Journal of Applied Social Psychology*, 20: 984–1025.

Rusbult, C. E., Lowery, D., Hubbard, M. L., Maravankin, O. J., and Neises, M. (1988). Impact of employee mobility and employee performance on the allocation of rewards under conditions of constraint. *Journal of Personality and Social Psychology*, 54: 605–15.

Sagan, K., Pondel, M. and Andrisin, M. (1981). The effect of anticipated future interaction on reward allocation in same- and opposite-sex dyads. *Journal of Personality*, 49(4): 438–49.

Sampson, E. E. (1975). On justice as equality. *Journal of Social Issues*, 31: 45–64.

Sampson, E. E. (1980). Justice and social character. In G. Mikula (Ed.), *Justice in Social Interaction*, pp. 285–314. New York: Springer-Verlag.

Scholl, R. W., Cooper, E. A. and McKenna, J. F. (1987). Referent selection in determining equity perceptions: Differential effects on behavioral and attitudinal outcomes. *Personnel Psychology*, 40: 112–23.

Schmitt, D. R. and Marwell, G. (1972). Withdrawal and reward allocation as responses to inequity. *Journal of Experimental Social Psychology*, 8: 207–21.

Schmitt, M. and Montada, L. (1982). Determinanten erlebter Gerechtigkeit (Determinants of experienced justice). *Zeitschrift fuer Sozialpsychologie*, 13: 32–44.

Schuster, J. and Clark, B. (1970). Individual differences related to feelings about pay. *Personnel Psychology*, 23: 591–604.

Schwinger, T. (1980). Just allocations of goods: Decisions among three principles. In G. Mikula (Ed.), *Justice in Social Interaction: Experimental and Theoretical Contributions from Psychological Research*, pp. 95–126. New York: Springer.

Schwinger, T., Kayser, E. and Mueller, T. (1981). Was rechtfertigt ungleichhabige Güterverteilung? (Under which circumstances will unequal distribution of resources be taken to be just?) *Archiv für Psychologie*, 134: 303–14.

Schwinger, T. and Naehrer, W. (1983). *Prinzipien der gerechten Vergabe von interpersonalen Ressourcen in verschiedenen Sozialbeziehungen* (Principles of just allocation of interpersonal resources under various social circumstances). Universität Mannheim: SBF, 24.

Shapiro, E. G. (1975). Effect of expectation of future interaction on reward allocation in dyads: Equity or equality? *Journal of Personality and Social Psychology*, 31: 873–80.

Sheehan, E. P. (1988). *The effects of employee turnover on those who stay: An equity theory approach*. Doctoral dissertation, University of California, Santa Cruz.

Shirom, A. (1980). Foremen's comparison groups for equity assessment. *Journal of Occupational Behavior*, 1: 129–37.

Siegal, M. and Schwalb, D. (1985). Economic justice in adolescence: An Australian-Japanese comparison. *Journal of Economic Psychology*, 6: 313–26.

Simon, H. A. (1957). The compensation of executives. *Sociometry*, 20: 32–35.

Simpson, E. (1976). Socialist justice. *Ethics*, 87: 1–17.

Stake, J. E. (1983). Factors in reward distribution: Allocator motive, gender and Protestant ethic endorsement. *Journal of Personality and Social Psychology*, 44: 410–18.

Stolte, J. F. (1987a). The formation of justice norms. *American Sociological Review*, 52: 774–78.

Stolte, J. F. (1987b). Legitimacy, justice and productive exchange. In K. S. Cook (Ed.), *Social Exchange Theory*, pp. 190–208. Newburry Park, CA: Sage.

Stouffer, S. A. Lumsdaine, A., Lumsdaine, M. et al. (1949a). *The American Soldier* (vol. 2). Princeton, NJ: Princeton University Press.

Stouffer, S. A., Suchman, E. A, DeVinney, L. C., Star, S. A. and Williams, R. M. (1949b). *The American Soldier: Adjustments During Army Life* (vol. 1). Princeton, NJ: Princeton University Press.

Subbarao, A. V. and deCarufel, A. (1983). Pay secrecy and perceptions of fairness in a university environment. In G. Johns (Ed.), *Proceedings of the Administrative Science Association of Canada*, 4: 173–81.

Summers, T. P. (1988). Examination of sex differences in expectations of pay and perceptions of equity and pay. *Psychological Reports*, 62: 491–96.

Summers, T. P. and DeNisi, A. S. (1990). In search of Adams's other: Reexamination of referents used in the evaluation of pay. *Human Relations*, 43: 497–511.

Telly, C. S., French, W. L. and Scott, W. G. (1971). The relationship of inequity to turnover among hourly workers. *Administrative Science Quarterly*, 16: 162–74.

Thornton, D. A. and Arrowood, A. J. (1966). Self-evaluation, self-enhancement and the locus of social comparison. *Journal of Experimental Social Psychology*, Suppl. 1:27–31.

Thurow, L. C. (1975). *Generating Inequality: Mechanisms of Distribution in the U.S. Economy*. New York: Basic Books.

Tindale, R. S. and Davis, J. H. (1985). Individual and group award allocation decisions in two situational contexts: Effects of relative need and performance. *Journal of Personality and Social Psychology*, 48 1148–61.

Torgerson, W. S. (1958). *Theory and Methods of Scaling*. New York: Wiley.

Törnblom, K. Y. (1977a). Distributive justice: Typology and propositions. *Human Relations*. 30: 1–14.

Törnblom, K. Y. (1977b). Magnitude and source of compensation in two situations of distributive justice. *Acta Sociologica*, 20: 75–95.

Törnblom, K. Y. (1982). Reversal in preference responses to two types of injustice situations: A methodological contribution to equity theory. *Human Relations*, 35(11): 991–1014.

Törnblom, K. Y. (1988). Positive and negative allocations: A model for conflicting justice principles. In E. J. Lawler and B. Markovsky (Eds.), *Advances in Group Processes*, 5: 141–68. Greenwich, CT: JAI Press.

Törnblom, K. Y. and Foa, U. G. (1983). Choice of a distribution principle: Cross-cultural evidence on the effects of resources. *Acta Sociologica*, 26(2): 161–73.

Törnblom, K. Y. and Jonsson, D. R. (1985). Subrules of the equity and contribution principles: Their perceived fairness in distribution and retribution. *Social Psychology Quarterly*, 48: 249–61.

Törnblom, K. Y. and Jonsson, D. R. (1987). Distribution vs. retribution: The perceived justice of the contribution and equality principles for cooperative and competitive relationships. *Acta Sociologica*, 30: 25–52.

Törnblom, K. Y., Jonsson, D. R. and Foa, U. G. (1985). Nationality, resource class, and preferences among three allocation rules: Sweden vs. USA, *International Journal of Intercultural Relations*, 9: 51–77.

Tornow, W. W. (1971). The development and application of an input-outcome moderator test on the perception and reduction of inequity. *Organizational Behavior and Human Performance*, 6: 614–38.

Trist, E. L. and Bamforth, K. W. (1951). Some social and psychological consequences of the longwal method of coal-getting. *Human Relation*, 4: 3–38.

Turner, R. (1955). Reference groups of future oriented men. *Social Forces*, 34: 130–36.

Uray, H. (1976). Leistungsverursachung, Verantwortungszuschreibung und Gewinnaufteilung (Contribution, attribution of responsibility and reward allocation). *Zeitschrift für Sozialpsychologie*, 7: 69–80.

Utne, M. K. and Kidd, R. (1980). Equity and attribution. In G. Mikula (Ed.), *Justice in Social Interaction*, pp 63–94. New York: Springer.

Valentine, R. J. (1971). *The effect of group unity on reward allocation behavior*. Unpublished master's thesis, North Carolina State University.

Valenzi, E. R. and Andrews, I. R. (1971). Effect of hourly overpay and underpay inequity when tested with a new induction procedure. *Journal of Applied Psychology*, 55: 22–27.

Van-Knippenberg, A. and Van-Oers, H. (1984). Social identity and equity concerns in intergroup perceptions. *British Journal of Social Psychology*, 23(4): 351–61.

Vanneman, R. D. and Pettigrew, T. (1972). Race and relative deprivation in the urban United States. *Race*, 13: 461–86.

Vecchio, R. P. (1982). Predicting worker performance in inequitable settings. *Academy of Management Review*, 7: 103–10.

Vecchio, R. P. (1984). Models of psychological inequity. *Organizational Behavior and Human Performance*, 34: 266–82.

Von Grumbkow, J., Deen, E., Steensman, H. and Wilke, H. (1976). The effect of future interaction on the distribution of rewards. *European Journal of Social Psychology*, 6: 119–23.

Von Grumbkow, J. and Wilke, H. (1978). Extreme underpayment in a simple and complex comparison situation. *European Journal of Social Psychology*. 8: 129–33.

Vroom, V. (1964). *Work and Motivation*. New York: Wiley.

Wahba, M. A. (1972). Preferences among alternative forms of equity: The apportionment of coalition reward in the males and females. *Journal of Social Psychology*, 87: 107–15.

Walker, I. and Pettigrew, T. F. (1984). Relative deprivation theory: An overview and conceptual critique. *British Journal of Social Psychology*, 23: 301–10.

Wall, D. R. and Nolan, S. (1986). Perceptions of inequity, satisfaction and conflict in task oriented groups. *Human Relations*, 39: 1033–52.

Walster, E., Berscheid, E. and Walster, W. G. (1976). New directions in equity research. In L. Berkowitz and E. Walster (Eds.), *Advances in Experimental Social Psychology*, 9: 1–42. New York: Academic Press.

Walster, E., Walster, G. and Berscheid, E. (1978). *Equity Theory and Research*, Boston: Allyn and Bacon.

Watts, B. L., Messe, L. A. and Vallacher, R. R. (1982). Toward understanding sex differences in pay allocations: Agency communion and reward distribution behavior. *Sex Roles*, 12: 1175–88.

Weick, K. E. (1966). The concept of equity in the perception of pay. *Administrative Science Quarterly*, 11: 414–39.

Weick, K. Bougon, M. and Maruyama, G. (1976). The equity context. *Organizational Behavior and Human Performance*, 15: 32–65.

Weick, K. and Nesset, B. (1968). Preferences among forms of equity. *Organizational Behavior and Human Performance*, 3: 400–16.

Weinstein, A. G. and Holzbach, R. L. (1973). Impact of individual differences, reward distribution, and task structure on productivity in a simulated work environment. *Journal of Applied Psychology*, 58: 296–301.

Wheeler, L. (1966). Motivation as a determinant of upward comparison. *Journal of Experimental Social Psychology*, Suppl. 1: 27–31.

Wheeler, L., Shaver, K. L. et al. (1969). Factors determining choice of a comparison other. *Journal of Experimental Social Psychology*, 5: 219–32.

Wheeler, L. and Zuckerman, M. (1977). Commentary. In J. M. Suls and R. L. Miller (Eds.), *Social Comparison Processes: Theoretical and Empirical Perspectives*. pp. 335–58. New York: Wiley.

White, M. (1981). *Pay Conflict*. London: MacMillan.

Wiener, Y. (1970). The effects of "task-" and "ego-oriented" performance on two kinds of overcompensation inequity. *Organizational Behavior and Human Performance*, 5: 191–208.

Wilke, H. and Steur, T. (1972). Overpayment: Perceived qualifications and financial compensation. *European Journal of Social Psychology*, 2: 273–84.

Williams, R. M. (1975). Relative deprivation. In L. A. Coser (Ed.), *The Idea of Social Structure: Papers in Honor of R. K. Merton*. pp. 355–78. New York: Harcourt Brace Jovanovich.

Witting, M. A., Marks, G. and Jones, G. A. (1981). The effect of luck versus effort attributions on reward allocation to self and others. *Personality and Social Psychology Research Bulletin*, 7: 71–78.

Zelditch, M., Berger, J., Anderson, B. and Cohen, R. P. (1970). Equitable comparisons. *Pacific Sociological Review*, 13: 19–26.

Zelditch, M., Berger, J. and Cohen, B. P. (1966). Stability of organizational status structures. In J. Berger, M. Zelditch and B. Anderson (Eds.), *Sociological Theories in Progress* (vol. 1). pp. 269–94. Boston: Houghton Mifflin Co.

Ziemak, J. P. (1988). *Personal, internal and external equity: Multiple facets of pay fairness?* Doctoral dissertation, The Ohio State University.

Author Index

Subject Index

ABOUT THE AUTHOR

MIRIAM DORNSTEIN is senior lecturer in sociology at the University of Haifa, Israel. She has previously held positions as senior economist and senior economic adviser in government and at a publicly owned corporation. Her major research interests include the social psychology of economic and organizational behavior. Her publications in this field include *Boards of Directors under Public Owner-ship: A Comparative Perspective* and numerous scholarly articles. Her recent work has focused on the perceived fairness of pay and on related topics.